LANDCASTER PRESS

The Cherry Orchard[1]

A Comedy in Four Acts[2]

Anton Chekhov

Translated, Adapted, Edited and Annotated by

Thomas G. Jewusiak

The Cherry Orchard

Jacket Design by Mussorgsky

Cover Photo by yspbqh14

Printed by Jason Hand, Inc. on the Outer Banks

"Chekhov is the bearer of the greatest banner that has been raised in the thousand years of Russian history, the banner of a true, humane, Russian democracy, of Russian freedom, of the dignity of the Russian man."

Words of a fictional character, Leonid Madyarov, in Vasily Grossman's, *Life and Fate*

Copyright © August 22, 2017   Thomas G. Jewusiak

All rights reserved. No part of this book may be reproduced in any form without the written consent of the author. Professionals and amateurs are hereby notified that this material, being fully protected under the Copyright Laws of the United States and all other countries of the Berne and Universal Copyright Conventions, is subject to royalty. All rights, including but not limited to, professional, amateur, recording, motion picture, recitation, lecturing, public reading, including educational institutions, radio and television broadcasting, are expressly reserved.

This is a work of translation, adaption, editing and annotation. Any resemblance to any persons or fictional characters or any other works, except Chekhov's, is entirely coincidental.

First Paperback Edition

10th Printing

The Cherry Orchard

Chekhov, Anton

Translated, Adapted, Edited and Annotated by

Jewusiak, Thomas G.

ISBN-10:0-9970967-9-9

ISBN-13:978-0-9970967-9-8

Parts of this work were written in old growth ancient virgin forests. While the author was living in the woods, he hurt no old trees in any way.

LANDCASTER PRESS
West Palm Beach
LandcasterPress.com
LandcasterPress@aol.com

RUSSIAN NAMES

Mastering Russian naming customs is essential to understanding the nature and subtlety of personal relationships, their gradation and intensity. It is the smallest price to pay and worth the effort. Formal address in Russian consists of the first name and the patronymic. When used together, the name and patronymic serve as "Mr.," "Miss," and "Mrs.," signifying the speaker's respect. Russian's middle names, the patronymic, represent the father's first name with a suffix. The suffix depends on whether the bearer is a man or a woman: ovich for sons; ovna for daughters. Anton Pavlovich Chekhov's first name is Anton, and his patronymic is Pavlovich, Pavel being his father's first name. Chekhov's sister's name and patronymic name is Maria Pavlovna. Chekhov is the family name, the last name. However, the feminine variant of the last name is different from its male variant. The last name of Chekhov's sister is Chekhova thus designating that it is the name of a woman. In Russian culture the first name, patronymic and last name are the full proper name as used in official documents. The first name and patronymic are used when addressing somebody formally. First and patronymic names are not used when addressing one's children, parents, or close relatives. In the prerevolutionary Russia of Chekhov's plays, masters do not address their servants by both their name and patronymic; they use either the first name or the patronymic. Using both would transgress class boundaries. However, servants may use first name and patronymic in addressing one another.

In addition to this formal mode of addressing one another, Russians have a multitude of inventive and endearing nicknames and diminutives. For example, in *Ivanov*, the hero, Nikolai Ivanov, calls his wife Aniuta but not Anushka both diminutives of Anna. Alexandra, another character in *Ivanov*, is called by several diminutives: Sasha, Shura, Shurochka. Ivan can be Vanya, Ivasha, Isha, Ishuta, Iva, Vanyukha, Vanyusha, Vanyura, or Vanyuta. In *Three Sisters*, the nanny, Anfisa, calls one of the sisters Arinushka and the other Oliushka; endearing folk versions of Irina and Olga, respectively. Maria, Mariushka, Marusia, Mania, Mosia and Masha are all variations of the same name. These nicknames or "pet names," are formed by adding diminutive endings to the first name which can be added in almost endless variations, signifying warmth, emotional intimacy, sympathy or they can be scornful or patronizing. A first-degree diminutive is common in the family circle. For example, Gaev calls his sister by the diminutive "Lyuba," for "Lyubov." Most of the servants are called by their pet names: "Dunyasha" for "Avdotya" and "Yasha" (whose formal first name is not even given in the cast list). These informal names are entirely unlike nicknames in America which are often associated with the decadent rich or with ignorant yokels. Uncle Vanya cannot and should not be translated as "Uncle Johnny".

Lyubov Andreyevna's foster daughter is usually called "Varya" instead of the more formal "Vavara," a form of address that tends to equate her with the servants.

When the servants call Lopakhin "Ermolay Alekseyevich" (Ermolay Son-of-Aleksey), they show him respect because he is a rich man; his wealth elevates his social standing in spite of his humble peasant origins or perhaps they respect him for who he is rather than who he has become.

Russians rarely use surnames, which serve primarily to identify a family connection, a famous personage or to introduce complete strangers. Sometimes using a last name alone is a sign of disrespect. While perhaps not consciously insulting, most of the characters in *The Cherry Orchard* call Epikhodov by his last name, suggesting their superior attitude toward him.

First names are used only by one's intimate friends and family, but can always be used by anyone when speaking to children and servants.

Charlotta is a German name; her Russian patronymic Ivanovna does not mean that her father's name was necessarily Ivan: Russians occasionally use that patronymic when the father's name is so un-Russian as to resist Russification or when the father's name is unknown.

CHARACTERS

LYUBÓV[3] ANDRÉYEVNA RANÉVSKAYA[4] (Lyúba), a landowner

ÁNYA (Ánechka), her daughter, seventeen years old

VÁRYA (Varvára Mikháilovna), her foster[5] daughter, twenty-four years old (or twenty-two[6])

LEONÍD ANDRÉYEVICH GÁEV[7] (Lyónya), Ranevskaya's brother

ERMOLÁI[8] ALEXÉYEVICH LOPÁKHIN[9] (Alexéich), a merchant

PYÓTR SERGÉEVICH TROFÍMOV (Pétya), a student

BORÍS BORÍSOVICH SIMEÓNOV-PÍSHCHIK, a landowner [10]

CHARLÓTTA IVÁNOVNA (no last name), a governess [11]

SEMYÓN PANTELÉEVICH EPIKHÓDOV, a clerk, bookkeeper

DUNYÁSHA (Avdótya Fyódorvna Kozoédova), a maid

FIERS[12][13] (Nikolaevich), a servant, eighty-seven years old

YÁSHA, a young servant[14]

A PASSERBY[15].

THE STATIONMASTER

A POSTAL CLERK

GUESTS

SERVANTS

The action takes place on L. A. Ranevskaya's estate.[16]
[17]

ACT ONE

A room still called[18] the children's room.[19] One of the doors leads to Anya's room. Daybreak, the sun will rise soon. It is already May, the cherry trees are in bloom, but it is chilly. There is a morning frost in the orchard. The windows in the room are closed.

Enter Dunyasha with a candle and Lopakhin with a book in his hand.[20] [21] [22]

LOPAKHIN:

> God be praised[23], the train's come in. What time is it?[24]

DUNYASHA:

> Almost two.[25] [26]*(Blows out the candle)* It's light out already.

LOPAKHIN:

> How late was the train? Two hours at least. *(Yawns and stretches)* I'm a fine one. A fool . . . that's me. I come all this way just to meet them at the station, and sleep right through it[27] . . . Fell right asleep sitting up in my chair.[28] What a shame . . . Why didn't you wake me up?[29]

DUNYASHA:

> I thought you'd gone.[30] *(Listens)* There, I think I hear them coming.

LOPAKHIN:

(Listening) No . . . They've got to pick up their luggage and one thing and another . . .

Pause.

Lyubov Andreyevna's been living abroad for five years. I don't know what she's like now . . . what to expect. She's a good person.³¹ Easy to get along with, unaffected.³² I remember when I was a boy, five or six,³³ my father, who is at rest . . . he kept a general store then, right here, in the village . . . punched me in the face with his fist . . . made my nose bleed . . . We had come here to the house together for some reason or another, and he was a little drunk³⁴. Lyubov Andreyevna, I can see her now before my eyes, as if it were yesterday, so young, so slender, she took me to the washstand, right here, in this very room, in the nursery. "Don't cry, little muzhik,³⁵" she said, "It will heal in time for your wedding day . . ."³⁶ ³⁷ ³⁸ ³⁹

Pause.

"Little muzhik". . . It's true . . . my father who is at rest, was a Muzhik, a real peasant, but look at me now: white waist coat and yellow high-button shoes.⁴⁰ Like a pig loose in a fine pastry shop . . .⁴¹ Oh, I'm rich, all right; I've got tons of money. But deep down you can see I'm still a peasant through and through . . .⁴² *(He leafs through the book.)* I tried to read this book but didn't understand a word of it ⁴³ ⁴⁴ . . . I read myself to sleep. (Pause.) ⁴⁵

DUNYASHA:

>The dogs have been up all night.[46] They know their masters are coming home.[47] [48]

LOPAKHIN:

>What's the matter, Dunyasha? Your . . .

DUNYASHA:

>My hands are shaking. I think I'm going to faint.

LOPAKHIN:

>You're a very delicate flower, aren't you? And dressing like the young lady. And the way you fix up your hair . . . just like a lady. It's not appropriate. You should know your place. You should remember who you are.[49] [50]

(Enter EPIKHODOV[51] carrying a bunch of flowers. He is wearing a short jacket and highly polished boots that squeak loudly.[52] On his way into the room he drops the flowers.[53])

EPIKHODOV:

>(picking up the flowers). Here, the gardener sent these. He told me you're to put them in the dining room.[54] (He hands DUNYASHA the flowers.)

LOPAKHIN:

>And bring me some kvass.[55] [56]

DUNYASHA.

> Yes, sir. *(She exits.)*

EPIKHODOV:

> It's three degrees below freezing out,[57][58] and the cherry trees are all flowering. I can't say I approve of our climate. *(sighs.)* I just cannot. It's not what you might call conducive to health. Now, Ermolay Alekseyevich, if you will allow me to communicate to you[59]: I bought these boots the day before yesterday, and . . . let me beg to assure you . . . they squeak so badly that it's unbearable. What can I grease them with for the squeak?

LOPAKHIN:

> Leave me alone. I'm sick of you.[60]

EPIKHODOV:

> Every day some new misfortune happens to me. And I don't complain, I've grown accustomed to it, I even smile right through it. *(Exits)*

Enter Dunyasha, serves Lopakhin his kvass.

EPIKHODOV:

> I'm going now.

(He bumps into a chair, which falls over)

> There . . . *(As if triumphantly)* There, you see what I mean? It proves my point. What a victim

of circumstance, by the way, if you'll pardon my expression . . . It's simply extraordinary!

(Exits)

DUNYASHA:

I just have to tell you, Ermolay Alekseyevich, Epikhodov has proposed to me.

LOPAKHIN:

Has he though?[61]

DUNYASHA:

I really don't know what to do . . . He's nice enough, a quiet man but once he gets to talking you can't understand a word of it. What he says is sweet and full of feeling but you can't understand it. I even like him, a little and he's madly in love with me. But he's an unfortunate man. Everyday it's something else. We make fun of him; they call him "Twenty-Two Misfortunes."[62]

LOPAKHIN:

(Listens) There, I think I hear them coming...

DUNYASHA:

They're coming! What's the matter with me? I'm shivering.

LOPAKHIN:

Yes, it's really them. Let's go and meet them. I wonder if she'll recognize me?[63] It's been five years now.

DUNYASHA:

(Agitated) I'm going to faint . . . Oh my dear, I'm going to faint!

Two carriages are heard driving up to the house. Lopakhin and Dunyasha exit quickly. The stage is empty. Noise starts in the adjoining rooms. Fiers, who went to the station to meet Lyubov Andreyevna,[64] hurries across the stage, leaning on his walking stick; he is wearing old-fashioned footman's livery and a top hat[65] and mumbling to himself, but it is impossible to understand what he's saying. The noise backstage grows louder and louder. A voice says: "Let's go through here..."[66] Lyubov Andreyevna, Anya and Charlotta Ivanovna, with a little dog on a leash, enter; they are all dressed in traveling clothes. They are followed by Varya, wearing a long overcoat and head scarf[67] (babushka?), Gaev, Simeonov-Pishchik, Lopakhin, Dunyasha carrying a bundle and an umbrella, servants with the luggage. They all walk through the room.

ANYA[68]:

Let's go through here.[69] Do you remember what room this is, mama?

LYUBOV ANDREYEVNA:

(Joyfully, through tears[70] [71]*)* The "nursery"[72] [73]!

VARYA:

It's so cold. My hands are freezing. *(To Lyubov Andreyevna)* Your rooms, the white one and the violet one, are the same way they used to be when you left them, Mamochka.

LYUBOV ANDREYEVNA:

The nursery, my dear, precious room . . . I slept here when I was a little girl . . . *(Weeps)* And now I'm like a little girl again[74] . . . *(She kisses her brother, then Varya, then her brother again)* And Varya's the same as she always was[75], just like a nun.[76] [77] And I recognized Dunyasha [78]. . . *(She kisses Dunyasha)*

GAEV:

The train was two hours late. What do you think of that for punctuality? Everything's mismanaged.

CHARLOTTA:

(To Pishchik) My dog eats nuts.[79] [80]

PISHCHIK[81]:

(Surprised) That so?

Exit all but Anya and Dunyasha

DUNYASHA:

We've waited so long to see you again [82]...
(She takes Anya's coat and hat)

ANYA:

Four nights on the train and I didn't sleep at all
... I'm so frozen now.

DUNYASHA:

You left during Lent, there was still snow on
the ground, too, and frost, but now? Oh, Anya,
sweet Anya! *(Laughs, kisses her)* We've waited
so long to see you again, my joy, my angel ... I
can't wait to tell you; I'm so excited ...

ANYA:

(entirely without enthusiam) Always something.
What is it now?[83]

DUNYASHA:

Epikhodov, you know who I mean, the estate
clerk. He proposed to me just after Holy
Week.[84]

ANYA:

That's all you ever talk about ... *(Straightens
her hair)* I lost all my hairpins ... *(She is so
tired she is unable to keep her balance as she
walks.)*

DUNYASHA:

I just don't know what to think. He loves me,
he loves me so very much.

ANYA:

> *(Looks through the door to her own room, tenderly)* My room, my windows, as if I've never been away. I'm home! Tomorrow morning I'll get up and run out into the orchard . . . Oh, if only I could sleep! I didn't sleep the whole trip, I was too exhausted . . . too worried to sleep.

DUNYASHA:

> Pyotr Sergeyevich got here three days ago.

ANYA:

> *(Joyfully)* Petya!

DUNYASHA:

> He's sleeping in the bathhouse.[85] That's where he wanted to stay. He didn't want to cause any trouble. I'm afraid to be an imposition, he said. *(Looking at her pocket watch[86])* I wanted to wake him up, but Varvara Mikhailovna told me not to. "No, let him sleep", that's what she told me.

Varya enters with a bunch of keys hanging from her belt. [87]

VARYA:

> Dunyasha, coffee, quick . . . Mamochka's asking for coffee.[88]

DUNYASHA:

> This very minute. *(Exits)*

VARYA:

> God be praised, you've come back. You're home again. *(Caressingly)* My darling's come home! My beautiful one has come back home!

ANYA:

> I've had a terrible time of it.

VARYA:

> I can just imagine!

ANYA:

> We left during Holy Week. It was cold then. Charlotta wouldn't shut up the whole trip, and did magic tricks[89] with her cards. Why on earth did you saddle me with Charlotta . . .

VARYA:

> You couldn't have gone alone, darling. Not at seventeen!

ANYA:

> Anyway, we got to Paris. It was cold, snowing. My French is dreadful. Mama lived on the fifth [sixth] floor [90], I walk all the way up, there are some French people there, ladies, an ancient Catholic priest,[91] with a book. Tobacco smoke everywhere, no place to sit, depressing[92] and uncomfortable. I suddenly felt so sorry for Mama, so very sorry, I took her head in my arms, and held it, pressed it to me, and

couldn't let go. Mama just kept hugging me and crying . . .

VARYA

(Through tears) I don't want to hear, don't . . . stop . . . enough.

ANYA:

She had already sold her dacha near Menton,[93] she had nothing left, nothing . . . and I had nothing, not a kopeck, we barely made it home. And Mama doesn't understand! Whenever we ate at a station restaurant, she orders the most expensive things and tips each waiter a whole ruble. Charlotta does the same. And Yasha orders a full serving. It's just awful. Mama has this lackey[94], Yasha, we've brought him with us.[95] . .[96]

VARYA:

I saw the creature.

ANYA:

Well, so, how is everything going? Have you kept up with the payments on the mortgage?

VARYA:

What with?

ANYA:

My God, my God . . .

VARYA:

The estate goes up for sale in August[97] . . .

ANYA:

My God . . .

LOPAKHIN:

(Peeks through the door and moos like cow[98]) Mooo [99] *(Exits)*

VARYA:

(Through tears) Oh, I could give it to him . . . *(Shakes her fist)*

ANYA:

(Embraces Varya) Varya, has he proposed?[100] *(Varya shakes her head no)* But he does love you . . . Why don't the two of you have it out between you? What are you both waiting for?

VARYA:

I don't think it'll come to anything. He's much too busy . . . he's got no time[101] to bother with me . . . he pays no attention, doesn't seem to notice me. I'm through; God be with him . . . I can't stand to even look at him . . . Everybody talks about our wedding, everybody congratulates me, and he looks like he's going to propose, but in fact there's nothing, it's all like a dream . . . [Sometimes I'm scared. I don't know what to do with myself . . .][102] *(In a different tone)* Your brooch looks like a bumblebee.

ANYA:

(Sadly) Mama bought it for me.[103] *(Goes to her room, talks gaily, childishly)* I flew over Paris in a hot-air balloon.[104]

VARYA:

My darling's come home! My beautiful angel's come home!

Dunyasha has now returned with the coffee pot and is preparing coffee.

(Varya is standing by the door to Anya's room)

All day long I do my chores, working around the house[105], and dream and dream. If only we could marry you off to a rich man I'd be at rest then[106], and I'd take myself to a hermitage, then to Kiev . . . to Moscow, and go from holy place to holy place . . . on and on. What bliss![107]

ANYA:

The birds are singing in the orchard. What time is it?

VARYA:

It's after two. It's time to go to sleep, my darling. *(Going into Anya's room)* What bliss!

Enter Yasha with a lap blanket and a traveling bag.

YASHA:

(Walks across the stage) May I pass through here ?

DUNYASHA:

I would never have recognized you, Yasha. You've changed so much being abroad . . .

YASHA:

Hm . . . And who might you be?

DUNYASHA:

I was no bigger than so high when you left . . . (Shows height from the floor) Dunyasha, Fyodor Kozoedov's daughter. Don't you remember me?

YASHA:

Hm . . . A lovely little cucumber[108]. (Looks around then puts his arms around her; she cries out and drops a saucer. Yasha quickly exits)

VARYA:

(In the doorway, displeased) What's going on in here?

DUNYASHA:

(Through tears) I broke a saucer[109] . . .

VARYA:

A fortunate sign.

ANYA:

(Coming out of her room) Someone should warn Mama that Petya's here . . .

VARYA:

I gave orders not to wake him up.

ANYA:

(Pensively) It's been six years now. First father died, then a month later my brother Grisha[110] drowned in the river . . . only seven years old . . . my beautiful brother. Mama couldn't bear it, she ran away, abandoned everything, left without once looking back . . . (Shudders) I understand her so well, if only she knew.

Pause.

Since Petya Trofimov was Grisha's tutor . . . he might bring back memories . . .

Enter Fiers wearing a jacket and white waistcoat.

FIERS:

(Approaches the coffee pot, preoccupied)

Madam will have her coffee here... (Puts on white gloves) Is the coffee ready? (Sternly, to Dunyasha) You there! Where's the cream?

DUNYASHA:

Oh, my God... (Exits quickly)

FIERS:

(Fussing over the coffee pot) Eh, you numbskull . . .[111] *(Mutters to himself)* So, they're home from Paris are they . . . There was a time the master went to Paris . . . by post-chaise[112] . . . *(Laughs)*

VARYA:

What is it, Fiers?

FIERS:

How may I be of service? *(Joyfully)* My lady has come home! How I've waited but never thought I'd live to see the day. Now I can die . . . *(Weeps from joy)*

~~VARYA: You foolish man. You're so silly~~ [113]

Lyubov Andreyevna, Gaev, Lopakhin and Simeonov-Pishchik enter. Simeonov-Pishchik is wearing a long waisted jacket of fine broadcloth and full broad trousers[114]. Gaev, as he enters, makes the motions of playing billiards.[115]

LYUBOV ANDREYEVNA:

How does it go? Wait I remember . . . Yellow into the corner! Double into the side!

GAEV:

Cut shot into the corner![116] Once upon a time we both slept in this very room, sister, and now I'm already fifty-one, strange though it may seem . . .

LOPAKHIN:

Yes, time goes by.

GAEV:

Whom? (What's that?) [117] [118]

LOPAKHIN:

I said, time goes by. [119]

GAEV:

The place smells of patchouli. [120]

ANYA:

I'm going to sleep. Good night, Mama. *(Kisses LYUBOV ANDREYEVNA)*

LYUBOV ANDREYEVNA:

Blindingly beauteous child of mine. [121] *(Kisses her hands)* Are you glad you're home? I don't think I shall ever descend to the earth.

ANYA:

Good night, Uncle.

GAEV:

(Kisses her face and hands) May God be with you. You look just like your mother! *(To his sister)* You looked just like her when you were that young, Lyuba.

Anya gives her hand to Lopakhin and Pishchik, exits, closing the door behind her. [122]

LYUBOV ANDREYEVNA:

She's exhausted.[123]

PISHCHIK:

It must have been a long trip.

VARYA:

(To Lopakhin and Pishchik) Well, gentlemen? It's nearly three, time for you to go.

LYUBOV ANDREYEVNA:

(Laughs) You're still the same, Varya.[124] *(Pulls her to herself and kisses her)* I'll finish my coffee, then we'll all go together.[125] [126]

(Fiers puts a little cushion under her feet.) Thank you, dearest. I've gotten used to coffee.[127] I drink it day and night. Thank you, my dear old man[128]. *(She kisses Fiers)*

VARYA:

I've got to see that they've brought all the luggage in . . . *(Exits)*

LYUBOV ANDREYEVNA:

Is it really me sitting right here? *(Laughs)* I want to jump up and wave my arms around. *(Covers her face with her hands)* What if I'm only dreaming this! Let God be my witness, I love my motherland, love it tenderly but I couldn't stand to look out at it from the train, I was crying too much. *(Through tears)* But I must have my coffee,[129] first. Thank you, Fiers, thank you, my dear old man. I'm so glad you're still alive.[130]

FIERS:

Two days ago.

GAEV:

He's hard of hearing.[131]

LOPAKHIN:

I've got to go. I've got to catch the five o'clock train to Kharkov. This is really disappointing![132] I wanted to have a good look at you, a chance to talk a little . . . You're as lovely as ever.

PISHCHIK:

Even got prettier . . . Dressed up Parisian-style . . . "I've lost my cart with all four wheels."[133] [134]

LOPAKHIN:

Your brother, Leonid Andreevich here, goes around calling me a Kulak, a tightfisted peasant[135], but I don't care, it's all the same[136] to me.

Let him talk. All I want is for you to believe me like you did before, that your wonderful, gentle eyes look at me and trust me like they did before. Merciful God! My father was your grandfather's serf, and your father's, but you,

you personally, once did so much for me[137] that you've made me forget all that painful past and love you like one of my own flesh and blood [138]... more than one of my own flesh and blood. [139]

LYUBOV ANDREYEVNA:

I can't sit still, I just can't, it's impossible... *(Jumps up and paces about in great excitement)* This happiness is too much for me... Go ahead and laugh at me, I know I'm so silly... My dear little bookcase... *(Kisses the bookcase)* My little table.[140]

GAEV:

Nyanya[141] died while you were away?

LYUBOV ANDREYEVNA:

(Sits down and drinks her coffee) Yes, God rest her soul. They told me in a letter.[142]

GAEV:

And Anastasy is dead. Cross-eyed Petrushka left me and now is working in town at the police chief's. *(Takes a box of fruit drop candies from his pocket, puts one into his mouth and sucks on it[143])*

PISHCHIK:

My dear daughter, Dashenka... sends you her regards...[144]

LOPAKHIN:

I would like to say something very nice and it will cheer you up.[145] *(Looks at his watch)* I've got to go now, there's no time[146] to talk . . .[147] well, so, here it is in a word or two. As you already know, your cherry orchard is going to be sold off to pay your debts, the auction is fixed for August 22nd, but don't you worry, my dear lady, you can sleep peacefully,[148] there's a way out of this . . . Here's my plan. Please, attention please! Your estate is only twenty versts [fifteen miles] from town, the railroad passes very close by, and if the cherry orchard and the land by the river is subdivided into building lots and leased out for dachas, you'll have an income of at least twenty-five thousand a year.[149]

GAEV:

Pardon me, but that's utter nonsense!

LYUBOV ANDREYEVNA:

I don't quite understand what you're saying, Ermolai Alexyevich.

LOPAKHIN:

You will charge the summer people, at the very least, a yearly rent of twenty-five rubles for every desyatina[150] [two and a half acres] of land, and if you advertise right now, I'll bet anything you like that by autumn you won't have a single free lot left, it'll all be snapped right up. In short, I congratulate you, you're saved. The orchard is beautifully situated, the river's deep.[151] Though, of course, there'll have to be some clearing away, some cleaning up . . . for instance, you'll have to tear down the old buildings, like this house, which no longer has any use,[152] and cut down[153] the cherry orchard.

LYUBOV ANDREYEVNA:

Cut it down? My dear, forgive me, but you don't understand anything at all. If there's one thing in the whole province[154] that's interesting, even remarkable, it can only be our cherry orchard.[155]

LOPAKHIN:

The only remarkable thing about this orchard is that it's very big. It produces cherries only every other year, and even then you don't know what to do with them, nobody buys them.

GAEV:

I will have you know . . . this orchard is even mentioned in the *Encyclopedia*.[156]

LOPAKHIN:

(Glancing at his watch) Unless we can come up with a solid plan, both the cherry orchard and the entire estate will be sold at auction on August 22nd. Make up your minds! There's no other way out, I swear to you. None. None.

FIERS:

In the olden days, forty or fifty years ago, they'd dry the cherries, soak them, marinate them... made them into juice, and preserves, and we used to . . .

GAEV:

Be quiet, Fiers.[157]

FIERS:

And we used to send wagonloads of dried cherries off to Moscow and Kharkov. And made money at it. And those dried cherries were soft, juicy, sweet, fragrant . . . They knew a way to do it . . .

LYUBOV ANDREYEVNA:

So what happened? Where is that way now?

FIERS:

Everything forgotten.[158] Nobody remembers.

PISHCHIK:

(To Lyubov Andreyevna) How are things in Paris? Eh? Did you eat any frogs?

LYUBOV ANDREYEVNA:

No, I ate crocodiles.[159]

PISHCHIK:

Just imagine that . . .

LOPAKHIN:

Up until now, there were just landlords and peasants here in the country, but now we have these dacha people[160]. All the towns, even the smallest ones, are surrounded by dachas now. And it's certain to happen that in ten or twenty years the dacha people will multiply and begin to work. Today they only drink tea on their verandas, but it might just happen that they start gardening and farming on their two and a half acres, and then your cherry orchard will become happy, rich and luxurious.

GAEV:

(Indignantly, offended) What utter nonsense!

Varya and Yasha enter.

VARYA:

Two telegrams came for you, Mamochka. *(Chooses a key and with a ringing[161] noise opens the old bookcase)*

Here they are.

LYUBOV ANDREYEVNA:

From Paris. *(Tears up the telegrams[162] without reading them)* I'm done with Paris . . .

GAEV:

Do you have any idea how old this bookcase is, Lyuba?[163] Last week I pulled out the lower drawer[164], and saw some numbers burnt into it. This bookcase was made exactly one hundred years ago. How about that? Eh? We could celebrate its centenary. It's an inanimate object, but still, you have to admit, it's a fine bookcase.

PISHCHIK:

(Surprised) A hundred years . . . Can you imagine that . . .?

GAEV:

Yes . . . That's quite something . . . *(Touches the bookcase)* Dear, revered bookcase! I salute your existence, which for more than a hundred years now has been dedicated to the bright ideals of justice and virtue. Your silent summons to fruitful work[165] has never wavered in those hundred years, sustaining courage in the generations of our family line, *(through tears)* faith in a better future, and cultivating in us the ideals of the good and of social self-awareness.[166] [167]

Pause.

LOPAKHIN:

Aye, well . . .

LYUBOV ANDREYEVNA:

You're the same as ever[168], Lyonya.

GAEV:

(Slightly embarrassed) Carom into the right corner! Cut shot into the side!

LOPAKHIN:

(Glancing at his watch)

    Well, time for me to go.

YASHA:

    (Offering Lyubov Andreyevna medicine) Perhaps it would be a good time to take your pills[169] . . .

PISCHIK:

    You shouldn't take any medicines, my darling . . . It does no good; no harm either . . . Let me have them . . . my dear. *(Takes the pills, places all of them into the palm of his hand, blows on them, puts them in his mouth, and washes them down with some kvass)* There![170]

LYUBOV ANDREYEVNA:

    (Frightened) You've gone crazy!

PISCHIK:

    I swallowed all the pills.

LOPAKHIN:

    What a glutton! *(All laugh.)*

FIERS:

    His excellency[171] came to visit us during Holy Week and ate half a bucket of our pickled cucumbers . . . *(Mumbles)*

LYUBOV ANDREYEVNA:

What did he say?

VARYA:

He's been mumbling for three years. We're used to it.

YASHA:

Second childhood.

Charlotta Ivanovna, dressed in white, very thin and tightly corseted, with a lorgnette dangling at her waist,[172] walks across the stage.[173]

LOPAKHIN:

Excuse me, Charlotta Ivanovna, I haven't had the opportunity to welcome you back. *(Tries to kiss her hand)*

CHARLOTTA:

(Taking her hand away)

If I let you kiss my hand, then you'll be after my elbow, then my shoulder . . . [174]

LOPAKHIN:

I'm out of luck today. *(All laugh.)* Show us your magic, Charlotta Ivanovna! [175]

LYUBOV ANDREYEVNA:

Charlotta, show us your magic[176]

CHARLOTTA:

No I won't. I wish to sleep. *(Goes out)*

LOPAKHIN:

We'll see each other in three weeks. *(Kisses Lyubov Andreyevna's hand)* Good-bye for now. It's time for me to go. *(To Gaev)* I'll be suing you.[177] *(Exchanges kisses on the cheeks with Pischik)*[178] I'll be suing you. *(Gives his hand to Varya, then to Fiers and to Yasha)*[179] I don't want to go. *(To Lyubov Andreyevna)* Should you make up your mind on the dachas, let me know, and I'll get you a loan of fifty thousand or so. Think it over, seriously.

VARYA:

(Crossly) Go if you're going!

LOPAKHIN:

I'm going, I'm going . . . *(Goes out)*

GAEV:

What a boor[180]. Actually, pardon me . . . Her *beau*[181]; Varya's going to marry him.

VARYA:

Uncle, you talk too much . . . about nothing.

LYUBOV ANDREYEVNA:

It's all the same[182], Varya? I'll be very glad for you. He's a good man.[183] [184]

PISCHIK:

He is, to tell the truth . . . a most worthy man . . . And my Dashenka . . . says the same thing . . . She says many different things.[185] *(Snores, but wakes up immediately)*[186] But still, my esteemed madam, lend me . . . two hundred and forty rubles . . . to pay off the interest on my mortgage tomorrow . . .[187]

VARYA:

(Frightened) No, we don't have it! We don't have it.

LYUBOV ANDREYEVNA:

As a matter of fact, I've got nothing, nothing at all.

PISCHIK:

You'll find some. *(Laughs)* I never lose hope. It happens like this: just when I thought all was lost and I was ruined, they built a railroad across my land . . . and they paid me for it. Something else will come up, if not today, then tomorrow. Maybe Dashenka will win two hundred thousand . . . she's got a lottery ticket.

LYUBOV ANDREYEVNA:

We've finished our coffee . . . now we can go to rest.

FIERS:

(Brushing off Gaev's suit and speaking in a scolding tone) You've put on the wrong trousers again. What am I to do with you!

VARYA:

(Quietly) Anya's asleep. *(Quietly opens the window)* The sun's up already; it's not cold. Look, Mamochka, what wonderful trees! And, my goodness, the air! The starlings[188] are singing!

GAEV:

(Opens the other window) The orchard's all white. You remember, don't you, Lyuba? This long avenue of trees goes straight all the way, straight like a stretched-out belt; it gleams on moonlit nights. Do you remember? You haven't forgotten?

LYUBOV ANDREYEVNA:

(Looks at the orchard through the window) Oh, my childhood, my innocence! I used to sleep in this nursery, looked out from these windows into the orchard, awakened happy every morning, and it was just the same back then; nothing has changed. *(Laughs with joy)* All, all white! Oh, my orchard! After a dark and rainy fall and a cold winter, you're young again, full of joy, and the heavenly angels haven't forsaken you [189]. . . If only I could lift the heavy stone off my chest and off my shoulders[190], if only I could forget my past![191]

GAEV:

> Yes, and they'll sell off the orchard to pay off our debts,[192] as strange as that may seem . . .

LYUBOV ANDREYEVNA:

> Look, our dead Mama is walking in the orchard . . . in a white dress! *(Laughs with joy)* There, it's her.

GAEV:

> Where?[193]

VARYA:

> God be with you, Mamochka.

LYUBOV ANDREYEVNA:

> There's no one there, I imagined it. On the right, as the path leads to the summer-house, there's a small white tree bending down; it looks like a woman . . .

Enter Trofimov wearing glasses and a shabby student uniform.[194] [195]

LYUBOV ANDREYEVNA:

> What a marvelous orchard! This mass of white flowers, the azure sky . . .

TROFIMOV:

> Lyubov Andreyevna! *(She looks round at him.)* I only wanted to bow to you, to pay my respects, and then I'll go away. *(Kisses her hand heartily)*

I was told to wait until morning, but I didn't have the patience . . . *(Lyubov Andreyevna looks at him, perplexed.)* [196]

VARYA:

(Through tears) This is Petya Trofimov . . .

TROFIMOV:

Petya Trofimov, the former tutor to your Grisha . . . Have I changed so much?

Lyubov Andreyevna embraces him and sobs softly.

GAEV:

(Embarrassed) That's enough, enough, Lyuba.

VARYA:

(Crying) Petya, I told you to wait until tomorrow.

LYUBOV ANDREYEVNA:

My Grisha . . . my boy . . . Grisha . . . my son . . .

VARYA:

There's nothing we can do about it, Mamochka. It's the will of God. [197]

TROFIMOV:

(Softly, through tears) Don't, please don't . . .

LYUBOV ANDREYEVNA:

> *(Crying softly)* My boy died, he drowned . . . For what? For what, tell me that, my friend? *(More quietly)* Anya is asleep in there and I'm speaking so loud . . . making such a racket . . . What is the matter with you, Petya? Why have you become so ugly? Why have you grown so old?[198] [199]

TROFIMOV:

> In the train an old peasant woman called me a "Shabby Gentleman".[200]

LYUBOV ANDREYEVNA:

> You were just a boy then, a handsome student, and now your hair is thin and these glasses. Are you still a student, really? *(Goes to the door)*

TROFIMOV:

> I'll probably always be a student. [201]

LYUBOV ANDREYEVNA:

> *(Kisses her brother, then Varya)* Well, go to sleep . . . You, too, have grown old, Leonid.

PISCHIK:

> *(Follows her)* So, time for bed . . . Oh, my gout! I'll stay over for the night . . . If only, perhaps Lyubov Andreyevna, dear, I could get . . . two hundred- and forty-rubles tomorrow morning . . .

GAEV:

    Tired old tune.

PISCHIK:

    Two hundred and forty rubles . . . to pay the interest on my mortgage.

LYUBOV ANDREYEVNA:

    I don't have any money, my dear.

PISCHIK:

    I'll pay it back, dear . . . A trifling sum . . .

LYUBOV ANDREYEVNA:

    Well, all right, what can I do, Leonid will give it to you . . . Give it to him, Leonid

GAEV:

    I'll give it to him all right![202] [*"pow" unsaid, with a swing*]

LYUBOV ANDREYEVNA:

    What else can we do? Give it to him. He needs it . . . He'll pay it back.

Lyubov Andreyevna, Trofimov, Pischik, and Fiers exit. Gaev, Varya, and Yasha remain on stage.

GAEV:

    My sister hasn't lost her habit of throwing money away. *(To Yasha so no one else hears)*

Get out of here, young man, you smell from the ladies[203].

YASHA:

(Grinning): You're still the same. Just like you always were, Leonid Andreyevich.

GAEV:

What was that? *(To Varya)* What did he just say?

VARYA:

(To Yasha) Your mother's come from the country; she's been sitting in the servants' quarters since yesterday, she's come to see you[204]...

YASHA:

God should help the woman?

VARYA:

You should be ashamed of yourself.

YASHA:

What's so important! Couldn't she come tomorrow? *(Goes out)*

VARYA:

Mamochka's the same as she always was. She hasn't changed. If she had her way she'd give everything away.

GAEV:

> Yes . . . *(pause)* When many different cures are prescribed to treat a particular sickness, it means that the sickness is incurable. I think and think, wrack my brains and I come up with all sorts of remedies which means that I have none. It would be nice to inherit a fortune from somebody. It would be nice to marry off our Anya to a rich man; it would be nice to go to Yaroslavl[205] and try our fortune with our aunt the Countess. After all, our aunt is very, very rich.

VARYA:

> *(Weeps)*: If God would only help us.

GAEV:

> Stop crying[206]. Our aunt's very rich, but she doesn't like us. In the first place, my sister married a lawyer, not a nobleman[207] . . .

(Anya appears in the doorway)

> Not a nobleman, you understand, and it's not as if she conducts herself virtuously. She's fine and kind and charming, and I love her very much, but no matter what extenuating circumstances you allow for, you have to face up to the fact that she's a slut[208], she exudes it, you can feel it in her slightest movement.[209]

VARYA:

> *(Whispers)* Anya's standing in the doorway.[210]

GAEV:

What did you say? *(pause)* That's odd; I just got something in my right eye . . . I can't see well out of it. And Thursday, when I was at the district court . . .

Enter Anya.

VARYA:

Anya, why aren't you sleeping?

ANYA:

I can't fall asleep. I just can't.

GAEV:

My little sweetheart! *(Kisses Anya's face and hands)* My child . . . *(Through tears)* You're not my niece, you're my angel, you're everything to me . . . Believe me, you must believe me . . .

ANYA:

I believe you, Uncle. We all love you and respect you . . . but, Uncle dear, you need to keep quiet, just keep quiet. What were you saying just now about my Mama, about your own sister? Why did you say that?

GAEV:

Yes, yes . . . *(Covers his face with her hand)* Yes, really, it's an awful thing to say. Oh, my God, oh, my God, save me! And today I made a speech to a bookcase . . . So stupid! And it's only after I'd finished that I understood how really stupid it was.

VARYA:

Dear Uncle, yes, you really ought to keep quiet. Just keep quiet, just be.

ANYA:

You'd feel better about yourself if only you'd keep quiet.

GAEV:

I'll keep quiet. *(Kisses their hands)* I'll keep quiet. But let's talk about this business. On Thursday I was at the district court, and I met a group of friends there, and we started talking about this and that and one thing and another, and I think it might be possible to secure a loan against the promissory note to pay off the interest to the bank.

VARYA:

If only God would help us!

GAEV:

I'll go there Tuesday to the court and I'll bring it up again. *(To Varya)* Stop crying. *(To Anya)* Your mother will talk to Lopakhin, he won't refuse her[211], of course . . . And you, as soon as you are all rested up, you'll go to Yaroslavl to visit the countess, your great aunt.[212] So you see, we'll attack it from all three fronts and it's a done deal. We'll pay off the interest, I'm sure of it . . . *(Puts a fruit drop candy in his mouth)* I swear to you, on my word of honor, the estate will not be sold! (Excited) I swear by my happiness! Here's my hand on it. You may call me a dishonorable worthless piece of trash[213] if I permit that auction to take place! I swear to you with the whole of my being!

ANYA:

(Calm again and in a good mood)

You are so nice and so very clever! *(Embraces her uncle)* Now I feel at rest! I'm much more at rest now. I'm happy!

Enter Fiers.

FIERS:

(Reproachfully) Leonid Andreyevich, have you no fear of God? When are you going to bed?

GAEV:

Right away, right away. You can go, Fiers. All right, I'll get undressed by myself this time. Well, children, "nighty night" . . . I'll give you all the details tomorrow, but now go to bed. *(Kisses Anya and Varya)* I'm a man of the eighties[214] . . . You don't say much good about those days but, still, I can tell you I suffered plenty for my convictions. It's not for nothing the peasant loves me so much[215], I can assure you of that. You've got to know your peasant! You've got to know how . . .

ANYA:

You're at it again, Uncle!

VARYA:

Please be quiet, dear Uncle!

FIERS:

(Angrily) Leonid Andreyich!216

GAEV:

Coming, coming . . . Go to bed now. Off the two sides and into the center! I'll sink the white one . . .

(Exists. Fiers, hobbling along, follows after him)

ANYA:

I'm so much more at rest now. I don't want to go to Yaroslavl, I don't like my great aunt but still, I'm at rest now. Thanks to you, Uncle. (Sits down)

VARYA:

You must go to sleep. I'm going. We had an unpleasant incident here while you were gone. In the old servants' hall as you know, where only the old servants live, Yefimusha, Polya, Evstigney, and Karp, too. They started letting some crooks and beggars in for the night there—and I didn't say anything about it. But then I heard they were spreading rumors that I said they must be fed nothing but peas porridge. Out of stinginess, if you please . . . And it was all Evstigney's doing . . . Very well, I thought, if that's how things are going to be, I was going to fix him good. So I send for Evstigney . . . *(Yawns)* He comes in . . . "How could you say such things" I say to him, "Evstigney . . . you are an idiot" . . . *(Looking at Anya)* Anya, dear! *(pause)* She's asleep! . . . *(Takes Anya's arm)* Let's go beddy-bye . . . Come . . . *(Leads her along)* My darling's asleep! Come . . .

They go into Anya's room. In the distance, far beyond the orchard, a shepherd plays[217] his reed pipe.[218] Trofimov crosses the stage and stops upon seeing Varya and Anya.

VARYA:

> Shh . . . She's asleep . . . asleep . . . Let's go, my darling.

ANYA:

> *(Softly, half-asleep)* I'm so tired . . . I keep hearing bells . . . Dear Uncle . . . Mama and Uncle . . .

VARYA:

> Let's go, my dear, let's go[219] . . . *(Goes into Anya's room)*

TROFIMOV *(Tenderly)*: My sunshine! My springtime![220]

Curtain

ACT TWO[221]

An open field. An old, long-ago abandoned, chapel[222] leaning over to one side; next to it a well and some large stones, which seem to have been tombstones[223] in the past[224], and an old bench. A road to Gaev's manor house[225] can be seen. On one side poplars rise ominously casting shadows . . . and then the beginning of the cherry orchard. A row of telegraph poles in the distance, and on the horizon, way in the distance—one can just make out a big town, visible only on very clear sunny days. The sun is about to set.[226]

Charlotta, Yasha, and Dunyasha are sitting on the bench; Epikhodov stands nearby strumming a sad song on a guitar; they are all sitting, lost in thought. Charlotta wears a man's old peaked cap with a visor; she has taken a rifle[227] [228]off her shoulder and is adjusting the buckle on the strap.

CHARLOTTA:

(Deep in thought) I don't have real identity papers[229]; I don't know how old I am; but I feel like a young girl.[230] When I was a young girl, my Papa and Mama went around to country fairs[231] putting on shows, very good ones, and I

would perform the salto mortale[232] and all sorts of tricks. And when Papa and Mama died, a German gentlewoman took me home with her, adopted me[233] and had me educated. I liked it. I grew up and became a governess. But where I came from and who I am, I have no clue[234] . . . Who my parents were, very likely they weren't even married . . . I don't know.[235] *(Takes a cucumber out of her pocket and eats it)*[236] I don't know anything. *(pause)* I feel so much like talking to someone, but there is no one . . . I don't have anyone.[237] [238]

EPIKHODOV:

(Strumming the guitar and singing) "Who am I in this hectic world, What are friends or foes to me . . ."[239] [240]How nice it is to play the mandolin!

DUNYASHA:

That's a guitar, not a mandolin. *(Looks in a pocket mirror and powders her face.)*

EPIKHODOV:

For a man who's lovesick, it's a mandolin. *(Sings)* "If only our hearts could burn with requited love from thee . . ." *Yasha sings along, too.*

CHARLOTTA:

It's awful the way these people break into song without the least encouragement.²⁴¹ . . . Ugh! Like hyenas.

DUNYASHA:

(To Yasha) You are so lucky to have been abroad.

YASHA:

Yes, of course. I cannot disagree with you on that account. *(Yawns and lights a cigar)*

EPIKHODOV:

That's comprehensible. Abroad everything has already reached its completion.

YASHA:

That goes without saying.

EPIKHODOV:

I'm intelligent, a cultivated, evolved person, I've read different remarkable books, but I cannot figure out the direction I wish to take, whether I should live or whether I should shoot myself; but in any event, if the inclination moves me, I always go armed with a revolver. Here it is . . . *(Shows a revolver)*²⁴²

CHARLOTTA:

I'm done. I've had enough. I'll go now. *(Slings the rifle over her shoulder)* You, Epikhodov, are a very intelligent man and a very frightening man.243 Women must be crazy for you. Brrr! *(goes)* These intellectuals are such idiots, there's nobody to talk to, nobody . . . I'm always alone, and I've nobody at all . . . and who I am or why I am, I don't have a clue . . . *(Exits slowly)*

EPIKHODOV:

Speaking on my own behalf, not touching upon other subjects, I must express myself about myself, by the way, fate treats me pitilessly, like a storm tosses a small ship. If, let us say, I'm mistaken, then why should I wake up this morning, as an example, to find a gigantic spider on my chest . . . This big. *(Uses both hands to show the size)* And also, I take some kvass to quench my thirst, and there on the bottom of the glass there's something disgusting, like a cockroach. *(pause)* Have you read Buckle?244 245*(pause)* I would like to trouble you, Avdotiya Fedorovna, with a couple of words.

DUNYASHA:

You may speak.

EPIKHODOV:

Preferably in private . . . *(Sighs)*

DUNYASHA:

(*Embarrassed*) All right, then . . . only first bring me my cape²⁴⁶ . . . It's near the bookcase . . . it's a bit damp out here . . .

EPIKHODOV:

All right, madam . . . I'll go get it . . . Now I know what to do with my revolver . . . *(Takes the guitar and walks off strumming it)*

YASHA:

Twenty-two Misfortunes! A stupid man, confidentially between you and me. *(Yawns)*

DUNYASHA:

God, I hope he doesn't shoot himself. *(pause)* I've become so nervous, so anxious; I'm upset all the time. I was still a little girl when they brought me to live with the masters, in the big house²⁴⁷, and I'm disconnected now from the common life, and my hands are so white and soft like a lady's. I'm so sensitive and delicate, overbred; everything frightens me . . . I'm so frightened. And, Yasha, if you lead me on and throw me over, I don't know what it would do to my nerves.

YASHA:

(Kisses her) A juicy cucumber! Of course, every girl must know her place;²⁴⁸ there's nothing I dislike more than a girl who behaves improperly.

DUNYASHA:

I'm madly in love with you; you're so educated, and can talk about anything. *(pause)*

YASHA:

(Yawns) Yes, madam . . . In my opinion if a girl says she loves you, then she's already without morals. *(pause)* It's nice to smoke a cigar in the fresh open air . . . (Listens) Somebody's coming . . . It's the masters . . .

Dunyasha suddenly hugs him.

YASHA:

Go home, as if you went for a swim in the river. Take this path, otherwise you'll run into them and they might think that I was out with you. I couldn't stand them thinking that sort of thing.

DUNYASHA:

(Coughing softly) I've got a headache from that cigar . . . *(She leaves)*

Yasha remains, sitting alone near the chapel.

Enter Lyubov Andreyevna, Gaev, and Lopakhin.

LOPAKHIN:

You have to make up your mind once and for all, time is running out. To put it simply. Will you lease your land for dachas or not? Just say the word: yes or no? Answer me one word!

LYUBOV ANDREYEVNA:

Who's been smoking revolting cigars here . . .
(Sits down)

GAEV:

Since they built the train it's so convenient now. [249]*(Sits down)* We can go to town just to have lunch[250] . . . the yellow ball to the middle! I wouldn't mind going in and playing one game . . .

(She looks vexed)

LYUBOV ANDREYEVNA:

You will have time later.

LOPAKHIN:

Yes or no? *(pleadingly)* Give me your answer!

GAEV:

(Yawning) What was that?

LYUBOV ANDREYEVNA:

(Looks in her purse) I had a lot of money yesterday, but so little today. My poor Varya, feeds everybody milk soup to economize; in the kitchen, the old people eat only peas porridge, and I spend my money so stupidly. *(Drops the purse, scattering gold coins)* There, the coins gone all over the place[251] . . . *(annoyed)*

YASHA:

Allow me, I'll pick them up. *(picks up the coins)*[252]

LYUBOV ANDREYEVNA.

Thank you so much, Yasha. And why did we go to lunch to that place . . .? That nasty restaurant of yours with its trashy music, the tablecloths smell of soap . . . Why do we drink so much, Lionya? Why do we eat so much? Why do we talk so much? And at the restaurant today you talked too much, and all of it out of place. About the seventies . . . about the Decadents.[253] And who do you talk to? The waiters . . . about the Decadents!

LOPAKHIN:

Yes.

GAEV:

(Waves his hand) Obviously, I'm incorrigible . . . *(annoyed by Yasha)* Why . . . why are you always cavorting about in front of me?

YASHA:

(laughs) You break me up . . . The sound of your voice makes me laugh, I can't help it.

GAEV:

(to his sister) Either he goes or I go[254] . . .

LYUBOV ANDREYEVNA:

Go away, Yasha, run along . . .

YASHA:

> *(Gives Lyubov Andreyevna her purse.)* I'm leaving, right away. *(can barely keep from laughing)* Right this minute. *(Exits.)*

LOPAKHIN:

> The rich Derigánov is coming to buy your estate. He's coming himself, personally to the auction. That's what they tell me.

LYUBOV ANDREYEVNA:

> And where did you hear that?

LOPAKHIN:

> The whole town is talking about it.

GAEV:

> Our aunt in Yaroslavl promised to send money, but we don't know when or exactly how much . . .

LOPAKHIN:

> How much will she send? One hundred thousand? Two hundred thousand?

LYUBOV ANDREYEVNA:

> Well . . . Ten thousand . . . or fifteen, and for that we'll be thankful.

LOPAKHIN:

You'll forgive me, I've never met such scatterbrained frivolous people as the two of you, such unbusiness-like, peculiar people. I tell you in plain Russian that your estate will be sold, and you still don't get it.

LYUBOV ANDREYEVNA:

What can we do? What can we do? Tell us what to do?

LOPAKHIN:

I tell you every day. Every day I tell you the very same thing over and over . . . Both the cherry orchard and the land by the river must be rented for dachas. Do it now, today, the auction is on top of you! Can't you get that into your heads? Decide, say the word, once and for all, that there will be dachas, then you'll get all the money you need, and then you'll be saved.

LYUBOV ANDREYEVNA:

Dachas and dacha people . . . it's all so vulgar,[255] forgive me.

GAEV:

I completely agree with you.

LOPAKHIN:

I'll either cry, or scream, or I'll fall down in a fit. I can't stand it! You're driving me crazy! *(To Gaev.)* You're an old lady!

GAEV:

Who? What did you say?

LOPAKHIN:

I said you're an old lady! *(starts to leave)*

LYUBOV ANDREYEVNA:

(Frightened) No, please don't leave, my dear man. I beg of you. Maybe we'll think of something!

LOPAKHIN:

Think? Think? What is there to think about?

LYUBOV ANDREYEVNA:

Please don't go away. I beg you. It's more fun with you here [256]. . . *(pause)* I keep waiting for something to happen, as if the house is going to fall down around our ears.

GAEV:

(deep in thought) A bank shot to the corner . . . a crosier into the middle . . .

LYUBOV ANDREYEVNA:

I have sinned, so much . . .

LOPAKHIN:

Sinned? In what way have you sinned?[257]

GAEV:

(Puts a fruit drop candy in his mouth) They say that I've eaten up my fortune in fruit drop candy.[258] *(Laughs)*

LYUBOV ANDREYEVNA:

Oh, my sins . . . I've always squandered money uncontrollably, like a mad woman, and married a man who made no money at all, who made nothing but debts. My husband died from champagne . . . he drank heavily. . . and unfortunately, I fell in love with another man, chased off after him, and then it happened . . . my first punishment, a blow straight to the head . . . my little boy drowned, here, in this very river . . . and I went abroad, never meaning to return, never to see this river again . . . I shut my eyes and ran, I forgot myself, but my lover chased after me . . . pitiless, so coarse. I bought a dacha[259] near Mentone because that's where he got sick, and for three years I never rested day or night. This sick man wore me down, drained me and my heart dried up. And last year, when the villa was sold to pay off my debts, I went to Paris, and there he robbed me, then abandoned me, took up with another woman, I tried to poison myself . . . So silly, so humiliating . . . And suddenly I was drawn back to Russia, to my country, to my little girl . . . *(wipes away tears)* Lord, dear God, have mercy on me, forgive me my sins! Don't punish me anymore! *(takes a telegram out of her pocket)* I got this today from Paris . . . He begs for forgiveness, begs me to return . . .

(tears the telegram to pieces) I think I hear music? *(listens)*

GAEV:

That is our famous Jewish orchestra. You remember . . . four violins, a flute, and a double-bass.

LYUBOV ANDREYEVNA:

So, they still exist?²⁶⁰ We should hire them sometime, throw a little party²⁶¹.

LOPAKHIN:

(listens) I don't hear it²⁶² . . . *(sings softly)* "For the right price even Germans will make a Russian French." *(laughs)* I saw a play at the theatre last night, very funny. ²⁶³

LYUBOV ANDREYEVNA:

There was probably nothing funny in it at all. Instead of looking at plays,²⁶⁴ you should take a look at yourself, at how you act instead. How dull your lives are . . . What rubbish you talk . . . about nothing whatsoever.²⁶⁵

LOPAKHIN:

It's true. Let's face it, the lives we lead are idiotic, preposterous . . . *(pause)* My father was a peasant, an idiot; he understood nothing, taught me nothing, and only beat me with a stick when he was drunk. The point is that I am just as much of a loudmouth and I'm an idiot just like he was. I was taught nothing; my handwriting is awful. I'm ashamed to let people see it! I write like a pig.[266]

LYUBOV ANDREYEVNA:

You need to get married, my friend.

LOPAKHIN:

Yes . . . That's true enough.

LYUBOV ANDREYEVNA:

To our Varya? She's a very nice girl.

LOPAKHIN:

True

LYUBOV ANDREYEVNA:

She came to me from peasant stock[267], she can work the whole day long, but most importantly, she loves you. And you yourself have been fond of her for a long time now.[268]

LOPAKHIN:

And why not? I'm not against it. . . She's a nice girl.

(pause)

GAEV:

I've been offered a position at the bank. Six thousand a year . . . Have you heard?

LYUBOV ANDREYEVNA:

>You at a bank? Please . . . You stay where you are.

Enter Fiers bringing an overcoat

FIERS:

>*(To Gaev)* Pray sir, put it on, it's damp out here.

GAEV:

>*(Putting it on)* You're a nuisance, old man.

FIERS:

>Never mind that . . . You went off this morning without even letting me know you left. *(Looking carefully over Gaev)*

LYUBOV ANDREYEVNA:

>You've grown so old, Fiers!

FIERS:

>As you wish.

LOPAKHIN:

>She says: "You've grown so old".

FIERS:

>I've been alive a long time. They arranged a marriage for me before your father was even thought of[269] . . . *(Laughs)* I was the head valet when the freedom came.[270] Only I didn't agree

to be freed and I stayed with the masters . . . *(pause)* I remember everybody was happy when the freedom came, but why they were happy, they didn't know themselves.

LOPAKHIN:

Absolutely, thing were much better back then, the good life. And then there were those floggings.

FIERS:

(Not hearing) To be sure, those were the days. Peasants had their masters, and masters had their peasants. But now everyone's mixed up and you don't know what's what or who's who.[271]

GAEV:

Be quiet, Fiers. I'm going to town tomorrow. I've been promised an introduction to meet a certain general who could let us have a loan against a promissory note.

LOPAKHIN:

Nothing will come of it. And you won't pay off the mortgage interest, you can mark my word.

LYUBOV ANDREYEVNA:

He's delirious. The only general is the general in his head.

Enter Trofimov, Anya, and Varya

GAEV:

    Here come the children.

ANYA:

    And Mama's here.

LYUBOV ANDREYEVNA:

    (Tenderly) Come, come, my darlings . . . *(Embracing Anya and Varya)* If you both only knew how much I love you. Sit down next to me, right here.[272]   *(They sit down)*

LOPAKHIN:

    Our eternal student is always walking with the ladies.

TROFIMOV:

    It's none of your business.

LOPAKHIN:

    He'll be fifty soon and still a student.

TROFIMOV:

    I'm fed up with your idiotic jokes.

LOPAKHIN:

    Why are you getting so upset? Oddball.

TROFIMOV:

    Why can't you just leave me alone?[273]

LOPAKHIN:

> *(Laughs)* May I ask? What's your opinion of me?

TROFIMOV:

> My opinion of you, Ermolai Alexeyevich, is that you are a rich man, and you'll be a millionaire soon. You are necessary to balance nature . . . like a predator that eats up everything in its way . . .
>
> *All laugh*

VARYA:

> Can't you talk about the planets, instead, Petya.

LYUBOV ANDREYEVNA:

> No, let's continue yesterday's discussion!

TROFIMOV:

> About what?

GAEV:

> About the "proud man".[274]

TROFIMOV:

> Yesterday we talked for a long time but we didn't settle anything[275]. The way you look at it, the proud man has something mystical about him. Maybe you are right, the way you look at it without trying to be too clever, but then what

room is there for pride? What sense does it make, when physiologically speaking, man is such a poor specimen, physiologically and the vast majority of human beings are coarse and stupid, and profoundly miserable? We have to stop admiring ourselves so much. The only thing to do is work.

GAEV:

But we all die, in the end, no matter what.276

TROFIMOV:

Are you so sure of that? And what does that mean . . . to die? Maybe a man has a hundred senses and with death only five that we know of die with him, but the other ninety-five live on.

LYUBOV ANDREYEVNA:

How very clever you are, Petya . . .

LOPAKHIN:

(Ironically) Very clever!

TROFIMOV:

Humanity marches forward perfecting its power. Things that seem unachievable to us now will someday be familiar, possible. We must work and help all we can those who are searching for the truth. Here, in Russia only a very few of us really work. The vast majority of the intelligentsia that I know search for nothing, do nothing, and have no capacity for hard work. They call themselves the intelligentsia, but they talk down to their servants[277] as if they were children[278] and talk to their peasants as if they were animals. They don't study; they don't read, not anything serious; and they do absolutely nothing; all they do is talk... about science, and they understand little about art.

And they all look so grim, with such stern faces, and talk about such significant things, but while they go on philosophizing[279], right in front of them, the people who work[280] are eating swill, sleeping without proper bedding, thirty or forty to a room, and everywhere bedbugs, stench[281], dampness, moral degradation . . . And obviously, all our pretty talk is only to distract ourselves and others too. So where are the crèches[282] we hear so much about, where are the libraries? They only exist in fiction, in novels not in the real world. What we have got is dirt, vulgarity, and Asiaticism[283] [284]. . . I'm afraid of these serious faces and I'm afraid of these serious conversations. It would be better if we all just shut up![285]

LOPAKHIN:

Would you believe, I get up a little past four every morning and work from morning till night, well, I deal constantly with money—my own and other people's— and dealing with money doing business reveals to me what people are really like. Just try to get something done, to work yourself at a business and you'll find out how few honest, decent people there really are. Sometimes, when I can't sleep, I think: "Lord, you give us vast forests, boundless fields, vast horizons and living in the middle of all this we ought to be giants ourselves . . ."

LYUBOV ANDREYEVNA:

You want giants now . . . Giants are only good in fairy tales and even there they frighten us.

Epikhodov crosses in the back of the stage softly, sadly playing his guitar.

LYUBOV ANDREYEVNA:

(Pensively) There goes Epikhodov . . .[286]

ANYA:

(Pensively) There goes Epikhodov . . .[287] [288]

GAEV:

The sun has gone down[289], ladies and gentlemen.

TROFIMOV:

Yes.

GAEV:

(Not loudly, as if softly declaiming) Oh, nature, glorious nature, you shine with eternal light, beautiful and unsympathetic; you whom we

call Mother; you unite within yourself both life and death; you give life and you take life away . . .²⁹⁰ ²⁹¹ ²⁹²

VARYA:

(Imploringly) Uncle, dear!

ANYA:

Uncle, you're at it again!

TROFIMOV:

You'd do better to shoot the yellow to the middle with a bank.

GAEV:

I am quiet, I am quiet.

*They all sit lost in their thoughts. Silence. Only Fiers's mumbling is heard. Suddenly a faraway sound is heard, as if coming from the sky, a string snapping; the sound dies mournfully.*²⁹³

LYUBOV ANDREYEVNA: What was that?

LOPAKHIN:

I don't know. Maybe a cable snapping, a bucket breaking loose somewhere far away . . . in the mines. But somewhere very far away.²⁹⁴

GAEV:

Or maybe it's a bird of some kind . . . like a heron.

TROFIMOV:

> Or an owl . . .

LYUBOV ANDREYEVNA:

(Shudders) I can't say why but I don't like it.

pause

FIERS:

> Before the misfortune, it was like that; an owl screeched[295] and a samovar kept humming all day and all night.

GAEV:

> Before what misfortune?

FIERS:

> Before the freedom.[296]

pause

LYUBOV ANDREYEVNA:

> Come, my friends, we have to be going in; it's getting dark. *(To Anya)* You have tears in your eyes . . . What is it, my little girl? *(Embraces her)*

ANYA.

> It's alright, Mama. It's nothing

TROFIMOV:

> Someone's coming.

*Enter Passerby in an old white worn out peaked cap and overcoat. He is a little drunk.*²⁹⁷

PASSERBY:

> Would you be so kind as to tell me if I may I cross through here to get to the station?

GAEV:

> You may. Take this same road.²⁹⁸

PASSERBY:²⁹⁹

> I thank you from the very bottom of my heart. *(After coughing)* Lovely weather . . . *(Recites)* "Brother, long-suffering brother! Go down to the Volga, whose groan . . ."³⁰⁰ *(To Varya)*
>
> Mademoiselle, please give a hungry Russian thirty kopecks . . .

Varya is frightened, she screams.

LOPAKHIN:

> *(Angrily)* A person's allowed to be rude only so far as they're allowed! (Or perhaps "Even where you come from there must be a thing called manners.")³⁰¹ ³⁰²

LYUBOV ANDREYEVNA

> *(Startled, unnerved)* Take this . . . here you are . . . *(Feels in her purse)* I have no silver . . . No matter, here's gold (ten rubles). . .³⁰³

PASSERBY:

I am most profoundly obliged to you.

(Exits)

Laughter.

VARYA:

(Frightened) I'm going, I'm going . . . Oh, Mamochka, at home there's nothing for the servants to eat, and you give him your gold.

LYUBOV ANDREYEVNA:

What on earth are we going to do with me, I'm such a silly fool? At home I'll give you everything I've got. Ermolai Alexeyevich, won't you lend me some more, won't you? . . .

LOPAKHIN:

I am at your humble service.

LYUBOV ANDREYEVNA:

Let's go, ladies and gentlemen; it's time. And Varya, while sitting here we've made a match[304] for you;[305] so congratulations.[306]

VARYA:

(Through tears): Don't make jokes about it, Mama.[307]

LOPAKHIN:

Okhmeliya,[308] get thee to a nunnery . . .[309] [310] [311]

GAEV:

My hands are yearning to play; I haven't played billiards in a long time.³¹²

LOPAKHIN:

Okhmeliya, oh, nymph, in thy orisons³¹³ be all my sins remembered.³¹⁴

LYUBOV ANDREYEVNA:

Let's go, ladies and gentlemen. It's nearly suppertime.

VARYA:

That man gave me a fright. My heart's still pounding.

LOPAKHIN:

Let me remind you, ladies and gentlemen, that on August 22nd ³¹⁵, the cherry orchard will be sold. Think about it . . . Think . . .

All leave with the exception of Trofimov and Anya.

ANYA:

(Laughing) We ought to be thankful that the passerby³¹⁶ frightened Varya, at least now we're alone.

TROFIMOV:

Varya's afraid that we're suddenly going to fall in love with each other. She's been following us around for days. What her narrow-mind can't understand is that we're above love. The whole meaning and purpose of our lives is to break free from all the petty illusions, which prevents us from being happy and free. Forward! On. We march forward triumphantly towards a bright blazing star out there in the distance! Forward! In step together, my friends!³¹⁷

ANYA:

(Clapping her hands) How beautifully you talk.³¹⁸

pause

It's heavenly here today!

TROFIMOV:

Yes, the weather is wonderful.

ANYA:

What have you done to me, Petya, that I don't love the cherry orchard like I used to? I loved it so tenderly, and I used to think there was no finer place in the whole world than this orchard of ours.

TROFIMOV:

All Russia is our orchard³¹⁹. The whole country is so big and beautiful and there are so many wonderful places in it.

pause

Anya, just think: Your grandfather, and his father and his father's father and all your ancestors owned serfs; <u>they owned living souls. Can't you see the human beings looking out at you from every cherry, from every leaf and every tree trunk</u> in the orchard? <u>Can't you hear their voices crying out to you . . .? The sound is awful. They owned living souls, which caused the degeneration</u>[320] <u>of every one of us . . . those who lived before and those who are living now . . . so that your mother and you and your uncle don't even notice that you're living under the weight of that debt</u>[321], <u>you're living off those people; at the expense of those people who weren't even allowed to darken your</u> <u>doorway</u>[322] . . . We're two hundred years behind the times, we have nothing yet, no clear attitude to the past history we live under, we philosophize, talk, talk, talk, wallow in our misery and whine and whine, or drown ourselves in vodka. But in order to really live in this present, we need to redeem our past, atone and make a clean break, only then can we redeem ourselves, by suffering and by relentless, ceaseless hard work.[323] Remember, Anya.[324]

ANYA:

The house we live in hasn't been our house for a long time now. I'm going to leave it, I give you my word of honor.[325]

TROFIMOV:

If you have the keys[326], throw them down the well and walk, walk away. Be as free as the wind.

ANYA:

> *(Thrilled)* How beautifully you talk.[327] [328]

TROFIMOV:

> Put your faith in me and listen, Anya, put your faith in me! I'm not thirty yet, I'm young and I'm still a student, but I've already experienced so much! In winter, I'm half-starved, sick, full of fear, poor as a beggar, tossed every which way by fate! And yet my soul has always, every minute of the day and night been flooded . . . haunted by unexplainable premonitions, mysterious visions of a happy future. Happiness[329] is coming, it is coming, Anya, I can see happiness coming . . .[330]

ANYA:

> *(Pensively)* The moon is rising.[331]

Epikhodov is heard playing his guitar. It's the same gloomy song. The moon rises. Somewhere near the poplars Varya is looking for Anya and calls out "Anya, where are you?"

TROFIMOV:

> Yes, the moon is rising.

(pause)

> There it is, happiness too is rising, here it comes; closer and closer, and I can hear its footsteps already.[332] And if we don't see it and

never see its face, what does it matter? Others will see it!

Varya's voice: "Anya! Where are you?"

TROFIMOV:

That Varya again! *(Angrily)* It's exasperating!

ANYA:

Well? Let's go down to the river.³³³ It's nice there.³³⁴

TROFIMOV:

Let's go.

(They go)

*Varya's voice: "Anya! Anya!"*³³⁵

Curtain.

ACT THREE

A drawing room separated from a ballroom³³⁶ by an archway³³⁷. The chandelier is lighted. Sounds of the Jewish orchestra³³⁸, the one mentioned in Act Two, are coming from the entryway. Evening. In the ballroom³³⁹—they are dancing grand-rond.³⁴⁰ Simyonov-Pischik's voice:

"Promenade à une paire!"

Coming into the drawing room: the First pair are Pischik and Charlotta Ivanovna; the second, Trofimov and Lyubov Andreyevna; the third, Anya and the Post Office Clerk; the fourth, Varya and the Stationmaster[341], and so on. Varya is crying quietly and wiping away the tears as she dances. Dunyasha is in the last pair. They cross the drawing room and

Pischik shouts:

> "Grand-rond, balancez!" and "Les cavaliers à genoux et remerciez vos dames!"[342]

Fiers, in swallowtail jacket,[343] is bringing in a tray with seltzer water. Enter Pischik and Trofimov from the ballroom.

PISCHIK:

> I've got high blood pressure and I've had two strokes already. It's hard for me to dance, but, as they say, when running with the pack you've got to wag your tail whether you can bark or not. I'm as strong as a horse. My late father, a real comedian, God rest his soul, used to say that our ancient family of Simyonov-Pischik was descended from the very horse that Caligula made senator . . .[344] *(Sits down)* But the trouble is we have no money! A hungry dog believes only in meat. *(Snores and wakes up again immediately)* That's me . . . I think about nothing but money . . .

TROFIMOV:

> You know . . . you are built just like a horse.

PISCHIK:

> Well and why not . . . a horse is a good beast... you can sell a horse . . .

In the next room the sounds of a billiard game can be heard. Varya appears in the hallway under the arch.

TROFIMOV:

> *(Teasing)* Madame Lopakhina! Madame Lopakhina!

VARYA:

> *(Angrily)* Shabby gentleman!

TROFIMOV:

> Yes, I am a "Shabby Gentleman" and I'm proud of it!

VARYA:

> *(Brooding, with bitterness)* We've hired musicians, but how are we going to pay them?
>
> *(Goes out)*

TROFIMOV:

> *(To Pischik)* During your life, if the energy you spent trying to borrow money to pay off the mortgage interest had been used for something constructive, then you would've been able to move the world on its axis.

PISCHIK:

Nietzsche . . . the philosopher . . . the greatest, the most renowned man . . . a man of gigantic intellect, writes that it's perfectly all right to make counterfeit bank notes. [345]

TROFIMOV:

You've read Nietzsche?[346]

PISCHIK:

Well . . . my daughter Dashenka told me about him[347]. Now I'm in such an impossible position I might have to forge bank notes as my only way out . . . Three hundred and ten rubles are due the day after tomorrow . . . I've got one hundred and thirty already . . . *(Feels his pockets, nervously)* The money is gone! I've lost the money! *(Through tears)* Where's the money? *(Joyfully)* Oh . . . here it is . . . I've found it . . . in the lining right where I put it . . . I'm soaking wet with sweat . . . I gave myself quite a fright.

Enter Lyubov Andreyevna and Charlotta Ivanovna.

LYUBOV ANDREYEVNA:

(Humming the Lezginka[348] dance tune) Why isn't Leonid back yet? What's he doing in town?

(To Dunyasha)

Dunyasha, offer the musicians some tea...

TROFIMOV:

The auction probably never took place.

LYUBOV ANDREYEVNA:

> We summoned the musicians at the worst possible time and a celebration ball is totally out of place[349] . . . Well, never mind . . .

(Sits down and sings softly)

CHARLOTTA:

> *(Gives a deck of cards to Pischik to examine)* Take these cards. Think of a card, any card. [350]

PISCHIK:

> Got it.

CHARLOTTA:

> Now shuffle the deck. Very good, now. Give it back to me, oh my dear Herr Pischik. Ein, zwei, drei![351] Now look and you'll see in your side pocket . . .

PISCHIK:

> *(Pulls a card out of his pocket)* Eight of spades, absolutely right! *(Amazed)* Can you imagine that![352]

CHARLOTTA:

> *(To Trofimov while holding the deck of cards in the palm of her hand)* Now tell me, quick what is the top card.[353]

TROFIMOV:

> What? Well, the queen of spades[354].

CHARLOTTA:

Right! *(To Pischik)* Well? What's the top card?

PISCHIK:

The ace of hearts.

CHARLOTTA:

Right! *(Claps her hands and the cards disappear)* What beautiful weather we have today.

(A mysterious woman's voice answers her, as if coming from under the floor)

("Oh, yes, the weather is wonderful, my lady.") You are so good, my ideal . . .

The voice: *"I like you very much too."*355 356

STATIONMASTER:

(Applauds) Madame the Ventriloquist, bravo!

PISCHIK:

(Amazed) Imagine that! My most charming, bewitching Charlotta Ivanovna357 . . . I've totally fallen in love . . .

CHARLOTTA:

In love? *(Shrugging her shoulders)* As if you were capable of love?358 *Guter Mensch aber schlechter Musikant.*359 360 361

TROFIMOV:

(Slaps Pischik on the shoulder) Good old horse.

CHARLOTTA:

May I have your attention please! One more magic trick. *(Takes a robe off a chair)* Here's a very fine robe, I wish to sell it . . . *(Shakes it)* What am I offered?

PISCHIK:

(Amazed) Imagine that!

CHARLOTTA:

Ein, zwei, drei. *(She lifts up the robe quickly. Anya is standing behind it; she curtsies and runs to her mother, hugs her and runs back to the ballroom; the audience is delighted.)*

LYUBOV ANDREYEVNA

(Applauds) Bravo, bravo!

CHARLOTTA:

Once again! Ein, zwei, drei!

(Lifts the robe. Varya stands behind it and takes a bow)[362]

PISCHIK:

(Surprized) Imagine that!

CHARLOTTA:

The end!

(Throws the robe at Pischik, curtseys and runs into the ballroom)

PISCHIK:

> *(Hurries after her)* What an enchantress . . . An enchantress, that's what you are? You are? *(Exits)*

LYUBOV ANDREYEVNA:

> Why isn't Leonid back yet? What's he doing in town so long, I can't understand! Everything must be over by now. Either the estates been sold or the auction was called off, why keep us in suspense all this time!

VARYA:

> *(Trying to comfort her)* Uncle, dear, bought it. I'm sure he must have.

TROFIMOV: *(Sarcastically)* Yes, of course he did.

VARYA:

> Great aunt sent him her power of attorney to buy it in her name and transfer the debt to her. She's doing this for Anya. And I'm sure, with God's help, Uncle will buy it.

LYUBOV ANDREYEVNA:

> The Yaroslavl grandmother sent fifteen thousand rubles to buy the property in her name—she doesn't trust us—and that's not enough money to even pay the interest. *(Covers*

her face with her hands) My fate, my future is being decided today, my fate . . .

TROFIMOV:

(Teasing Varya) Madame Lopakhina!

VARYA:

(Angrily) Eternal student![363] They've thrown you out of the university twice already.

LYUBOV ANDREYEVNA:

Why are you so upset, Varya? He's teasing you about Lopakhin; so let him? You can marry Lopakhin if you want to, he's a good and interesting man . . . You don't have to if you don't want to, sweetheart; nobody's trying to force you[364] . . .

VARYA:

To be honest, Mamochka, I take this seriously. He's a good man, and I like him.

LYUBOV ANDREYEVNA:

Then marry him. What are you waiting for? . . . I don't understand!

VARYA:

I can't exactly propose to him myself, Mamochka. For two years now, everybody's been talking to me about the marriage; everybody, but he either says nothing, or jokes about it. I understand, he's getting rich; he's busy with work, and he can't be bothered with me. If I had money, even a little, even if only a hundred rubles, I'd quit everything and go as far away as possible. I'd enter a convent.

TROFIMOV:

Sounds wonderful!

VARYA:

(To Trofimov) Students are supposed to be intelligent but you must show how terribly witty you are! *(Softly with tears in her voice)* You've gotten so ugly,³⁶⁵ Petya, How old you've grown! *(To Lubov Andreyevna, no longer crying)* I can't stand still for one moment, Mamochka. I have to do something to keep me busy all the time.

Enter Yasha.

YASHA:

(Barely able to keep from laughing) Epikhodov broke a billiard cue . . . *(Exits)*

VARYA:

What is Epikhodov doing here? Who told him he could play billiards? I can't make any sense out of these people . . . ³⁶⁶ *(Exits)*

LYUBOV ANDREYEVNA:

Don't tease her, Petya. She's heartbroken even without being teased.

TROFIMOV:

But she's very eager to stick her nose where it doesn't belong . . . in other people's business. All summer long she's been pestering Anya and me, giving us no rest, afraid we might fall in love with each other. What business is that of hers? I never gave her a reason to suspect me; I'm not so vulgar. Anya and me, we are above love!

LYUBOV ANDREYEVNA:

While I'm supposed to be beneath love. *(Greatly agitated)* Why isn't Leonid back? If only I knew whether the estate's been sold or not? That misfortune seems so terrible that it just couldn't happen, I can't stand to think about it, I'm at my wit's end . . . I might scream out loud . . . or do something really stupid. Help me, Petya. Keep talking, just keep on talking . . .

TROFIMOV:

Whether the estate's been sold today or not, what does it really matter? It was all over a long time ago, there's no turning back now; the path is grown over and closed now. Calm down, dear soul. And don't deceive yourself. For just once in your whole life look at truth straight in the eye.

LYUBOV ANDREYEVNA:

What? Can you make out what is true from what is not true? I seem to have lost my sight. I see nothing. You look forward so boldly but isn't that because you can't see what's in front of you, but tell me, galubchik[367], isn't that because you're not old enough yet to have suffered[368] because of your problems? You look boldly forward because you can't foresee or expect anything terrible ever happening, because life is still hidden from your young eyes? You're more honest, braver, and deeper than we are, but just think about it and try to be more generous, even if just a tiny little bit, and spare me. I was born here, my father, my mother, and my grandfather all lived here, I love this house, and I can't imagine my life without the cherry orchard, and if it must be sold sell me along[369] with it . . .

(Embraces Trofimov, kisses him on the forehead)

LYUBOV ANDREYEVNA:

After all, my little boy drowned here . . . *(Cries)* Good, kind man, take pity on me.

TROFIMOV:

I feel for you with all my heart[370].

LYUBOV ANDREYEVNA:

But that should have been said differently. You need to say it differently, differently . . . *(Takes out a handkerchief, and a telegram falls on the floor)* My heart is heavy today, you can't imagine. I can't stand this noise, and my heart trembles at every sound, I'm trembling all over, and yet I can't go to my room: the sound of the silence frightens me, I'm frightened of being by myself. Don't condemn me, Petya . . . I love you as if you were my own flesh and blood. I'd gladly give Anya to you in marriage, honestly, I would; but please, golubchick, you must go back and complete your studies and take your degree. You don't do anything; Fate tosses you from place to place; don't you see how strange this is . . . Don't you see? Isn't it so? And you must do something about that beard of yours if you can even call it a beard . . . make it grow or something . . .[371] *(Laughs)* You look so funny!

TROFIMOV:

(Picking up the telegram) I don't pretend to be beautiful.

LYUBOV ANDREYEVNA:

The telegram's from Paris. I get one every day. One yesterday, one today. That crazy man is sick again, he's in terrible shape . . . He begs me to forgive him, begs me to come back, and I suppose I should go to Paris to be with him. Petya, I see you're frowning, but what else can I do, my dear boy, if he's ill, he's lonely, and he's unhappy, and who else is there to take care of him, who will stop him from making a fool of himself and who will give him his medicine on time? And why should I hide it; why should I make a secret of it. I love him. I love, I love him . . . He's a millstone around my neck and he's dragging me down to the bottom with him it, but I love this millstone of mine and can't live without it. *(Squeezes Trofimov's hand)* Don't think I'm bad, Petya, and don't talk to me the way you do, don't . . .

TROFIMOV:

(Through tears) Forgive me for being so frank, but for God's sake, the man is robbing you!³⁷²

LYUBOV ANDREYEVNA:

No, no, no, you mustn't talk like that! *(Covers her ears with her hands)*

TROFIMOV:

But he's a scoundrel; you're the only one who doesn't see it! He's a petty scoundrel³⁷³, a nonentity³⁷⁴ . . .

LYUBOV ANDREYEVNA:

(Angry, but in control) You're twenty-six or twenty-seven, but you are still gymnasium second class!³⁷⁵

TROFIMOV:

S'that so.

LYUBOV ANDREYEVNA:

You should be a man by now . . . at your age you should understand what it is to be in love. You should be in love yourself!³⁷⁶ *(Sternly)* Yes! You think you're being so innocently pure? You are just a prude, a sissy, silly geek, a pervert . . .

TROFIMOV:

(In horror) What is she saying?!

LYUBOV ANDREYEVNA:

"I'm above love!" You're not above love, you're what our Fiers calls a numbskull. [377] Imagine a man at your age never having had a mistress . . .

TROFIMOV:

(Horrified) This is awful! What is she saying? *(Walks quickly toward the ballroom, clutching his head)* This is awful . . . I can't take it, I've got to get out of here . . . *(Exits, but comes back at once)* "All is over between us,"[378] *(Exits into the entryway)*

LYUBOV ANDREYEVNA:

(Shouts after him): Petya, wait! Don't be silly, I was only joking! Petya!

There is the sound of footsteps going up the stairs then the sound of someone falling down the stairs followed by a crash. Anya and Varya scream; then a burst of laughter is heard.

LYUBOV ANDREYEVNA:

What's happened?

Anya runs in

ANYA:

>Petya fell down the stairs! *(Runs out)*

LYUBOV ANDREYEVNA:

>What an oddball, this Petya . . .

Stationmaster:

(stops in the middle of the drawing room and recites)

>"The Wanton Woman" [379] by A. Tolstoy:
>
>>A swarming crowd: gay laughter's clang,
>>
>>The crash of gongs, the lutes' clear twang,
>>
>>Flowers and green'ry scattered round...

The guests listen to him but as soon as he delivers a few lines, the strains of a waltz reach them coming from the entrance hall, and the recitation abruptly stops. Everybody then dances. Trofimov, Anya, Varya, and Lyubov Andreyevna enter from the hall.

LYUBOV ANDREYEVNA:

>Please, Petya . . . poor pure heart . . . please forgive me . . . Let's dance . . . *(She dances with Trofimov)* [380]

Anya and Varya dance.

Enter Fiers and leans his walking stick by a side door.

Yasha has also entered from the drawing room and is looking at the dancers.

YASHA:

How's it going, grandfather[381]?

FIERS:

Not feeling so good. In the old days, generals and barons, and admirals used to dance at our balls, and now who are we stuck with, the postman and the stationmaster, and even they aren't all that anxious to grace our halls. I'm feeling weak. The old Master, their grandfather, would give us all sealing wax when we got sick. I took sealing wax every day for twenty years now, maybe more. Maybe that's what keeps me alive.[382]

YASHA:

I'm sick of you, grandpa. *(Yawns)* Hurry up and die, why don't you.

FIERS:

Get away with you . . . another numbskull! *(Mumbling to himself)*

Trofimov and Lyubov Andreyevna dance in the ballroom, then in the drawing room.

LYUBOV ANDREYEVNA:

Merci. I'll think I'll sit down for a while . . .

(Sits down) I'm tired.

Enter Anya

ANYA:

> *(Enter, shaken up)* A man in the kitchen just said that the cherry orchard was sold today.

LYUBOV ANDREYEVNA:

> Sold? Who bought it?

ANYA.

> He didn't say who bought it. He's gone now.

(Anya dances with Trofimov dancing into the ballroom)

YASHA:

> Some old man muttering. A stranger, not from here.

FIERS:

> And Leonid Andreyich isn't back; hasn't come back yet and wearing only a light overcoat; he's going to catch cold. Oh, these young people . . . they don't know anything.

LYUBOV ANDREYEVNA:

> The suspense is killing me. Go, Yasha, go and find out who bought it.

YASHA:

> But the man, he's gone . . . he left a long time ago. *(Laughs)*

LYUBOV ANDREYEVNA:

(Slightly annoyed) What's so funny? What are you laughing about?³⁸³ ³⁸⁴

YASHA:

Epikhodov . . . he's so funny. What an idiot. Twenty-two Misfortunes.

LYUBOV ANDREYEVNA:

Fiers, if the estate is sold, where will you go?

FIERS:

Wherever you tell me to go.

LYUBOV ANDREYEVNA:

You don't look so good. Are you sick? Why don't you go and lie down and rest.

FIERS:

Sure . . . *(In total seriousness)* I go to bed, and who'd do the serving, who'll take charge, give the orders, without me? There's no one in the house but me. ³⁸⁵

YASHA:

(To Lyubov Andreyevna) Lyubov Andreyevna, may I ask a favor of you, please? If you go back to Paris again, please take me with you; I implore you, please. I can't stay here anymore. *(Looking around, sotto voce)* Is there any use in talking about it? You can see for yourself: the country is uncivilized, the people have no morals, and the boredom, and the food they

serve in the kitchen is uneatable, and on top of it all, here's old Fiers always going about, stumbling, interrupting with his nonsense. Please take me with you!

Enter Pischik

PISCHIK:

May I have the pleasure . . . of this little waltz, my ravishing lady . . . *(Lyubov Andreyevna stands up, takes his arm)* My charmer, all the same, I must ask you for one hundred and eighty rubles . . . Just you wait and see . . . *(He dances)* Just one hundred and eighty . . .

(They waltz into the ballroom)

YASHA:

(Sings softly) "Can't you see that my heart is breaking . . . ?"[386] [387]

In the ballroom, a figure wearing a gray top hat and baggy checked trousers is jumping and waving her arms about; there are cries of:

"Bravo, Charlotta Ivanovna!"[388]

DUNYASHA:

(Stops to powder her face) The young mistress told me to dance . . . there're a lot of gentlemen and not enough ladies to go around . . . but the dancing makes my head spin, and my heart's pounding, Fiers Nikolayevich, the postman said

something to me just now that took my breath away. (*The music grows faint*)

FIERS:

So what did he say to you?

DUNYASHA:

He says, "You're like a flower."

YASHA:

(Yawns) The ignorance of these people takes my breath away . . . *(He exits)*

DUNYASHA:

Like a flower . . . I'm such a delicate girl; I just love when someone speaks such tender words to me.

FIERS:

Those pretty words will be your undoing.

Enter Epikhodov

EPIKHODOV:

Avdotiya Fedorovna, you've been avoiding me me . . . as if I were some kind of insect or something. *(Sighs)* This life! Life.

DUNYASHA:

What do you want from me?

EPIKHODOV:

Undoubtedly, perhaps you are right. *(Sighs)* But, on the other hand, if you regard it from a certain point of view, then you, if you will permit the expression, forgive my frankness, you have led me on, reduced me to a wretched state of mind. I know I'm doomed to some misfortune . . . every day a new misfortune, but I've gotten used to it a long time ago, and I face my fate with a smile. You gave me your word, and even if I . . .

DUNYASHA:

Please, May we talk about this some other time, but for now, please leave me in peace. I'm dreaming now. *(Plays with her fan)*

EPIKHODOV:

I have a misfortune every day, and, if I may say so, I smile, and even laugh at times.

Varya comes in from the ballroom talking first to Epikhodov

VARYA:

What are you still here, Semyon? You have no respect. *(To Dunyasha)* You may go now, Dunyasha. *(To Epikhodov)* First, you play billiards and break a cue, and then you wander about the drawing room like one of the invited guests!

EPIKHODOV:

You, if I may express myself thus, have no authority over me to lecture me in this manner.³⁸⁹

VARYA:

I'm not pulling rank on you, I'm only talking to you: All you ever do is wander around and never do any work. Why do we need a clerk at all; there's nothing to clerk.

EPIKHODOV:

(Offended) The only people qualified to judge my working or wandering or eating or billiards are those in authority³⁹⁰ and wiser heads than yours.³⁹¹

VARYA:

How dare you talk to me like that! *(Furious)* How dare you. Are you saying I'm not wise enough for you? Get out of here! This instant!

EPIKHODOV:

(Cowed) I must ask you to be more delicate in expressing yourself.

VARYA:

(Losing herself) Get out this instant! Get out! Out!

(He goes to the door, she follows)

Twenty-two Misfortunes! Get out of my sight! Don't set foot in this house again. I never want to see you again!

Epikhodov has gone out; his voice can be heard outside:

I shall lodge a complaint against you to those in authority.

VARYA:

So you're coming back in again?

(Picks up the walking stick, which Fiers had left leaning by the door)

Come on, come on, I'll show you a thing or two . . . So you're coming in? Are you coming? Well, then, take that.

(She swings the stick[392] as Lopakhin enters)

LOPAKHIN:

I am much obliged.

VARYA:

(Angrily but with irony) Sorry!

LOPAKHIN:

Never mind. Much obliged for a warm welcome.

VARYA:

Don't mention it. *(Walks away, then looks back, asking gently)* Did I hurt you?

LOPAKHIN:

> No, I'll be all right. I'll have an enormous bump, though.393 394

Voices from the ballroom:

> Lopakhin is back! Ermolai Alexeyevich!

PISCHIK:

> Long have we waited. Long have we wondered. *(Kisses Lopakhin)* I smell a whiff of cognac on you, my dearest friend. But we have been having a party ourselves.

Enter Lyubov Andreyevna

LYUBOV ANDREYEVNA:

> Is that you, Ermolai Alexeyevich? What took so long? Where's Leonid?

LOPAKHIN:

> Leonid Andreyevich came back with me, he's coming . . .

LYUBOV ANDREYEVNA:

> *(Excited)* Well, and . . . what happened? Was there an auction? Speak to us!395

LOPAKHIN:

> *(Embarrassed, <u>afraid</u> of showing his happiness)* 396The auction was over by four o'clock . . . We missed our train, and had to wait for the nine-

thirty. *(Sighs heavily)* Oh! My head's spinning a little . . .³⁹⁷

Enter Gaev. In his right hand he is holding his parcels, with his left he wipes away his tears.

LYUBOV ANDREYEVNA:

> Lionya, and? Lionya, well? *(Impatiently, in tears)* Quickly, tell us, for the sake of God . . .

GAEV:

> *(Says nothing to her, only waves his hand; to Fiers, crying)* Here, take them . . . Here are anchovies, Kertch herring . . .³⁹⁸ I haven't eaten all day . . . Oh, what I've been through today!

The door to the billiard room is open; the clicking of the balls is heard, and Yasha's³⁹⁹ voice:

> "Seven and eighteen!"

Gaev's facial expression changes, and he is no longer crying.

> I'm awfully tired. Fiers, bring me a change of clothes.

(Exits through the ballroom to his room; Fiers follows him)

PISCHIK:

> What happened at the auction? Tell us!

LYUBOV ANDREYEVNA:

> Was the cherry orchard sold?

LOPAKHIN:

It was sold.

LYUBOV ANDREYEVNA:

Who bought it?

LOPAKHIN:

I bought it.[400] *(Pause)*

Lyubov Andreyevna is overwhelmed; she would have fallen if she hadn't been standing by an armchair and table. Varya takes the keys from her belt, throws them on the floor[401] *in the middle of the drawing room and exits.*[402]

LOPAKHIN:

I bought it! Wait, ladies and gentlemen, if you would be so kind, I still can't think straight, I can't speak . . . *(Laughs)* We got to the auction. Deriganov was already there. Leonid Andreyevich had fifteen thousand and Deriganov started the bidding at thirty thousand over and above the debt. I could see what he means to do, so I take him on and put down forty . . . He put down forty-five thousand. I made it fifty-five. He jumps by fives, I by tens . . . Well, suddenly it's over. I put down ninety thousand over and above the debt,[403] and I got it. The cherry orchard is mine! Mine! *(Laughs out loud.)* My God, Lord God in Heaven, the cherry orchard is mine![404] Tell me that I'm drunk, that I'm out of my mind, Tell me this is all a dream...[405] *(Stamps his feet.)* Do not laugh at me. If only my father and grandfather could see me now, could rise from their graves and see what has become of me, how their Ermolay, beaten, half-illiterate Ermolay, who ran around barefoot in the winter, how this very same Ermolay bought the estate, the most beautiful estate in the whole world.[406] [407] I bought the estate where my grandfather and father were slaves, where they weren't even allowed to go into the kitchen. I must be dreaming, I must be making it up out of my imagination, it only seems to be . . . "This is the fruit of your imagination, a dark delusion wrapped in the mists of ignorance". . .[408] *(Picks up the keys, smiling tenderly)* She threw down the keys, she wants to show that she's no longer the housekeeper [housewife] here . . . *(Jingles the keys)* Well, that's alright with me.[409] *(The orchestra is heard tuning up.)* Hey musicians, play, play, I want to hear your music, me![410] Everyone, come see, look at how Ermolay Lopakhin will take the axe to the cherry trees, how the trees will tumble down and shake the ground! We'll erect dachas and our grandchildren and their grandchildren will discover a new life . . . Play musicians, play, play for me![411] [412]*(The music plays. Lyubov Andreyevna has collapsed into a chair and is weeping bitterly.)*

(To Lyubov Andreyevna reproachfully)

Why, oh why didn't you listen to me? It's too late now, my poor, good woman, you can't go back again . . . what is done is done and can't be undone.[413] *(With tears)* If only this was all over and done with, if only our, awkward[414], unhappy[415] life would change quickly! [416] [417] [418] [419]

PISHCHIK:

(Takes Lopakhin by the arm, in a whisper.) She's crying. Let's go into the hall, leave her alone . . . Come on, let's go . . . (Takes him by the arm and leads him into the hall)[420]

LOPAKHIN:

What's going on? Loud and clear; Music, strike up! Let everything be as I want it to be! *(With irony.)* Here comes the new landlord, the new owner of the cherry orchard is here! *(He bumps into a small table, <u>nearly</u> knocking over some candlesticks.[421])*

I can pay for it all.

(Exits with Pishchik)

There is no one in the hall and drawing room except Lyubov Andreyevna, who huddles in her chair, and weeps bitterly. The orchestra plays softly.

Quickly Anya and Trofimov enter. Anya goes to her mother and kneels in front of her. Trofimov remains standing at the entrance to the ballroom.

ANYA:

Mama . . . Mama, are you crying? My dear, kind, my good Mama, my beautiful Mama, I love you . . . I bless you. The cherry orchard is sold, it's gone, that's true, true, but don't cry, Mama, You still have your life ahead of you, you still have your good, pure heart . . . Come with me away. Come away from here, my darling, come! . . . We'll plant a new orchard, more wonderful than this one, you'll see, you'll understand, and joy, tranquil deep joy will fill your heart, like the rays of the setting sun, and you'll smile again, Mama! Come, my dear! Come! . . .[422] [423]

Curtain

ACT FOUR[424]

The same set as the First Act. There are no curtains in the windows, or paintings on the walls, there is some furniture remaining, which is stacked to one corner, as if it is to be sold. It feels empty. Near the door to the outside and upstage there are suitcases, traveling bundles, etc. piled up. To the left, the door is open, and from there the voices of Varya and Anya can be heard.

Lopakhin stands waiting. Yasha holds a tray with glasses, filled with champagne.[425] In the hallway, Epikhodov is tying up a box. Far offstage there is a low hum of voices like rumbling. The peasants have come to say goodbye.

The voice of Gaev:

"Thank you, my brothers, thank you."

YASHA:

> The peasants have come to say goodbye. I am of the opinion, Ermolay Alekseyevich, they mean well but they don't understand much.[426]

The humming voices die down.

Lyubov Andreyevna and Gaev enter from the hallway; she does not cry, but she is pale, her lips are twitching, she cannot speak.

GAEV:

> You gave them your purse, Lyuba. You shouldn't have! You shouldn't have!

LYUBOV ANDREYEVNA:

> I couldn't help it! I couldn't help it!

(They both exit.)

LOPAKHIN:

> *(At the door, calling after them)* Please, I most humbly beg you! Have a toast of champagne to say our goodbyes. I didn't think to bring any from town and I only found one bottle at the station. Please! *(Pause)* What's the matter, ladies and gentlemen! Don't you want to drink with me? *(Walks away from the door)* If I'd known, I wouldn't have bought it. Well, I won't have any either. *(Yasha carefully puts the tray on the table)* Drink up yourself, Yasha, you at least have some. Nobody else wants any.

YASHA:

> Greeting to those who are departing!⁴²⁷ Good luck to those who stay! *(Drinks)* This isn't real champagne, you can take my word of it.

LOPAKHIN:

> Eight rubles a bottle. *(Pause)* It's cold as hell here.

YASHA:

> No point in lighting the fires, since we're leaving.⁴²⁸ *(Laughs)*

LOPAKHIN:

> What are you laughing at?

YASHA:

> I'm just happy.

LOPAKHIN:

> Here we are and it's already October, but it might as well be summer it's so sunny and it's calm like summer. Good weather for building. *(Looking at his watch, at the door)* Ladies and gentlemen, don't forget that forty six minutes is all that remain before the train goes! That means that in twenty minutes you have to leave for the station.⁴²⁹ So hurry up, it's time.

(Trofimov in a coat enters from the outside)

TROFIMOV:

It's time to go. The horses are harnessed. Where are my galoshes. They're gone. *(Through the door)* Anya, my galoshes have disappeared! I couldn't find them anywhere!

LOPAKHIN:

I'm going to Kharkov. I'm taking the same train as you. I'll spend the whole winter in Kharkov. I'm worn out hanging around with you people here all this time . . . I'm worn out doing nothing . . . nothing[430]. I can't live without work, I don't know what to do with my hands. They just hang there like they belong to someone else.

TROFIMOV:

We'll be leaving, so you can get back to your own useful work again[431] in the real world.

LOPAKHIN:

Come on. Drink a glass with me.[432]

TROFIMOV:

I'm not going to.

LOPAKHIN:

So you'll be going to Moscow now?

TROFIMOV:

Yes, I'll see them off in town and tomorrow I'll go to Moscow.

LOPAKHIN:

>Yes . . . Well, the professors, no doubt, have stopped giving their lectures waiting for you to come back!

TROFIMOV:

>Why don't you mind your own business.

LOPAKHIN:

>How many years have you been studying at the university?

TROFIMOV:

>Why not think up something more original, that's getting tired and stale. *(Looks for his galoshes)* [433] You know, we may never see each other again[434], so allow me to give you just one piece of advice as we say goodbye: don't wave your arms about so much![435] Break that stupid habit . . . waving your arms[436]. And this too . . . building dachas and expecting the residents to till the soil that's just another pipe dream[437]; it's just more of the same waving your arms around . . . But anyway, <u>I still like you. You have fine, sensitive fingers,[438] like an artist, and on the inside, deep down, you are a fine, tender soul</u> . . .[439]

LOPAKHIN:

>*(Embraces him)* Goodbye, my friend. Thank you for everything. Let me give you some money for the road just in case you need it.

TROFIMOV:

Why should I? I don't need it.

LOPAKHIN:

But you don't have any money!

TROFIMOV:

Yes, I have. Thank you. I got some for a translation.[440] Here it is, in my pocket. *(Anxiously)* But where are my galoshes.

VARYA:

(From the other room) Take these filthy galoshes! *(She throws a pair of rubber galoshes on stage)*

TROFIMOV:

Why are you so upset, Varya? Hmmm . . . These aren't my galoshes!

LOPAKHIN:

I planted two thousand seven hundred acres[441] of poppies in the spring and now I've made forty thousand clear profit. But when my poppies were in bloom, what a sight it was to behold.[442] So, like I said, I made forty thousand and I'm offering you a loan[443] because I can afford it. Why turn your nose up at it? I'm a peasant, a muzhik . . . I put it to you straight.

TROFIMOV:

Your father was a muzhik, mine . . . a pharmacist, and what has that got to do with anything.

(Lopakhin takes out his wallet) Stop. Put it away, put it away . . . Even if you gave me two hundred thousand, I wouldn't take it.[444] I'm a free man. The things that mean so much to you, you rich and you poor alike, mean nothing to me, no more than this fluff, thistledown blowing around in the wind. I can get along without you; I can make my own. I can pass you by. I am strong and proud. Humanity is marching toward the highest truth, toward the highest happiness possible on earth, and I am in the vanguard,[445] marching in the very front ranks.[446]

LOPAKHIN:

Will you get there?

TROFIMOV:

I will get there. *(Pause.)* I will get there myself or I'll show others the way to get there.

The sound of the axe chopping down trees is heard in the distance.

LOPAKHIN:

Well, goodbye, galubchik[447] . . . Time for me to go.[448] We look down our noses at each other, we talk past each other, but life goes its own way.[449] When I work for a long time without a break, then my thoughts rest, and give me the feeling that I actually know what life is all about.⁴⁵⁰ But, brother, how many people are there in Russia, who don't know what they're doing or why they're doing it. Well, it gets down to the same thing, but that's not the crux of the matter. Leonid Andreyevich, they say, has gotten a position, he'll work in the bank. Six thousand a year . . . [Only he probably won't last long, he's too lazy]. . .⁴⁵¹

ANYA:

(At the door.) Mama wondered if you wouldn't wait till she's gone before chopping down the cherry trees.⁴⁵²

TROFIMOV:

(To Lopakhin) Really, have you no tact?⁴⁵³ *(Exits through the hallway)*

LOPAKHIN:

[I'll stop them immediately . . . The fools should have waited!]⁴⁵⁴

(Follows Trofimov off)

ANYA:

Did they take Fiers to the hospital?

YASHA:

I told them to do it this morning. I think they must have done it.

ANYA:

(To Epikhodov, who crosses through the ballroom)

> Semyon Panteleyevich[455], find out, please, if they have taken Fiers to the hospital.

YASHA:

> *(Offended)* I told Yégor[456] this morning. How many times will you ask me?

EPIKHODOV:

> Ancient Fiers, I have concluded, is beyond repair. It is time he found union with his forefathers. I can only envy him. *(Puts a suitcase down on a hatbox and crushes it.)* There, you see. What did I tell you? *(Exits)*

YASHA:

> *(Sarcastically)* Twenty-Two Misfortunes.

~~EPIKHODOV.~~

> ~~Well, it could have happened to anybody~~.[457] ~~(Exits.)~~

VARYA:

> *(Behind the door)* Did they take Fiers to the hospital?[458]

ANYA:

> Yes they did.

VARYA:

Why didn't they take the letter to the doctor with them at the same time?

ANYA:

We'll have to send it on after them... *(Exits)*

VARYA:

(From the neighboring room) Where's Yasha? Tell him his mother's come to say goodbye to him.[459]

YASHA:

(Waves his arm as if to brush her off) This is beyond my patience.

Dunyasha has been fussing with the baggage the whole time; now that Yasha is alone, she goes up to him.

DUNYASHA:

You might at least look at me once, Yasha. You're leaving . . . deserting me . . . *(Cries and flings her arms around his neck)*

YASHA:

Why are you crying? *(Drinks champagne.)* In six days I'll be back in Paris. Tomorrow we'll take the express train and off we'll go in a cloud of dust. I can hardly believe it. Vive la France[460] . . . I don't like it here, I can't live here. That's the way it is. I've seen enough of this ignorance . . . I've had it! *(Drinks champagne)*[461] Why cry?

If you've been a good girl, you wouldn't have anything to cry about.⁴⁶²

DUNYASHA:

(Powders her nose, looking in a hand mirror) Send me a letter from Paris. After all, I loved you, Yasha, loved you so much!⁴⁶³ ~~I'm such a delicate creature, Yasha~~!

YASHA:

They're coming this way! *(Pretending to fuss over the suitcases, sings quietly.)* ~~"Oh wilt thou grasp the stirrings of my soul . . ."~~

Enter Lyubov Andreyevna, Gaev, Anya, and Charlotta Ivanovna.

GAEV:

We have to go. Not much time left. *(glowering at Yasha, speaking so only he can hear.)* You smell of sex, of the ladies?⁴⁶⁴

LYUBOV ANDREYEVNA:

In about ten [five] minutes we must take our seats in the carriages . . . *(Looks around the room)* Goodbye, dear old house, old grandfather.⁴⁶⁵ The winter will pass, spring will come, but you will no longer be, they will smash you up. These walls have seen so much! [If they could only speak to us.] *(Kisses her daughter warmly)* My treasure⁴⁶⁶, you are radiant, your eyes are sparkling like diamonds. Are you happy? Very happy?

ANYA:

Very! A new life, a new beginning, Mama!

GAEV:

(Happily) True, everything's alright now. Before the sale of the cherry orchard, all of us worried and suffered so much, and then, when the question was finally decided, once and for all, everyone calmed down, even became cheerful . . . I'm a banker now, I'm a financier[467] . . . Yellow ball into the center, and you, say what you like Lyuba, somehow you look better, no doubt about it.

LYUBOV ANDREYEVNA:

Yes. My nerves are calmer, that's true. *(They help her on with her hat and coat)* I sleep well. Bring out my things, Yasha. It's time. *(To Anya)* My little girl, we'll see each other again soon . . . I'm going to Paris, to live there on the money your great aunt from Yaroslavl sent to buy the estate. God bless your great aunt! But that money won't last long.[468]

ANYA:

Mama, you'll come back soon, soon . . . Won't you Mama? I'll study and take my school exams, and then I'll go to work and help you.[469] Mama, we'll read all kinds of books together.[470] Won't we? *(Kisses her mother's hands)* We'll read on autumn evenings, we'll read through lots of books, and a new, wonderful world will open up before us . . . *(dreamily)* Mama, come back[471] . . .

LYUBOV ANDREYEVNA:

I'll come back, I'll come, my golden one.[472] *(Hugs her daughter.)*

(Enter Lopakhin and Charlotta quietly singing a little song)

GAEV:

Lucky Charlotta, she's singing!

CHARLOTTA:

(Picks up a bundle and holds it to look like a baby wrapped in a blanket) My little baby, lullaby, lullaby . . . *(The baby's crying is heard: "Wa! Wa! ...")* Quiet, my pretty one, my dear little boy.[473] *("Wa! . . . Wa! ...")* You're breaking my heart. *(She throws the bundle down)*[474]

Please, find me a place. I can't go on like this.[475]

LOPAKHIN:

We'll find you a place, Charlotta Ivanovna, don't be afraid.[476]

GAEV:

They're all abandoning us;[477] Varya's going away . . . All of a sudden nobody needs us.

CHARLOTTA:

I've got nowhere to live in town. It's time to go away. *(Hums)* What difference does it make . . .

Enter Pishchik

LOPAKHIN:

God's gift!⁴⁷⁸

PISHCHIK:

Oy, let me catch my breath . . . I'm done in . . . My most noble friends . . . Give me some water . . .

GAEV:

Here for money, no doubt. Your humble servant, but I flee temptation . . . *(Exits)*

PISHCHIK:

I haven't been here for quite some time . . . My beauteous lady . . . *(To Lopakhin)* I'm so glad you're here . . . How wonderful to see you . . . A person with an immense intellect . . . Take this . . . It's for you . . . *(Hands Lopakhin some money)* Four hundred rubles . . . Now all I owe you is eight hundred forty . . .⁴⁷⁹

LOPAKHIN:

(Shrugs his shoulders in bewilderment) I must be dreaming . . . Where did you get it from?⁴⁸⁰

PISHCHIK:

Wait a moment . . . It's hot in here⁴⁸¹ . . . The most extraordinary thing happened. Some Englishmen came to see me and found some kind of white clay on my land . . .⁴⁸² *(To Lyubov Andreyevna)* And for you four hundred . . . You beautiful, amazing woman . . . *(Hands her money)* The rest will come later. *(Drinks some water)* Just now a young man in the train told me that a great philosopher has been advising people to jump off their roofs. Jump. That's his whole message. *(Amazed)* Can you imagine that? More water!

LOPAKHIN:

Who are these Englishmen?⁴⁸³

PISHCHIK:

I leased them the piece of the land with the clay⁴⁸⁴ on it for twenty-four years. And now, excuse me, I'm very busy . . . I'll tell you later . . . I'm going to Znóikov . . . and to Kardamónov . . . I owe everybody . . . *(Drinks the water)* Best of health to you all ⁴⁸⁵ . . . I'll be back on Thursday . . .⁴⁸⁶

LYUBOV ANDREYEVNA:

We're leaving for town today, and tomorrow I'm going abroad . . .

PISHCHIK:

What? *(Alarmed)* What are you going to town for? Oh, yes, I see the furniture . . . suitcases . .

. Well, never mind . . . *(Through tears)* Never mind . . . People of great intellect . . . these Englishmen . . . It's alright . . . Be happy . . . With God's help . . . Never mind . . . All good things must come to an end . . . *(Kisses Lyubov Andreyevna's hand)* And if news reaches that my end has come, remember that . . . that very same horse, and say, "Once there lived on this earth a certain so and so . . . a Simeonov-Pishchik . . . May God rest his soul". . .[487] Wonderful weather . . . Yes . . . *(Exits overcome with emotion, but immediately returns and says at the door)* Dashenka sends her regards! *(Exits)*

LYUBOV ANDREYEVNA:

Now we can leave. I'm leaving with two worries. The first . . . old Fiers is sick. *(Looking at her watch)* We still have five minutes.

ANYA:

Mama, they already took Fiers to the hospital. Yasha sent him off this morning.[488]

LYUBOV ANDREYEVNA:

My second worry is Varya. She's used to getting up early and working,[489] [490]and now without work she's like a fish out of water. She's getting thin, getting pale, and she cries all the time,[491] poor thing . . . *(Pause)*

You know very well, Ermolay Alekseyevich, that I've dreamed of giving her away to you in marriage, and everyone believed that you would marry her. *(Whispers to Anya, then nods to Charlotta; both exit.)* She loves you, you're fond of her, and I don't know, I don't know why you avoid each other. I don't understand!

LOPAKHIN:

To tell you the truth I don't understand it either. It's all so strange . . . If there's still time, I'm ready to do it right now . . . Let's finish this off immediately, and be done with it. [But without you I feel that I will never propose to her.]492

LYUBOV ANDREYEVNA:

Excellent. After all, you only need a minute. I'll call her right now . . .

LOPAKHIN:

We even have champagne, right here! *(Looking at the glasses)* They're empty, someone's drunk it all. *(Yasha hiccups)*

That's what's known as really putting it away . . .

LYUBOV ANDREYEVNA:

(In a lively manner) Wonderful. We'll leave you . . . Yasha, allez!493 I'll call her . . . *(At the door)* Varya, drop everything and come here. Come on at once! *(Exits with Yasha)*494

LOPAKHIN:

(Looking at his watch) Yes . . . *(Pause)*

Behind the door, a stifled laugh, whispers, finally Varya enters

VARYA:

(Looking through the baggage for a long time) It's strange, I can't seem to find . . .

LOPAKHIN:

What are you looking for?

VARYA:

I packed it myself and I can't remember where. *(Pause)*

LOPAKHIN:

Where will you go, Varvara Mikhailovna?[495]

VARYA:

Me? To the Ragúlins . . . I agreed to run the house for them . . . A housekeeper, I guess you'd call it.

LOPAKHIN:

That's in Yáshnevo, isn't it? That's about forty-three miles.[496] *(Pause)*

So life in this house is over.[497]

VARYA:

(Examining the baggage) Where can it be . . .? Maybe I put it in the trunk . . . Yes, life in this

house is over . . .⁴⁹⁸ There won't be any anymore, ever . . .⁴⁹⁹

LOPAKHIN:

I'm going to Kharkov right now . . . on the next train. I have a lot of business there. I'm leaving Epikhodov here in charge of the property . . . I've hired him.⁵⁰⁰

VARYA:

You have?⁵⁰¹ ⁵⁰²

LOPAKHIN:

Last year at this time we had snow already, if you remember, and now it's calm, sunny. Only it's cold . . . Three degrees below freezing.⁵⁰³

VARYA:

I didn't look. *(Pause)* Actually, our thermometer is broken.⁵⁰⁴ *(Pause)*

A voice at the door from outside:

"Ermolay Alekseyevich . . ." ⁵⁰⁵

LOPAKHIN:

(As if he had been waiting for this call) Right away! *(Exits quickly)* ⁵⁰⁶

Varya sits on the floor, puts her head on a bundle tied up with a scarf, and quietly sobs, The door opens, Lyubov Andreyevna enters cautiously.

LYUBOV ANDREYEVNA:

Well? (Pause.)⁵⁰⁷ We must go now.

VARYA:

(No longer crying, wipes her eyes) Yes, it's time, Mamochka. I'll make it to the Ragulins today, that is if I don't miss the train . . .

LYUBOV ANDREYEVNA:

(At the door) Anya, put on your coat!

*Enter Anya, then Gaev, Charlotta Ivanovna; Gaev wears a heavy cloth overcoat with a hood.*⁵⁰⁸ *Servants and coachmen come in. Epikhodov busies himself near the baggage.*

LYUBOV ANDREYEVNA:

Now we can go.

ANYA:

(Joyfully) We can go!

GAEV:

My friends, my dears, my darling ones! As we leave this house forever, how can I stand silent, how can I refrain from expressing in way of farewell, those emotions which now well up within my whole being . . .

ANYA:

(Pleadingly) Uncle!

VARYA:

Dear Uncle, don't!

GAEV:

(Despondently) Yellow ball, rebound to the center . . . I'll be quiet . . .

Enter Trofimov, then Lopakhin

TROFIMOV:

Well, ladies and gentlemen. It's time to go!

LOPAKHIN:

Epikhodov, my coat.[509]

LYUBOV ANDREYEVNA:

I must sit down for just one more minute.[510] I feel as if I've never seen what the walls of this house look like, what the ceilings are like, and now I look at them with such a hunger as if I see them for the first time and with such tender love . . .

GAEV:

I remember when I was six years old, on Trinity Sunday;[511] I sat at this window and watched my father go off to church . . .

LYUBOV ANDREYEVNA:

Is everything ready? Have we taken all the luggage?

LOPAKHIN:

I think you've got everything. Everything's set. *(To Epikhodov, putting on his coat.)* Make sure, Epikhodov, that you keep things straight.

EPIKHODOV:

(Talks in a hoarse voice) Don't you worry, Ermolay Alekseyevich!

LOPAKHIN:

What's wrong with your voice?

EPIKHODOV:

I just drank some water and swallowed something in it.[512]

YASHA:

(With contempt) The ignorance . . .

LYUBOV ANDREYEVNA:

We'll go and not a living soul will be left behind . . .[513]

LOPAKHIN:

Until spring.

VARYA:

(Pulling an umbrella out of a bundle in a way that looks as if she were going to hit someone; Lopakhin pretends to be afraid.[514]) Don't be silly. What are you doing . . . What . . . I didn't mean to . . .

TROFIMOV:

> Ladies and gentlemen, we must go to the carriages . . . It's time! The train will be arriving any minute!

VARYA:

> Petya, here, your galoshes are right here, near this suitcase. *(With tears in her eyes)* They're so old, so dirty . . .[515]

TROFIMOV:

> *(Pulling on the filthy galoshes)* Let's go, ladies and gentlemen![516]

GAEV:

(Deeply moved, afraid of crying)

> The train . . . The station . . . Cross shot into the middle, the cue ball rebounds to the corner . . .

LYUBOV ANDREYEVNA:

> Let's go!

LOPAKHIN:

> Everybody's here? Is anybody in there? *(locks the side door on the left)* I've got things stored in here so we have to lock it up. Let's go . . .

ANYA:

> Goodbye, house! Goodbye, old life!

TROFIMOV:

> Hello, new life . . . *(Exits with Anya)*

Varya looks around the room and exits without hurrying. Yasha and Charlotta with her dog, exit.

LOPAKHIN:

> Well then, until the spring comes.[517] Let's go, out this way[518], ladies and gentlemen . . .[519] Until we meet again . . .[520] *(Exits)*

Lyubov Andreyevna and Gaev remain together alone. They seem to have been waiting for this moment, and throw their arms around each other, but hold back their deepest sobs, crying quietly, afraid to be heard.

GAEV:

> *(In despair[521])* My sister, my sister.

LYUBOV ANDREYEVNA:

> Oh, my sweet, my tender, my beautiful orchard . . . My life, my youth, my happiness, farewell . . . Farewell . . .

Voice of ANYA, happily calling:

> "Mama . . ."

Voice of TROFIMOV, (happily, excitedly):

> "Haloo . . ."[522]

LYUBOV ANDREYEVNA:

This is the last time I'll see these walls, the windows . . . My dear mother loved to walk around this room . . .

GAEV:

My sister, my sister...[523]

Voice of Anya:

"Mama . . ."

Voice of Trofimov:

"Haloo . . ."

LYUBOV ANDREYEVNA:

We're coming . . . *(They exit)*

The stage is empty. A key is heard locking the door, then the carriages are heard driving off. It becomes quiet. In the silence the dull thud of the axe cutting into the cherry trees is heard, sounding lonely and sad. Footsteps are heard; Fiers appears at the door to the right. He is dressed, as always, in a jacket and a white waistcoat. On his feet he wears slippers. He is sick.[524]

FIERS:

(Approaches the door, tries the door handle) It's locked. They've gone... *(Sits on the couch)* They forgot about me . . . Nevermind . . . I'll just sit here for a while . . . I suppose Leonid Andreyevich didn't put on his fur coat, went out in the cloth coat . . . *(Heaves a sigh, worried)* And I didn't look after it. These

children![525] *(Mumbles something that cannot be understood)* Life is over as if I never lived it . . .[526] *(Lies down)* I'll lie down for a minute or so . . . You don't have your strength now, do you? Nothing's left, nothing . . . Ah you . . . Numbskull . . .[527] *(Lies motionless)*

(A distant sound is heard, as if coming from the sky... the sound of a snapping string, dying away mournfully.[528] The silence descends and is disturbed only by the faraway sound of the axe chopping down the trees[529] in the cherry orchard.[530])

Curtain

About Translations of Chekhov in General:

"Most of the published translations of Chekhov are done either by native Russians, whose English is often awkward and stilted, or by Russian scholars, whose English is often formal and unidiomatic. The others are "versions" or "adaptations" done by playwrights who know no Russian; they work either by comparing existing translations or by hiring a Russian to help them. Inevitably their sense of what Chekhov actually wrote is extremely attenuated. And when they are playwrights with a strong dramatic language of their own, Chekhov's style and nuance are usually subordinated to theirs." Paul Schmidt, Introduction to *The Plays of Anton Chekhov, A New Translation,* Harper Collins Publishers, 1997
Attenuate: "To reduce in force, value, amount, or degree; weaken." Schmidt is too gentle in his criticism.

"Dramatists remote from Chekhov's sensibility, language, and concerns, such as Pam Gems, Edward Bond, David Mamet, Trevor Griffiths, Lanford Wilson, David Hare, Brian Friel, and Richard Nelson, transmogrify him in new versions, refracting their own preoccupations. This need of the English-speaking playwright to wrestle Chekhov to the mat has become a rite of passage. There is something compulsively Oedipal in this recurrent grappling with the one universally admitted patriarch of the modern stage." Laurence Senelick, from the Introduction to *The Complete Plays, Anton Chekhov,* W. W. Norton & Company

"The literary psychoanalyst Gregory Zilboorg, initiating American readers into Russian drama in 1920, stated point blank that Chekhov was fundamentally untranslatable, more so even than Ostrovsky and Gorky. 'Chekhov's plays lose their chief element in translation into whatever other language: the particular harmony and rhythm of the original. The student must bear in mind that studying Chekhov's drama in English he actually studies only some elements of them, the rest being lost in a foreign language.' Gregory Zilboorg, "A course in Russian drama," The Drama (November 1920): 69. Quoted by Senelick in, *The Complete Plays, Anton Chekhov, Translated, Edited and Annotated by Laurence Senelick,* W. W. Norton & Company

Ian McKellen, in 1998:
"The big problem with Chekhov is that we don't do Chekhov we do translations of Chekhov. Very few translators, at least those I've worked with, work from the original. Instead they come from literal translations… It's constantly frustrating not to know how close you are to his intentions. I think it is a crucial question ..."
The Cambridge Companion to Chekhov, Cambridge, 2000, P. 122

"Nevertheless, the fact remains that Chekhov's plays frequently reach British [one can say the same about American] audiences via several layers of ignorance. Versions are created by writers unable to read Russian, and then staged by directors and actors, reviewed by critics, and received by audiences, nearly all of whom have no knowledge of the original Russian text." Gordon McVay, *Anton Chekhov: The Unbelieving Believer*

"… Once somebody or something becomes the object of a cult then even the craziest idea can be accepted without questioning. That is the explanation of why an English director does not hesitate to sit down with several translations of a Chekhov play and proceed to write his own 'version', for he is convinced that he knows what Chekhov *ought to have* written, and he manipulates his or somebody else's version of the play accordingly: gloom, despondency, a dialogue that makes no sense; a few Russian words scattered here and there, a general atmosphere of gloom and despair; and scenery that is the work of some celebrated stage designer and that by itself is sufficient to kill the play stone dead." Magarshack, David, *The Real Chekhov, An Introduction to Chekhov's Last Plays*, GEORGE ALLEN & UNWIN LTD London, 1972

Chekhov's Words

In an 1889 letter to Suvorin:
In addition to plenty of material and talent, one should have something else which is no less important. One should be mature—that is one thing; and for another the feeling of personal freedom is essential, and that feeling has only recently begun to develop in me. I used not to have it before; its place was successfully filled by my frivolity, carelessness, and lack of respect for my work.

What writers belonging to the upper class have received from nature for nothing, the lower classes acquire at the forfeiture of their youth. Write a story of how a young man, the son of a serf, who has served in a shop, sung in a church choir, been at a high school and a university, who has been brought up to respect everyone of higher rank and position, to kiss priests' hands, to reverence other people's ideas, to be thankful for every morsel of bread, who has been many times beaten, who has trudged from one pupil to another without galoshes, who has been used to fighting, and tormenting animals, who has liked dining with his rich relations, and been hypocritical before God and men from the mere consciousness of his own insignificance—write how this young man squeezes the slave out of himself, drop by drop, and how waking one beautiful morning he feels that he has no longer a slave's blood in his veins but a real man's.

Letter to Suvorin:
My business, is merely to be talented, i.e., to know how to distinguish important statements from unimportant, how to throw light on the characters and to speak their language. Shcheglov-Leontyev blames me for finishing my story with the words: 'There's no making out anything in this world.' He thinks a writer

who is a good psychologist ought to be able to make it out, that is what he is a psychologist for. But I don't agree with him. It is time that writers, especially those who are artists, recognized that there is no making out anything in this world, as once Socrates recognized it, and Voltaire too.

Letter to Pleshcheyev, October, 1889:
I am afraid of those who look for a tendency between the lines, and who are determined to regard me as a liberal or as a conservative. I am not a liberal, not a conservative, not a believer in gradual progress, not a monk, not an indifferentist… I regard trade-marks and labels as a superstition. My holy of holies is the human body, health, intelligence, talent, inspiration, love, and the most absolute freedom - freedom from violence and lying, whatever forms they may take. This is the programme I would follow if I were a great artist.

Anton Chekhov's character Dmitry Silin in *Terror*
… I'm not much interested in such questions as the hereafter or the fate of humanity and I'm not much of a one for flights into the sublime either. What terrifies me most is just ordinary everyday routine, the thing none of us can escape … My living conditions and upbringing have imprisoned me in a closed circle of lies, I know … Worrying how to deceive myself and others every day without noticing that I'm doing so … that's my entire existence, I know that too, and I dread not being rid of this fraud until I'm in my grave.

Chekhov:
Vint (similar to both bridge and whist) has killed more people in Russia than all the epidemics of cholera, plague and typhus put together.

Chekhov:
"...may the devil take this philosophy of the great ones of this earth!... All the great sages are as despotic as generals, and as uncivil as generals, too, because they are convinced of their impunity."

Chekhov:
'It's only fools and charlatans who know everything and understand everything.'

Chekhov:
You abuse me for objectivity, calling it indifference to good and evil, lack of ideals and ideas, and so on. You would have me, when I describe horse-thieves, say: 'Stealing horses is an evil.' But that has been known for ages without my saying so.

On Chekhov

Tolstoy on Chekhov:
"He is a strange writer: he throws words about as if at random, and yet everything is alive. And what understanding. He never has any superfluous details; every one of them is either necessary or beautiful." from Aleksandr Borisovich Goldenveizer, *Talks with Tolstoy* Translated by S. S. Koteliansky and Virginia Woolf, The Hogarth Press, Richmond, England

Vladimir Nabokov:
"What really attracted the Russian reader was that in Chekhov's heroes he recognized the Russian idealist . . . a man who combined the deepest human decency of which man is capable with an almost ridiculous inability to put his ideals and principles

into action; a man devoted to moral beauty, the welfare of his people, the welfare of the universe, but unable in his private life to do anything useful; frittering away his provincial existence in a haze of utopian dreams; knowing exactly what is good, what is worthwhile living for, but at the same time sinking lower and lower in the mud of a humdrum existence, unhappy in love, hopelessly inefficient in everything—a good man who cannot make good." Vladimir Nabokov, *Lectures on Russian Literature,* London, 1981, p. 253.

"Chekhov managed to convey an impression of artistic beauty far surpassing that of writers who thought they knew what rich, beautiful prose was. He did it by keeping all his words in the same dim light of the same exact tint of gray, a tint between the color of an old fence and that of a low cloud. The variety of his moods, the flicker of his charming wit, the deeply artistic economy of characterization, the vivid detail, and the fade-out of human life--all peculiar Chekhovian features--are enhanced by being suffused and surrounded by a faintly iridescent verbal haziness." Vladimir Nabokov, Lectures on Russian Literature, London, 1981 P. 253

Chekhov's character Professor Nikolai Stepanovich of "A Dreary Story", (a story which Thomas Mann loved: "… for it is my favorite among all Chekhov's stories, an outstandingly fascinating work which for gentleness, sadness, and strangeness has no equal in the literary world."):

"As for serious treatises in Russian on sociology, for instance, on art, and so on, I do not read them simply from timidity. In my childhood and early youth, I had for some reason a terror of doorkeepers and attendants at the theatre, and that terror has remained with me to this day. It is said that we are only afraid of what we do not understand. And, indeed, it is very difficult to understand why doorkeepers and theatre attendants are so dignified, haughty, and majestically rude. I feel exactly the same terror when I read serious articles. Their extraordinary dignity, their bantering lordly tone, their familiar manner to foreign authors, their ability to split straws with dignity-   all that is beyond my understanding."

from *Winesburg, Ohio*, *The Book of the Grotesque*   by Sherwood Anderson:
"That in the beginning when the world was young there were a great many thoughts but no such thing as a truth. Man made the truths himself and each truth was a composite of a great many vague thoughts. All about in the world were the truths and they were all beautiful…

And then the people came along. Each as he appeared snatched up one of the truths and some who were quite strong snatched up a dozen of them.

It was the truths that made the people grotesques. The old man had quite an elaborate theory concerning the matter. It was his notion that the moment one of the people took one of the truths to himself, called it his truth, and tried to live his life by it, he became a grotesque and the truth he embraced became a falsehood."

Tennessee Williams:
"What writers influenced me as a young man? Chekhov! As a dramatist? Chekhov! As a story writer? Chekhov!"

Eudora Welty:
"Reading Chekhov was just like the angels singing to me."

Katherine Mansfield:
Katherine Mansfield consoled herself with thoughts of heaven, which for her, was the living presence of Chekhov:
> "I must start writing again... Ach, Tchekhov! Why are you dead! Why can't I talk to you - in a big, darkish room - at late evening - where the light is green from the waving trees outside. I'd like to write a series of Heavens: that would be one."

The Katherine Mansfield Notebooks, ed. Margaret Scott (Minneapolis, 2002)

Elizabeth Hardwick:
"The short stories of Chekhov are an inexhaustible treasury of humanity and wisdom. The naturalness of their form and the luminous simplicity of their turning away from the forced conclusion defined a large part of the modern tradition in short fiction."

Cynthia Ozick:
"Each story, no matter how allusive or broken-off, is nevertheless exhaustive--like the curve of a shard that implies not simply the form of the pitcher entire, but also the thirsts of its shattered civilization."

John Barth:
"Dr. Chekhov is a superb anatomist of the human heart and an utter master of his literary means. The details of scene and behavior, the emotions registered-- seldom bravura, typically muted and complex, often as surprising to the characters themselves as to the reader, but always right-- move, astonish, and delight us, line after line, story after story, volume after volume."

William Maxwell:

"It seems to be part of the human condition that a wall of glass separates one life from another. For Chekhov it did not exist... The greatest of his stories are, no matter how many times reread, always an experience that strikes deep into the soul and produces an alteration there."

Susan Sontag:
 "Chekhov is one of the few indispensable writers. His stories, which deluge us with feeling, make feeling more intelligent; more magnanimous. He is an artist of our moral maturity."

Shelby Foote asked Walker Percy if he had read "In the Ravine." He said he hadn't, and Foote said: " 'I'd rather have written *In the Ravine* than Moby Dick'. His eyebrows rose at this, as well they might, but he went home and read that great last long story-in which all the author's talents seem to be gathered together as naturally as a hand closing into a fist- and wound up in a state of exaltation similar to my own. Echoing Nabokov on Chekhov's near-miraculous combination of the funny and the sad, he shook his head in wonder. 'I don't know how it can be so pitiful and funny,' he wrote me later. 'I have to laugh out loud' "
Anton Chekhov's Short Stories Selections, Introduction by Shelby Foote, The Modern Library, NY. Lest we forget, Nabokov said "Things for him [Chekhov] were funny and sad at the same time, but you would not see their sadness if you did not see their fun, because both were linked up."

"Chekhov is the bearer of the greatest banner that has been raised in the thousand years of Russian history, the banner of a true, humane, Russian democracy, of Russian freedom, of the dignity of the Russian man." Words of a fictional character in Vasily Grossman's, *Life and Fate*, Жизнь и судьба, translated by Robert Chandler, New York, Perennial Library, 1987. Written in the 1950s, submitted for publication to Znamya magazine in

1960. The KGB seized the manuscripts, carbon copies, notebooks, and even the typewriter ribbons; however, two copies survived with friends. It was not published in Russia until 1988.

Paris Review - The Art of Fiction No. 76, Raymond Carver:
"Chekhov. I suppose he's the writer whose work I most admire… made me see things differently than I had ever before."
"Anyone who reads literature, anyone who believes, as one must in the transcendent power of art, sooner or later has to read Chekhov"
Fires, London, Pan, 1986, p. 24

The New York Times, February 15, 1981
A Storyteller's Shoptalk
RAYMOND CARVER:
"It's possible, in a poem or a short story, to write about commonplace things and objects using commonplace but precise language, and to endow those things - a chair, a window curtain, a fork, a stone, a woman's earring - with immense, even startling power. It is possible to write a line of seemingly innocuous dialogue and have it send a chill along the reader's spine - the source of artistic delight, as Nabokov would have it. That's the kind of writing that most interests me."

Leonard Cohen described his mother, a Russian Jew, with great affection as "Chekhovian"; "She laughed and wept deeply."
Harry Rasky, The Song of Leonard Cohen: Portrait of a Poet, a Friendship and a Film, Souvenir Press, 2001.
[Laughter and tears, often simultaneous, are not mutually exclusive].

Bibliography

Allain, Paul and Gottlieb, Vera editors of *The Cambridge Companion to Chekhov*, Cambridge University Press, 2000

Baehr, Stephen L., *The Machine in Chekhov's Garden: Progress and Pastoral in the Cherry Orchard,* The Slavic and East European Journal, Vol. 43, No. 1 (Spring, 1999), pp. 99-121, American Association of Teachers of Slavic and East European Languages

Balukhaty, S. D. "*The Cherry Orchard:* A Formalist Approach," in *Chekhov: A Collection of Critical Essays,* ed. Robert Louis Jackson, Prentice-Hall, Englewood Cliffs, N.J 1967

Barricelli, Jean Pierre, *Chekhov's great plays : a critical anthology,* New York : New York University Press, Gotham library of the New York University Press, 1981.

Beckerman, Bernard, *Dramatic Analysis and Literary Interpretation: The Cherry Orchard as Exemplum*, New Literary History, Vol. 2, No. 3, Performances in Drama, the Arts, and Society (Spring, 1971), pp. 391-406, The Johns Hopkins University Press

Belchikov, N. F., and others, eds., Anton Chekhov, Polnoe sobranie sochinenii ipisem v 30 tomakh, Moscow, 1974-83 (*Anton Chekhov, Collected Works and Letters in 30 Volumes, Moscow, 1974-83*)

Bentley, Eric, *Chekhov as Playwright* (Reconsiderations, No. XI)

The Kenyon Review, Kenyon College Vol. 11, No. 2 (Spring, 1949), pp. 226-250

Bergson, H., 'Laughter', in Sypher, W., ed., *Comedy*, Doubleday Anchor, New York, 1956

Bergson, H., *Laughter: An Essay on the Meaning of the Comic*, Macmillan and Co., London, 1935

Bloom, Harold, *Bloom's Modern Critical Views, ANTON CHEKHOV,* Edited and with an introduction, Yale University

Bloom, Harold, *Dramatists and Drama,* Chelsea House Publishers, Philadelphia, 2005

Borny, Geoffrey, *Interpreting Chekhov,* Chapter Title: *The Cherry Orchard: Complete Synthesis of Vision and Form*, ANU Press. (2006)

Braun, Edward. *The Cherry Orchard* in *The Cambridge Companion to Chekhov*, edited by Vera Gottlieb and Paul Allain, Cambridge University Press, 2000

Brandon, James R., *Toward a Middle-View of Chekhov*, Educational Theatre Journal. (December 1960), Johns Hopkins University Press. 12 (4): 270–275.

Brintlinger, Angela *The Cherry Orchard in the Twenty-First Century: New Adaptations and Versions,* with Carol Apollonio, Bloomington, IN: Slavica Publishers, 2012, 247–67.

Calderon, George, *Two plays by Tchekhof : the Seagull, the Cherry Orchard Translated with an Introduction and Notes* Grant Richards Ltd. London, 1912

Callow, Philip *Chekhov: The Hidden Ground* Ivan R. Dee.

Chudakov, Alexander, *Dr. Chekhov: a biographical essay (29 January 1860-15 July 1904)* in Allain, Paul and Gottlieb, Vera editors of *The Cambridge Companion to Chekhov*, Cambridge University Press, 2000

Columbus, Curt, *Chekhov: The Four Major Plays: Seagull, Uncle Vanya, Three Sisters, Cherry Orchard,* Ivan R. Dee, October 7, 2004

Corrigan, R., 'Stanislavski and the Playwright', in Corrigan, R., ed., *Theatre in the Twentieth Century*, Grove Press, New York, 1965

Corrigan, Robert W. "The Plays of Chekhov" re- printed in *The Context and Craft of Drama* , ed. Robert W. Corrigan and James L. Rosenberg, Chandler Publishing Company, San Francisco

Cross, A. G., *The Breaking Strings of Chekhov and Turgenev* The Slavonic and East European Review, Vol. 47, No. 109 pp. 510-513, the Modern Humanities Research Association and University College London, School of Slavonic and East European Studies, July, 1969

Deer, Irving, *Speech as Action in Chekhov's "The Cherry Orchard"* Educational Theatre Journal, Vol. 10, No. 1 pp. 30-34, Johns Hopkins University Press, March 1958

Ehre Milton, Translation with Introduction *Chekhov for the Stage: The Sea Gull, Uncle Vanya, The Three Sisters, The Cherry Orchard*, Northwestern University Press, December 9, 1992

Evdokimova, Svetlana, *What's so Funny about Losing One's Estate, or Infantilism in "The Cherry Orchard"*, The Slavic and East European Journal, Vol. 44, No. 4 (Winter, 2000), pp. 623-648, American Association of Teachers of Slavic and East European Languages

Fergusson, F., *The Idea of a Theater*, Doubleday Anchor, New York, 1953

Figes, Orlando, *A People's Tragedy; The Russian Revolution 1891-1924*, London, 1996

Flath, Carol, *Writing about Nothing: Chekhov's 'Ariadna' and the Narcissistic Narrator,* The Slavonic and East European Review, Vol. 77, No. 2 (Apr., 1999), pp. 223-239, The Modern Humanities Research Association and University College London School of Slavonic and East European Studies

Frayne, Michael, *Anton Chekhov, Plays, Introduction*, Methuen Publishing Ltd., London

Freedman, M., *'Chekhov's Morality of Work'*, Modern Drama, Vol. 5, No. 1, 1962.

Gassner, J., 'The Duality of Chekhov', in Bristow, E. K., *Anton Chekhov's Plays*, W. W. Norton, New York, 1977

Gerould, Daniel Charles, *The Cherry Orchard As A Comedy,* The Journal of General Education, Vol. 11, No. 2 (April 1958), pp. 109-122 Penn State University Press

Gillman, Richard, *CHEKHOV'S PLAYS An Opening into Eternity,* Yale University Press, New Haven and London

Gorky, Maxim, *Anton Chekhov: Fragments of Recollections,* B. W. Huebsch, Inc., 1921

Gottlieb, Vera and Allain, Paul, editors of *The Cambridge Companion to Chekhov*, Cambridge University Press, 2000

Gottlieb, Vera, 'Chekhov in Limbo: British Productions of the Plays of Chekhov', in Scolnicov, H. and Holland, P., eds, *The Play Out of Context: Transferring Plays from Culture to Culture,* Cambridge University Press, Cambridge, 1989

Griffiths, T., '*The Cherry Orchard:* A New English Version by Trevor Griffiths', in Miles, P., ed., *Chekhov on the British Stage*, Cambridge University Press, Cambridge, 1993, p. 163

Gruber, William E., "CHEKHOV'S ILLUSION OF INACTION." CLA Journal, vol. 20, no. 4, 1977, pp. 508–520.

Guthke, K. S., *Modern Tragi-Comedy*, Random House, New York, 1996

Hahn, Beverley, *Chekhov: A Study of the Major Stories and* Plays (Major European Authors Series) Cambridge University Press, May 5, 1977

Heim, Michael, translator with commentary by Simon Karlinsky *Letters of Anton Chekhov*, Harper & Row, New York

Heim, Michael Henry, *Anton Chekhov: The Essential Plays: The Seagull, Uncle Vanya, Three Sisters & The Cherry Orchard, Translated, with an Introduction and Notes, by Michael Henry Heim* (Modern Library Classics) Random House Publishing Group.

Hingley, Ronald, *A New Life of Anton Chekhov,* Knopf, New York, 1976

Jackson, Robert Louis, "What time Is It? Where Are We Going?", *Chekhov's The Cherry Orchard: The Story of a Verb* in Close Encounters, Essays on Russian Literature, Academic Studies Press. (2013)

Jackson, Robert Louis, originally in Russian under the title "Kotoryi chas? Kuda my idem? Vyshnevyi sad kak istoriia glagola," in the Moscow theater journal, Teatr. Literaturno-khudozhestvennyi zhurnal 2 (2006): 145–150.

Jones, W. Gareth, *Chekhov's Undercurrent of Time*
The Modern Language Review, Vol. 64, No. 1 (Jan., 1969), pp. 111-121 Modern Humanities Research Association

Kataev, Vladimir, *If Only We Could Know,* Translated by Harvey Pitcher, Ivan R, Dee, 2003

Latham, Jacqueline E. M. *"The Cherry Orchard" as Comedy*, Educational Theatre Journal, Vol. 10, No. 1 (Mar., 1958), pp. 21-29, The Johns Hopkins University Press

Le Blanc, Ronald D., *Two-And-Twenty Misfortunes: Epixodov, Farce, and the Subversive Nature of Laughter in Višnevyj sad,*

Linden, Anna L., *Chekhov vs. Gorkii and The Moscow Arts Theater*, Russian History, Vol. 18, No. 4 (WINTER 1991 / HIVER 1991), pp. 501-528, Brill

Lehrman, Alexander, *Anton Čechov's "Višnevyj sad". A Critical Edition of the Original Russian Text with an Introduction, a New Translation and Supplementary Materials*

Loehlin, James N., *Chekhov The Cherry Orchard*, CAMBRIDGE UNIVERSITY PRESS, Cambridge, New York, Melbourne, Madrid, Cape Town, Singapore, Sao Paulo, 2006

Magarshack, David, *Chekhov the Dramatist*, Eyre Methuen, London,
1980

Magarshack, David, *The Real Chekhov, An Introduction to Chekhov's Last Plays,* GEORGE ALLEN & UNWIN LTD London, 1972

Müller, H., *The Spirit of Tragedy*, Alfred A. Knopf, New York, 1956

Pevear, Richard, (Translator and Introduction) with Richard Nelson (Translator), Larissa Volokhonsky (Translator) *The Cherry Orchard by Anton Chekhov* (TCG Classic Russian Drama Series) Theatre Communications Group, August 3, 2015

Pitcher, Harvey, *The Chekhov Play: A New Interpretation*, Chatto and Windus, London, 1973

Pritchett, V.S, *Chekhov: A Spirit Set Free*, Viking, New York, 1989

Magarshack, David, *Chekhov the Dramatist,* Hill and Wang, New York, 1960

Magarshack, David, *THE REAL CHEKHOV, An Introduction to Chekhov's Last Plays,*
GEORGE ALLEN & UNWIN LTD, LONDON, 1972

McAfee, Helen, *Tchekhov, and the Spirit of the East*
The North American Review, Vol. 204, No. 729 (Aug., 1916), pp. 282-291 University of Northern Iowa

Meierkhold, Vsevolod, *The Naturalistic Theater and the Theater of Mood* from A Norton Critical Edition, *Anton Chekhov's Selected Plays*, edited by Laurence Senelick, W. W. Norton & Company New York, London, 2005

Moravcevich, N., *'The Dark Side of the Chekhovian Smile'*, Drama Survey, Vol. 5, No. 3, Winter 1996–7

Nabokov, Vladimir, *Lectures on Russian Literature*, London, 1981

Nabokov, Vladimir, *Strong Opinions*, New York: Vantage International, 1973

Parts, Lyudmilla, *The Chekhovian Intertext: Dialogue with a Classic*, 2nd Edition, Ohio State University Press, April 22, 2008

Parts, Lyudmilla, *Chekhov, Literature, and the Intelligentsia in Viacheslav Pietsukh's Stories*, The Slavic and East European Journal, Vol. 46, No. 2 (Summer, 2002), pp. 301-317 Published:

American Association of Teachers of Slavic and East European Languages

Rayfield, Donald, *Anton Chekhov: A Life*, Faber & Faber. Henry Holt & Co; 1st American edition, March 1998

Rayfield, Donald, *THE CHERRY ORCHARD Catastrophe and Comedy,* TWAYNE PUBLISHERS, NEW YORK, 1994

Remaley, Peter P., *Chekov's "The Cherry Orchard"* South Atlantic Bulletin, Vol. 38, No. 4 (Nov., 1973), pp. 16-20

Risso, Richard, *Chekhov: A View of the Basic Ironic Structures* from Jean Pierre Barricelli, *Chekhov's great plays: a critical anthology*, New York University Press, Gotham library of the New York University Press, New York, 1981

Schmidt, Paul, The Plays of Anton Chekhov, A New Translation, Harper Collins, 1997

Senderovich, Savely, *The Cherry Orchard: Chekhov's Last Testament* in *Bloom's Modern Critical Views, ANTON CHEKHOV,* Edited and with an introduction, Yale University

Sendich, Munir, *ANTON CHEKHOV IN ENGLISH: A Comprehensive Bibliography of Works About and By Him* (1889-1984) Russian Language Journal / Русский язык, Vol. 39, No. 132/134, (1985), pp. 227-379, American Councils for International Education

Senelick, Laurence, *The Chekhov Theatre: A Century of the Plays in Performance*, Cambridge University Press

Simmons, Ernest J. *Chekhov: A Biography,* Little, Brown, Boston and Toronto, 1962

Soloski, Alexis, Review of Lev Dodin's Maly Drama Theater production at the BAM in *The New York Times* Feb 18, 2016 *'The Cherry Orchard,' the Myopia of an Aristocratic Family*

Stepanov, A. D. Problemy kommunikatsii u Chekhova. Studia philologica. Iazyki slavianskoi kul'tury, Moscow, 2005

Styan, J. L., *The Idea of a Definitive Production: Chekhov in and out of Period,* Comparative Drama, Vol. 4, No. 3 (Fall 1970), pp. 177-196

Styan, J. L., 'The Delicate Balance: Audience Ambivalence in the Comedy of Shakespeare and Chekhov', Costerus, Vol. 2, 1972

Troyat, Henry, *Chekhov,* Dutton, New York, 1986

Tulloch, John, *Chekhov: A Structuralist Study*, Palgrave Macmillan, New York, 1980

Warner, P., *The Axe in Springtime (The Cherry Orchard)* Theoria: A Journal of Social and Political Theory, No. 10 (1958), pp. 41-57, Berghahn Books in association with the Faculty of Humanities, Development and Social Sciences, University of Kwa Zulu-Natal, South Africa

Wolf, Tobias, introduction to *Anton Chekhov, Five Plays*, translated by Maria Brodskaya, Stanford University Press, California

Worrall, Nick comp., *File on Chekhov,* Methuen, London and New York, 1986

End Notes

[1] According to Stanislavsky, Chekhov wavered between the pronunciations Vishnevy sad (accentuated on the first syllable, "an orchard of cherries") and Vishnyovy sad (accentuated on the second syllable, "a cherry orchard"). He chose the latter. "The former is a market garden, a plantation of cherry-trees, a profitable orchard which had value. But the latter offers no profit, it does nothing but preserve within itself and its snow-white blossoms the poetry of the life of the masters of olden times" (My Life in Art). Such an Orchard is beautiful but profitless. Alexander Lehrman [*Anton Cechov's Visnevyj sad. A Critical Edition of the Text with an Introduction, a New Translation and Supplementary Materials,* Otto Sanger, Munich 2009] who translates and analyses the original Russian text has a different take on this: Lehrman also questions where the stress should be placed in the play's title, but asserts that the current (Soviet and post-Soviet period) pronunciation, now nearly universally accepted, is incorrect. Thus, Vishnevy sad, which means "The Cherry-Colored Orchard," is contrary to Chekhov's intention in both stress and meaning, Vishnyovy sad, "The Orchard of Cherry Trees." This putative mispronunciation of the play title is attributed to Stanislavsky, who Lehrman insists did not understand what the correct usage should be: "The accent on the first syllable "cherry-tree" (adj.) is bookish, aristocratic, and archaically recherché, in contrast to the common accent on the second syllable, relating to the fruit (as in 'cherry pit') or its color. These stylistic and social facts are intimately connected with the attitudes and mores of the estate's owners, Lyubov Andreyevna Ranevskaya and her brother Leonid Gaev and so with the fate of the Cherry Orchard."

² (komediya v chetyrekh deystviyakh) This subtitle was used in the Marks edition of 1904. On the posters and publicity the play was called a drama. Chekhov never agreed: "Why is it that my play is persistently called a 'drama' in the posters and newspaper advertisements? Nemirovich- Danchenko and Stanislavsky see in my play something completely different from what I have written, and I am ready to stake my word that neither of them has read my play through attentively even once" (letter to Olga Knipper of April 10, 1904). In a letter to Madame Stanislavsky on September 15, 1903, Chekhov wrote of *The Cherry Orchard* that "the play has turned out not a drama, but a comedy, in parts even a farce [vodevii]." Chekhov states: "Stanislavski has ruined the play for me." In fact, the enmity was such that after Chekhov's death Vladimir Nemirovich-Danchenko, wrote to Stanislavsky: "We had already lost Chekhov after *The Cherry Orchard*. He would not have written anything more. [for The Moscow Art Theater]" His letter to Olga Knipper of September 21, 1903 echoes this sentiment: "The last act will be merry, and the whole play will be cheerful and light-hearted." J. L. Styan [*The Idea of a Definitive Production: Chekhov in and out of Period,* Comparative Drama, Vol. 4, No. 3, Fall 1970] qualifies Chekhov's insistence that "the last act will be merry" with a reminder that "it will be the surface gaiety of desperation." "This is not a comedy, not a farce, as you wrote," Stanislavsky stubbornly insisted to Chekhov who was then exhausted by and dying of tuberculosis: "It is a tragedy, whatever outlet for a better life you may have offered in the last act.... I hear you saying: 'Wait a minute, but this is a farce...' No, for an ordinary person this is a tragedy."
Maurice Valency [*The Breaking String: The Plays of Anton Chekhov,* New York, Oxford University Press, 1966] argues that it is "inconceivable that Chekhov was insensible to the tragic

implications of the situation he had created"... and Valency essentially concludes that Stanislavsky knew better: "It was precisely that blend of comedy and pathos with which, as it seemed to Chekhov, Stanislavsky was ruining his play that gave *The Cherry Orchard* its originality and freshness."

But Chekhov does not artificially divide his characters between the comic and the tragic, he does something more profound. As Karl Guthke comments: "... this device of internal character dichotomy realises its tragi-comic effect by exploring the two sides of the *dramatis persona* in such a way that they not only offset each other, but impart their aesthetic quality (comic and tragic respectively) to each other." K. S. Guthke, *Modern Tragi-Comedy*, Random House, New York, 1996, p. 84.

However, those who insist that *The Cherry Orchard* is a tragedy argue that Chekhov's opinion need not be accepted as definitive. Applying the theorizing of W. K. Wimsatt *[The Intentional Fallacy. From The Verbal Icon: Studies in the Meaning of Poetry. W.K. Wimsatt, Jr., and Monroe C. Beardsley. Lexington: University of Kentucky Press, 1954]* these critics insist that an author's intention and the effect of his actual work may not only be different but antithetical.

Daniel Gerould ["*The Cherry Orchard as a Comedy*," Journal of General Education, XI, 1958] states: "How could anyone possibly call a comedy a play in which the heroine's husband dies of drink, her son drowns, her lover deserts her, and she returns to the one thing in the world she loves her home and cherry orchard only to have them taken from her and destroyed, only to be turned out into the unfriendly world again, all alone? Furthermore, the other characters, who also love the orchard, are scattered at the end of the play, and the faithful old servant Firce is left behind, locked up in the deserted house perhaps to die. Wouldn't a person have to have a warped sense of humor to find this story comic?" Also, Gerould: "Won't it still be possible to assert that the spectacle of this group of foolish, bungling, impractical characters dispossessed and cast out into a world with which they are not fit to cope is not a comic one? A perceptive reader may be willing to grant that the characters are . . . incompetent... and that their actions are futile and inappropriate, but he will insist that the effect of seeing lonely, irresponsible people come to an unhappy end is one of sadness not comedy." While writing the play Chekhov predicted a farce [vodevii]. In 1901 after Three Sisters had just opened, Chekhov wrote to Olga Knipper, "The next play I write will definitely be funny, very funny - <u>at least in intention</u>." [TJ underlining] "At least in intention": Chekhov knew exactly what he was doing and understood that he would be subject to "misinterpretation". Stanislavsky writing to his sister Zinaida in September of 1903: "I imagine it will be something impossible on the weirdness and vulgarity of life. I only fear that instead of a farce again we shall have a great big tragedy. Even now he thinks *Three Sisters* a very merry little piece."

According to Anna L. Linden [*Chekhov vs Gorkii and The Moscow Arts Theater,* Russian History, Vol. 18, No. 4 Winter 1991, pp. 501-528 Published by Brill], Stanislavski's and Nemirovich-Danchenko's interpretation was also motivated by the bottom line. The audience's positive response to Chekhov's plays was anticipated by them because it was their intent to present and promote Chekhov as a melodramatic and fatalistic playwright. Knowing the taste of the audience, the two directors of the Moscow Art Theater, despite their empty talk about naturalism, developed a formula that stressed the sentimental subtext in the story line, designating a character to serve as a proponent of a particular ideology, preferably liberal, but still catering to the needs of the members of the audience. That pursuit of profit may have skewed their judgment. "[Chekhov]… always has a horror of stagy sentimentality in all its aspects. All actors displease him because of their tendency to exaggerate, overact, yield to melodramatic excesses, gesticulate wildly, and play to the gallery. He tried everything possible to oppose stupid ideas, stupid arguments put forward by actors to justify their bad acting, their excesses and their exaggeration; to oppose the narcissistic and masturbatory manifestation of their feelings, which keeps them from projecting themselves into the next moment." Peter Stein [*My Chekhov* from *A Norton Critical Edition, Anton Chekhov's Selected Plays*, W. W. Norton & Company New York, London] And Chekhov fully loathed this hamyness: "… [Stanislavsky's] … procedures were never naturalistic enough for the exacting Chekhov. Rather were they too flamboyant and excessively 'theatrical' in the traditional sense." Hingley P. XVIII (There is no over-acting like the over-acting of the so-called "method" [bastard descendants of Stanislavsky who was an unembarrassed ham himself] actors who seem to be on the verge of hysteria or complete mental breakdown; rivalling any stage ham of old in eating up the scenery, however "natural" they ironically claim to be.) Chekhov would have hated modern "method" actors with their incessant bits of "business", their manneristic excesses and their shameless scene stealing. Stanislavski in his dramatic depiction of Doctor Astrov finally cleansed the trivial inappropriate details he so loved, toned down his melodramatic overacting and relaxed; and this new Dr Astrov, to his surprise, resulted in a portrayal that was universally esteemed. He is said to have said to Olga Knipper in astonishment: "I do nothing and the public loves it." "I have seen many good performances and many great actors, but never have I experienced anything like it before. I realised what it was: here one believed everything; here was no trace of theatricality; it almost seemed that there were no actors on the stage and no previously contrived mise-en-scènes. Everything was so simple, just as in real life, but beneath this simplicity one became aware of the seething cauldron of human passions." (Leonidov, L., quoted in Magarshack, D., *Stanislavsky: A Life*, Faber and Faber, London, 1986, p. 192.) Chekhov's advice to the actors rehearsing in Karpov's St Petersburg production of *The Seagull*: "Above all, avoid theatricality. Try to be as simple as possible. Remember that they are all ordinary people." Anton Chekhov, quoted in Magarshack, D., *Chekhov the Dramatist*, p. 184.

Gerould concludes: "…the actions of the characters are inappropriate, inadequate, and irrelevant to the situation in which they find themselves and to the problem they face. It is for this reason that we can say the action of the play is purely a comic one and one of the most perfect comic plots ever created." Svetlana Evdokimova [*What's so Funny about Losing One's Estate, or Infantilism in "The Cherry Orchard"* The Slavic and East European Journal, Vol. 44, No. 4 (Winter, 2000), pp. 623-648, American Association of Teachers of Slavic and East European Languages]: "Clearly, the source of the comic lies not in the play's fabula or situation, not in what happens, but in how it happens and to whom it happens. The enigmatic, captivating, and almost mesmerising effect that *The Cherry Orchard* continues to exert on its audience is to be found in its good-humoured but foolish protagonists – both charming in their gullibility and pathetic in their utter confusion. But with the exception of several minor farcical characters, most of the play's characters cannot be classified as traditional comic types. … the play focuses on the universal childishness of Russian society, and the comic nature of the play's characters stems to a large extent from their infantilism."

"But to the eye of a dying man life, even at its most majestic, may reveal a degree of absurdity which is not readily apparent to those who expect to live forever. It is, very likely, this sense of the ultimate stupidity of the whole performance, on all its levels from the individual to the cosmic, that gives *The Cherry Orchard* its unique place in the social drama of our time." Maurice Valency

It is Valency who reminds us that Chekhov was anxious that his play not be presented as a "comedie larmoyante". "The danger was all too evident, and, as he feared, Stanislavsky's production did nothing to avert it. It is difficult, indeed, to see how, short of a dramatic miracle, the pathos of the situation could be disguised or diluted. With all its jokes, its slapstick, and comic flourishes, with all its expressions of hope for the future, *The Cherry Orchard* centers upon the sound of the breaking string." Comédie larmoyante (French: tearful comedy) was a genre of 18th century French sentimental comedy in which looming tragedy was resolved, amid reconciliations and tears. These plays, whether they ended "happily" or not, wanted the audience to experience a moral triumph earned through the suffering of these heroes and heroines. Comedy was no longer to provoke laughter, but instead tears. This form was meant to break the supposed distinction then existing between tragedy and comedy in French literature. But I doubt that this form created anything new in drama, it only debased and sentimentalized what was always inherent in the <u>best</u> comedy and tragedy.

There was, we must remember, the old Elizabethan designation "tragicomedies". [John Fletcher wrote in his preface to *The Faithful Shepherdess* (c. 1610), tragicomedy "wants deaths, which is enough to make it no tragedy, yet brings some near it, which is enough to make it no comedy"]

Gotthold Ephraim Lessing (January 1729 - February 15, 1781) German writer, dramatist and art critic, defined it as a mixture of emotions in which "seriousness stimulates laughter, and pain pleasure." Friedrich Dürrenmatt, (January 5, 1921 - December 14, 1990) the Swiss dramatist, suggested that tragicomedy was the inevitable genre for the twentieth century's dark comedy and the Theater of the Absurd.

Ronald Hingley [*The Cherry Orchard* in *Chekhov: Uncle Vanya and The Cherry Orchard*, New York, 1965] speaking of *Uncle Vanya* might just as well be speaking about *The Cherry Orchard:* "With *Uncle Vanya*, though, we shall do better to look neither for tragedy nor comedy, but to realize that we have <u>entered a strange anti-climactic, anti-romantic, anti-dramatic world such as had never existed on the stage before Chekhov, a world with its own laws, its own dimensions, its own brand of humour."</u> (TJ underlining)

"Chekhov, to sum up, transcended the superficiality that often adheres to optimistic literature and at the same time escaped the morbidity that besets pessimistic profundity; and he kept a characteristic balance in other important respects …
remembering especially the plain yet somehow elusive fact that there was ever sympathy in his comedy and some degree of comedy in his sympathy…" Gassner, J., 'The Duality of Chekhov', in Bristow, E. K., *Anton Chekhov's Plays*, W. W. Norton, NewYork, 1977, P. 410.

A 1977 New York Times Clive Barnes review of Serban's Beaumont production: "When you are both amused and touched something very special happens to our hearts—they are uplifted to the giddy, bitter laughter of the gods". Middleton Murry described *The Cherry Orchard* as, "a shower of laughing tears." Chekhov exercises a skill in bringing us to the height of pathos and then bursting it with laughter, at ourselves also for being taken in by the pathos. "And there is also an art of throwing a wet blanket upon sympathy at the very moment it might arise, the result being that the situation, though a serious one, is not taken seriously." Henri Bergson *[Laughter: An Essay on the Meaning of the Comic]*

When they approach art, the comic and the tragic appear indistinguishable and not only to Chekhov. But while we may laugh at Chekhov's characters, we are not detached from them but quite the contrary; we remain deeply sympathetic toward them. Ionesco wrote that the comic and tragic are merely two aspects of the same situation and "I have now reached the stage where it is hard to tell the one from the other".

Soren Kierkegaard, [*Concluding Unscientific Postscript to Philosophical Fragments,* University Bookshop, Reitzel, Copenhagen, 1846]: "Pathos that is not reinforced by the comic is illusion; the comic that is not reinforced by pathos is immaturity. Seen pathetically, a second has infinite value; seen comically, ten thousand years are a mere flash of foolery like yesterday; and yet time, in which the existing individual finds himself, is made up of such parts."

Harvey Pitcher states: "I am inclined to suspect that he himself (Chekhov) was never aware of tragic implications in *The Cherry Orchard*."

Though recognizing his personal warmth and kindness, there is in Chekhov an almost cosmic godlike stepping back from the travails and troubles of ordinary mortals, of watching, like an audience, which is why he may be so perfect a writer; he sees us more clearly than we see ourselves and laughs at our personal tendency to wallow in our own melodrama and indulge in self-pity. "Chekhov, like God, is sometimes seen as full of lovingkindness towards his characters, the only expression of which seems to be his supposedly wistful and elegiac view of the world." Michael Frayne [Introduction to his Translation *Chekhov Plays* Bloomsbury Methuen Drama, (July 14, 1988)] But Chekhov's god is more forgiving than even the Christian God; he refuses to hand down judgement from on high though he holds his characters to full account. "Chekhov's judgements were sure and final and terrible; but he did not make them with adverbs." Philip Hensher. I'm not so sure about final and terrible. Speaking of his play *Ivanov*, Chekhov wrote to his brother: "I wanted to be original... I did not portray a single villain or a single angel... did not blame nor exculpate anyone." David Edelstein: "... Chekhov [is] seen by writers like Janet Malcolm through the lens of Christianity, as someone who registered every human flaw but finally released his characters from judgment." "He will not comment on reality; he will permit reality to comment on itself." Brustein, *Chekhov, Anton. The Major Plays*, P. ix, Penguin Publishing Group.

However, this supposed refusal to pass judgement has been interpreted incorrectly as a cold dispassion. There is the quality of a detached yet dedicated scientific clinician, of the medical doctor that Chekhov primarily considered himself; who must stand back if only to see things clearly, to diagnose accurately. Zola, a writer Chekhov had read and commented upon, regarded the writer as a scientist conducting an autopsy (not a good image when you consider the subject is dead). Suvorin stated: "Chekhov is a man of flint and a cruel talent with his harsh objectivity. He's spoilt, his amour propre is enormous." [(French, "self-love"): "is a concept in the philosophy of Jean-Jacques Rousseau that esteem depends upon the opinion of others. Rousseau contrasts it with amour de soi, which also means 'self-love', but which does not involve seeing oneself as others see one. According to Rousseau, amour de soi is more primitive and is compatible with wholeness and happiness, while amour-propre is an unnatural form of self-love that arose only with the appearance of society and individuals' consequent ability to compare themselves with one another. Rousseau thought that amour-propre was subject to corruption, thereby causing vice and misery."]

Graham Greene said that there must be a 'splinter of ice in the heart of a writer' which allowed him to look dispassionately at tragedy and turn it into art; he might have added "and perhaps comedy". As Chekhov himself said to another writer: "When you want to touch a reader's heart, try to be colder. It gives their grief, as it were, a background against which it stands out in greater relief."

"For there is at all times something of the man of science about Chekhov, a quiet going about his business in which he is concerned more for the integrity of the facts and for their proper weighting in the narrative than for an audience who must be made to understand." Beverley Hahn [*Chekhov: A Study of the Major Stories and Plays* (Major European Authors Series) Cambridge University Press (May 5, 1977)]p. 9

"First, he [Chekhov] was a doctor, and the first lessons in philosophy he learnt were medical: not to become too involved in the suffering of the patient; to diagnose objectively. Chekhov has been the victim of savage attacks (especially during the Soviet era) for what was deemed his political and ideological 'neutrality' and the artistic 'inconclusiveness' of his writing." Chekhov's trip to study the penal colony of Sakhalin may have been a response to critics who said that he did not feel the human suffering he wrote about, that he was a pure artist and had no social conscience. Lev Shestov attacked Chekhov's "creation out of nothing" in 1908, for what he perceived to be the "absence of a definite point of view", and with it a lack of a positive message, which he regarded as Chekhov's moral failure. And this ludicrous thinking persists. *Melbourne Times* critic, Chris Boyd, speaking of a production of *Uncle Vanya* (Melbourne Times, 10 July 1991): "Though its portentous themes peal through the 20th century, one must first ask, is Chekhov really attempting to say anything?"

"Ambivalence is the source of all that is truly participatory in comedy. By promoting his thousand and one details at once our sympathy with his characters and our alienation from them, Chekhov has refashioned for proscenium arch drama the <u>time-honored ironies of the traditional aside</u>. For ambivalence as it flourishes in *The Cherry Orchard* reveals its author's sense of the playhouse as well as his sense of the play. Compensating us for the loss of an earlier participatory theatre, he must draw us into the world of the characters at one moment, into the illusory world through the arch, and at the <u>next push us back into our seats, more critical than before.</u> The tone of the play therefore constantly edges on satire, without being distinctively satirical. He divides us against ourselves and splits our attention in order to arouse us." J. L. Styan. TJ underlining

"Throughout *The Cherry Orchard* Chekhov places the action on a knife edge between laughter and tears; but he intends no neutral balance. He expects pathos to weigh on the side of the comic, not against it, and comedy, thus reinforced, to tilt decisively in favour of laughter." Richard Arthur Peace, *Chekhov: A Study of the Four Major Plays,* Yale Univ. Press (September 1983) p. 120

"The principle of permanently changing genre is all inclusive in *The Cherry Orchard*. Time and again the comic (the limited and relative) is deepened so that we feel sympathy, or, conversely, the serious is brought down to the level of obvious illogicality or repetition." Vladimir Kataev, *If Only We Could Know!: An Interpretation of Chekhov*, Ivan R. Dee, June 18, 2002.

A number of critics have remarked how profoundly Chekhov was influenced by the popular stage entertainments of the day, vaudeville and farce. "The vaudeville is an inalienable part of the creative work of Chekhov the dramatist, not separate and apart." Z. Paperny, *The Vaudevilles,* from A Norton Critical Edition, *Anton Chekhov's Selected Plays*, Laurence Senelick, W. W. Norton & Company, New York, London, 2005. "A full understanding of even such mature work as *The Cherry Orchard* is impaired if the operetta, music hall, and folkloric allusions go unmarked." Donald Rayfield, P.5.

Taganrog's theater presented the classics of the Russian stage, including Alexander Ostrovsky [generally considered the greatest representative of the Russian realistic period; authored 47 plays and "almost single-handedly created a Russian national repertoire."]; light opera such as Offenbach's *La Belle Helene*, also operettas by Suppe, Lehar, Lecocq; touring Italian opera companies, Sarasate, Liszt's pupil, Laura Carer; Tommaso Salvini sang the title role in Otello; a stage production of Uncle Tom's Cabin , Shakespeare, Sheridan's *School for Scandal*, Gribedov's *Woe from Wit*. During Chekhov's schooldays more than 340 different plays were performed there. "In those days we were all gripped by a theatrical fever… all our savings and pocket money went for gallery seats" reported a classmate and theater companion of Chekhov.

Taganrog was not entirely the backwater that Chekhov himself lamented. It has been described as more like a colonial capital than a provincial city. "Taganrog was the Russian equivalent of the Mediterranean French ports." Chudakov P.3. It was for a time a prosperous port with a wealthy foreign merchant class, primarily of Greeks, many of them "millionaires" but also Italians, French, English, Spanish, Armenians, Ukrainians, Jews, Tatars and Moldavians many of whom supported a thriving local theater. Chekhov's room over his father's shop overlooked the harbor, full, at the height of summer, with steamers and sailing ships. One could walk miles along the shore and see ships from Turkey, the Greek Archipelago, Italy, Spain: the San Antonio; the Sophia, the Ogios Gerasimos, the Movludi Bagri.

[3] Lyubov means love; the name is perhaps ironic; a kind of undiscriminating, sentimental, loose love characterizes her.

[4] Ivan Bunin, disdained the surname Ranevskaia as a name unknown among the aristocracy but rather a pseudonym a provincial actress would choose. Perhaps Chekhov intended Ranevskaia to be, like Zarechnaia in the *Sea Gull*, an actress, a poseur.

[5] This "daughter" relationship is informal. She was obviously never legally adopted; takes no direct part concerning the decisions on the sale of the estate; to our knowledge never attempts to convince Ranevskaya to listen to the man she loves, Lopakhin; in fact she never speaks of the "cherry orchard" as such and is treated not much better in the end than the loyal and trusty Fiers.

[6] (to Olga Knipper March 5,1903). "In *The Cherry Orchard* you will be playing Varvara or Varya, an adopted daughter, aged twenty-two."

[7] Gaev suggests gaer: buffoon, perhaps? Or maybe "I think he must have chosen the name Gayef for the faint flavour that it has of gdyer, a mountebank." Calderon *Two plays by Tchekhof : the Seagull, the Cherry Orchard.* But as Rayfield has correctly pointed out: these associations are unconvincing and irrelevant.

[8] Some critics have construed this name as particularly humble and rustic.

[9] According to L. M. Leonidov [Leonid Mironovich Leonidov, pseudonym of L.M. Volfenzon (May 22, 1873- August 6, 1941) Russian actor, director, and teacher who espoused the teachings of Konstantin Stanislavsky] Chekhov told him that Lopakhin outwardly should either be "like a merchant or like a medical

professor at Moscow University". "And later, at the rehearsals, after Act Three he said to me: 'Listen, Lopakhin doesn't shout. He is rich, and rich men never shout.'" "In fact, Lopakhin may be seen as a coarse self-portrait: he, like Chekhov, comes from peasant stock; he, like Chekhov, is the first generation of his family to 'make it.'" Michael Henry Heim [Simon Karlinsky and Michael Henry Heim *Anton Chekhov's Life and Thought: Selected Letters and Commentaries* Northwestern University Press (January 13, 1997)]

In a letter Chekhov's wrote to Olga Knipper, Oct. 30, 1903: "Lopakhin must be played, not by a loud mouth, there is no necessity to make him a merchant." In a letter to Stanislavsky also dated Oct. 30, 1903 Chekhov wrote: "When I was writing Lopakhin, I thought it was your role… Lopakhin, true, is a merchant, but he is a decent man in all regards; he must act in a dignified manner, as an educated person, without trifling or tricks, and thus I was thinking that this role, central in the play, would be a success by you." Bartlett 519. But Stanislavsky came from a very rich merchant family even though descended from the peasantry. Peter Holland sees Stanislavski "imposing the values of his own class on Chekhov's play" and "whose every instinct throughout his life was as reactionary as his theatre work was supposedly revolutionary and radical in its method".

I disagree with those critics who claim that Lopakhin shows no signs of an education; like Chekhov he was self-critical and self-deprecating. His misquotes of Hamlet are purposeful, showing a knowledge of Shakespeare's meaning.

"If Lopakhin, according to Chekhov, little resembles a merchant, then he definitely resembles someone else familiar to us… Lopakhin says: 'I bought the estate where my grandfather and my father were slaves, where they weren't even allowed to go into the kitchen.' If that resembles anybody, it is Chekhov himself, who made a lot of his family story, of the fact that his grandfather was a serf and his father a shop-keeper and a harsh disciplinarian in whose shop he himself worked as a boy. These facts loomed in Chekhov's mind so large that, as we know from his letters, they grew into his familial mythology." Savely Senderovich, *The Cherry Orchard: Chekhov's Last Testament* in *Bloom's Modern Critical Views, ANTON CHEKHOV,* Edited and with an introduction, Yale University Press

"Our grandfather was beaten by his masters… and the lowest of officials could smash him in the face." quoting Chekhov. Philip Callow, *Chekhov: The Hidden Ground,* Publisher: Ivan R. Dee, May 1, 1998

[10] Combines an ancient Russian name with a ridiculous one. A píshchik is a squeaking sound or the whistle used to make the squeaking voice of a traditional Ukrainian puppet, Petrushka, a kind of Punch. And so, we have the great Russian nobleman, perhaps descended from the powerful boyars, reduced to a squeaking puppet voice, a supplicant entreating money from his neighbors. Rayfield tells us that this name denotes a caricature, not a character. I disagree and find Pishchick compelling.

[11] She has a Germanic first name and a Russian patronymic.

[12] The old ex-serf is named after the obscure Orthodox Saint Thyrsus, martyred in 251.

[13] Rayfield maintains: "The name Firs, however, strikes a different resonance: the Russian version of the Greek Thyrses, it was a pastoral, pseudo-classical name that an eighteenth-century landowner would have found amusing to bestow on a serf. It bespeaks Firs's great age and anachronistic loyalties. It gives Firs a symbolic role of Time Past, the spirit of Antiquity by which the present can be assessed." Rayfield, Donald, THE CHERRY ORCHARD, Catastrophe and Comedy, TWAYNE PUBLISHERS, NEW YORK, 1994 P. 49. Rayfield seems to

forget the martyred saint which has very different associations. Tradition asserts that Thyrsus endured many tortures and was sentenced to be sawn in half. However, the saw did not penetrate; it became so heavy that the executioners could not use it.

[14] "…it has only one pernicious character, the self-important servant Yasha. Besides, Yasha is so vacuous that the consequences of his actions [are] two broken hearts…" Michael Henry Heim.

I think Yasha is more pathetically absurd than pernicious.

[15] "… the frightening and ill-omened "prokhozhii" (passerby). In him, as in Epikhodov, we find a member of the "khod" family, a "prokhozhii" (the word has as its etymological root, "khod"—motion, movement, going, etc.). Both the designation of the stranger as a "prokhozhii," one who is passing through, and his question, "Can I go straight through here to the station?" (Mogu li ia proiti zdes' priamo na stantsiu?), aptly awakens the underlying and disturbing theme of change or passage (prokhod)." Jackson P. 140

[16] But in the opening of Act Two Chekhov refers to the Gaev Manor House. Well, which is it? This is no oversight on Chekhov part. How has Ranevskaya managed to wrest control; of not just the estate. It is important to be reminded that this is, or was the Gaev family estate. Ranevskaya married a mere lawyer, a drunk, who not only sullied the great noble name but abetted the dissipation of the Gaev wealth. The question: why is Ranevskaya the master of the estate rather than Gaev? And there is no doubt than Gaev is subordinate to his sister. She allows Gaev to be humiliated not only by Lopakhin but even by her own lackey. The fact that he calls his sister a slut, that her every move exudes it, may be suggestive of deeper resentments, of a deeper story only implied.

[17] "It's an old manor house: once the life in it was very opulent, and this must be felt in the furnishings. Opulent and comfortable" (Chekhov to Olga Knipper, October 14, 1903) Why do so many productions indicate a dilapidated old mansion with rundown furnishings? Never once does Chekhov imply that the house is in disrepair. As Chekhov makes quite clear the family's financial difficulties haven't affected the furnishings which are luxurious, having been purchased long ago. This distortion traces back to Stanislavsky, who, totally ignoring Chekhov's insistence on a sense of richness and luxury presented a house in which the floors creak, the paint peels and plaster falls, a gross misrepresentation that carries on insistently to this day. Just as Ranevskaia is impeccably dressed in the latest Paris fashion, dines profligately in fine restaurants, we can assume that the house is beautifully maintained while peasant servants go hungry on peas porridge; Chekhov is making a point.

[18] "It _still_ goes by the name (do sikh por) of the "children's room". Why we may ask? There are no children or are there? The use of the word "'still' suggests a certain anomaly in the characters' perception of the room. Even though there are no more children on the estate, the room is still viewed as a 'children's room'…" Svetlana Evdokimova

"Is this a way of indicating that the house is stuck in the past? Or a suggestion that the family are in some form of retarded infancy? Or is it that Lyubov Andreyevna refuses to let her daughters grow up, perhaps as a way of staving off her own advancing age? Perhaps there is a hint of the dead Grisha, who after all would have been the last to occupy this room; has it been left unchanged as a sort of morbid memorial…" Loehlin, James N., *Chekhov, The Cherry Orchard,* CAMBRIDGE UNIVERSITY PRESS, Cambridge, New York, Melbourne, Madrid, Cape Town, Singapore, Sao Paulo, 2006, P. 9

[19] It is appropriate that the play begins and ends in the children's room, "nursery" (Russian: detskaia: detskaya is derived from an adjective which can also mean 'childlike', 'infantile' thus literally "the children's room") suggesting that these characters are essentially children and remain children even after seemingly calamitous events. A. R. Kugel wrote: "All the inhabitants of *The Cherry Orchard* are children and their behavior is childish."
In the manor houses of old Russia, the children's room was usually separated from the main part of the house from which the children were to some extent sequestered. In *The Cherry Orchard* the children's room has been opened up with the result that the children have taken over the house. Is there any hint of a memorial not only to the dead son Grisha but to themselves, indicating that the house and its occupants are trapped in a past of death from which they cannot escape? Why doesn't the room bring back memories of Grisha who presumably was its last occupant? Or even Anya? Instead it brings back memories of Ranevskaya's and Gaev's own childhood. This is their room, their memorial.

[20] In their fine dress the two of them, initially, could easily be mistaken for the masters of the house.

[21] And I think Chekhov wants to maintain the illusion of the lord and lady of the house until it is broken dramatically and surprisingly by the evolving play. Stanislavsky was dense to such sublety and misses the entire point: "To signal to the audience that Duniasha for all her fine clothes and delicate manners is a servant, Stanislavsky had her opening shutters, shutting the stove and wiping her nose on an apron. Similarly, Lopakhin's elegant dress ("white waistcoat, yellow suede shoes") and book in hand, as specified by Chekhov, are annulled by Stanislavsky having him enter disheveled, quietly cursing, smoking, spitting, picking

his teeth with a match, wiping the mist from the windowpane and dusting a chair with his overcoat." Rayfield P. 50

[22] Dunyasha with candle, Lopakhin with the book and Anya "I keep hearing bells". Varya's keys jangle like bells and Lopakhin picks them up and jingles them like holy bells. The phrase "bell, book and candle" refers to a Latin Christian method of excommunication by anathema, imposed on a person who had committed an exceptionally grievous sin. Part of the rite of anathema reads: "… we separate him from the society of all Christians, we exclude him from the bosom of our Holy Mother the Church [or Holy Mother Russia] in Heaven and on earth, we declare him excommunicated and anathematized and we judge him condemned to eternal fire with Satan and his angels and all the reprobate …" Is not Ranevskaya made anathema? Is not the entire play a ritual of anathema? Does she not proclaim: I have sinned, so much… oh my sins? She has killed her son, by neglect and will abandon her daughter the same way; she has squandered her substance, the cherry orchard which had been entrusted to her; destroys her patrimony; she "colludes", in Paris, with a Papist Roman priest who also possesses a book. [There was particularly bitter enmity between Papist Rome and Orthodoxy and Chekhov, although not practicing Russian Orthodoxy, disdained the Jesuits.] She is exiled from the possibility of the kingdom of heaven, exiled form the orchard, her Eden, from Holy Mother Russia itself, to wander in the world, an outcast. Quench the candle, close the book, ring the bell.

"Like Adam and Eve, the old nobility are expelled from their beautiful garden because of their 'sins.' Their own, superficial perception of these sins is mentioned several times. In Act II, for example, Ranevskaia states 'we have sinned a great deal …' and has a premonition that their manorial house will 'fall'" Stephen

L. Baehr, *The Machine in Chekhov's Garden: Progress and Pastoral in the Cherry Orchard*

[23] Slava Bogu: glory be to God or praise be to God. Although this may seem a stilted literal translation it captures the Christian Orthodox tradition which so imbued Russian culture; they initially invoked God with reverence, much as a devout Muslim would; although the phrases had become automatic, mouthed even by atheists. The phrase exists only in Russian, Belarusian, Ukrainian, and Bulgarian.

[24] These lines by Lopakhin predict two interconnected themes that haunt Chekhov's play: the arrival of progress signified by the train, the machina, intruding into the change resistant cherry orchard (or the cherry garden) of the old Russian nobility; and the forward movement of time, noticed but ignored or rather blocked out by this dying class. "Railroads fill the pages of Chekhov's stories and provide a metaphor for a world in flux—his art has been described as life seen from a moving railway car…" Milton Ehre, (Translator and Introduction) *Chekhov for the Stage: The Sea Gull, Uncle Vanya, The Three Sisters, The Cherry Orchard*, Northwestern University Press, December 9, 1992

Spencer Golub notes "… the major temporal dialogue in *The Cherry Orchard* is between the urban timetable of the railroad, which begins and ends the play, and the rural timetable of the agrarian seasonal cycle, which gives the play its act structure."

"Nor, for that matter, is it possible that Chekhov's plays can both quicken and deaden our sensitivity to the passing of time: 'A sense of time passing is certainly there in Chekhov's plays,' writes W. Gareth Jones; yet Corrigan claims that '… in spite of this frame of a time pattern, we have no real sense of time passing,' " William E. Gruber, "CHEKHOV'S ILLUSION OF INACTION." CLA Journal, vol. 20, no. 4, 1977, pp. 508–520. "In spite of a definite time framework in each of the plays - in fact, in spite of an extraordinary number of specific temporal reference points - we watch the plays with no real sense of time passing. But throughout the plays, we are often keenly aware of time having passed unawares. This distinction between our awareness of time passing, and of time having passed, is important, and must receive all possible emphasis." Gruber, P. 519.

"It is a play about time... penetrating and perceiving the imperceptible passage of time... The action never slackens; it is tense, solid, for, I repeat, every minute is full. Every minute has its own saturation, but not with dialogues, but silence, life itself passing." Jean-Louis Barrault

There is this profound sense of time moving ahead without us (identifying with the characters), with time wasted, of life itself wasted as if we had not lived. It is Fiers who utters profoundly at the end: "Life is over as if I never lived it." There is the quality of the cherry orchard being outside the bounds of time but of that "time" impinging upon it, intruding upon this unreal interlude in time and space, some never-never land, a magical kingdom disconnected but not immune from these constraints of time and place. Lopakhin, the interloper, always checking his watch, is always catching a train, though he loves the orchard: "the most beautiful estate in the whole world", he will chop it down to make it bloom again.

Chekhov cautiously but ambiguously sides with the "machina" but he loves the "garden" nonetheless; change though inexorable has a price. But there is danger of turning this, too, into melodrama. In David Mamet's production Gaev and Ranevskaya obliviously play with a toy train on the nursery floor while Lopakhin is proposing the solution to their problems. Tom Stoppard can't leave subtle suggestion alone; in his production (2009 adapted by Tom Stoppard and directed by Sam Mendes) the sound of the train repeatedly invades the orchard; he even adds a new stage direction at the end. Not content with the breaking string and the sounds of the ax he adds: "Then the distant sound of the train approaching." Chekhov would have been appalled. (To Olga Knipper November 23, 1903). "Stanislavsky wants to have a train going past in the second act. <u>He has to be stopped.</u> He also wants to have frogs and landrails." (TJ underlining) (To Stanislavsky November 23, 1903) "If it is possible to show a train without a noise, without the slightest sound, then by all means have it." Why not an absurdist, surreal production in which the train barrels right through the old manor house, utterly destroying it and old Fiers in the process and Yasha with an idiot grin waving Dunyasha's underwear from the window of the caboose as it passes through. This heavy-handedness has a long history. Eva Le Gallienne's production in the 1940s reduced *The Cherry Orchard* to a "tragicomedy in which the hero and villain were both aspects of progress and the victim was beauty."

David Magarshack [*The Real Chekhov: An Introduction to Chekhov's Last Plays* Allen & Unwin (June 8, 1972)] also sees in the play the destruction of beauty by those who are blind to it. "In *The Cherry Orchard* the trees that begin in blossom and end beneath the axe are everything that can ever be lost by mortal man - childhood, happiness, purpose, love, and all the brightness of life" Michael Frayne

What most critics fail to realize is how incredibly "fortunate" Gaev and Ranevskaya are. It is the train that would have "saved" them, if they allowed it to, giving new value to their estate, making it possible to save themselves, if at a price. But only Lopakhin recognizes this <u>good fortune.</u>

In a letter of March 27, 1894, to Suvorin, Chekhov, the grandson of a serf, rejects Tolstoyan philosophy and its opposition to progress: "Peasant blood flows in me and you can't surprise me with peasant virtues. Since childhood, I have believed in progress and cannot help doing so, since the difference between the time I was beaten and the time when they stopped beating me was huge ... Now something protests in me. Prudence and fairness tell me that there is more love for humanity in electricity and steam than in chastity and abstention from meat. War is an evil and the court system is an evil, but it doesn't follow that I should wear bast shoes and sleep on a stove alongside the hired hand and his wife."

[25] Stanislavsky placed the cherry orchard in either the Orel or the Kursk District, to the north of Kharkov (letter to Chekhov, 19 November 1903). There is no doubt that the shepherd's pan pipes playing at the end of Act One are indicative of the South. But Chekhov clearly tells us that it is daybreak, that the sun will rise soon and yet it is only 2 AM. The sun doesn't rise until after 5 in early May in the southern Ukraine. There isn't even any half-light at 2 AM. May and October aren't particularly cold months in the southern Ukraine. Are we in some never-never land, some magical kingdom disconnected from the constraints of place and time, closer in the heart to Russia's north with its half-light summer nights? Many Westerners think of Russia as a cold country which seems to imbue its literature, including Chekhov. "... the motif of a cold climate destroying the human physique and psyche is not accidental in his works." Emma Polotskaya. And it was the Russian north that captured Chekhov's soul. "Moscow for him was truly the holy land, the concentration of everything Chekhov loved in Russia ... even the grey misty days were dear to him, and filled his heart with pleasant feelings.'" S. Y. Yelpatyevsky eds., *Chekhov in the Memoirs of his Contemporaries*, Moscow, 1960. But Chekhov was born in the south on the warm Sea of Azov. Chekhov considered

Nemirovich-Danchenko, a Ukrainian, who had an estate, Neskuchnoe, in Ekaterinoslav province, a fellow "southerner". Why in the British premiere of *The Cherry Orchard*, did the actors wear fur coats and fur caps? Why is Fiers always reminding Gaev to dress warmly in his fur coat?

[26] Rayfield points out Chekhov's tendency for setting his action at times when the normal world is asleep.

[27] This is unlike the man of action that he is, so wedded to time and his watch; does he subconsciously purposefully fall asleep? Is he afraid they won't recognize him; won't welcome him, or more to the point couldn't care less? He has come to save them... from themselves. But Gaev and Ranevskaya don't want to be saved and certainly not by the son of a serf. Or was he left behind purposely and is he a less than welcomed "guest"?

[28] Lopakhin is self-deprecating and self-mocking as was Chekhov by most accounts. As Chekhov said himself: "Dissatisfaction with oneself is one of the fundamental qualities of every true talent." "Self-deprecation and self-mockery became a kind of armor [for Chekhov himself]" writes Philip Callow. However, Chekhov became a victim of this self-deprecation; fools taking him at his own word. As Thomas Mann observed: "… it seems to me that Chekhov was under-estimated for so long in western Europe, and in Russia too, because of his extremely sober, critical, and doubting attitude towards himself—a most disarming quality which however, far from inspiring respect, set a bad example to the world at large."

Although ridiculously self-conscious about his peasant origins Lopakhin reveals himself, as the play develops, as in some ways a finer "gentleman" than Gaev. Chekhov meant the major role of the peasant turned millionaire, Lopakhin, to be played by Stanislavsky. However, Stanislavsky, preferred the part of the incompetent aristocrat, Gaev, (closer to his own wealthy merchant roots) and he gave the role of Lopakhin, though much more important, to a lesser actor. Stanislavsky's reputed flair and charisma gave Gaev a gravitas that Chekhov did not envision. John Corbin of the New York Times (28 January 1923), when reviewing the preserved museum piece performed by the traveling MAT in New York realized that Stanislavsky was far too grand and imposing a figure to play Gaev: "it is fairly obvious that the Herculean presence of the director and his vigorous vibrant voice, so eloquent of an orderly mind and an unshakeable will, are ill-adapted to suggest the will-o'-the-wisp brain and uncontrolled moods of this attenuated aristocrat." Frank Rich in reviewing Peter Brook's 1988 production approvingly describes a more suitable interpretation and portrayal which accurately personifies Chekhov's intention: "As Lyubov's brother, Gaev - a forlorn representative of Czarist Russia's obsolete, decaying nobility - the Swedish actor Erland Josephson embodies the fossilized remains of a civilization. Elegant of bearing yet fuzzy of expression, his voice mellifluous yet childlike, he snaps into focus only when drifting into imaginary billiard games."

[29] Was he left behind purposely, an unwelcomed guest? It is only after he starts feeding Ranevskaya small amount of money for her to throw away that his presence seems more "welcomed".

[30] This is a strange thing to say. Where did she think he'd gone, to the station or just went away?

[31] I don't think it diminishes Chekhov's reputation to observe the often seemingly clumsy way in which he fills the play watcher in on the necessary background information. These characters are such inveterate, shameless speechmakers that we may overlook the fact that they often sound like a narrator or stage manager talking to themselves (or directly to the audience). Dunyasha doesn't seem to be listening; she's either heard it before or

doesn't care; but then again, these characters tend not to listen to each other. But along with giving us necessary, if disjointed, back story in these speeches, Chekhov also seems to reveal their innermost thoughts or perhaps their self-deception; we never receive the whole story or an entirely accurate one.

Stepanov, succinctly sums up: "… the intended message is conveyed and received imperfectly (if at all), people are self-absorbed, self-deceiving, self-justifying, and thus unresponsive to the demands, requests, complaints, etc., of others. Confessions are rarely sincere, sermonizing and preaching lack moral and intellectual authority, arguments are devoid of logic and marred by irritation… despite his belief in science, reason and social progress [Chekhov] remained essentially skeptical about the reliability of 'ideas' and information, the efficacy of human language to express emotions, and the possibilities of communication, sympathy and mutual understanding" Andrei D. Stepanov, Problemy kommunikatsii u Chekhova. Studia philologica. Iazyki slavianskoi kul'tury, Moscow, 2005. But as McVay notes, Stepanov overstates the case. Harold Pinter in speaking of himself could as well be speaking of Chekhov (The Sunday Times, March 4, 1962, London): "We have heard many times that tired, grimy phrase: 'Failure of communication', and this phrase has been fixed to my work quite consistently. I believe the contrary. I think that we communicate only too well, in our silence, in what is unsaid, and that what takes place is continual evasion, desperate rearguard attempts to keep ourselves to ourselves. Communication is too alarming. To enter into someone else's life is too frightening. To disclose to others the poverty within us is too fearsome a possibility."

"But to banish that other kind of solitary speaking [soliloquy], by which a man conveys to the audience <u>what is passing in his mind</u> when they could have no other means of learning it, is altogether a mistake. For what, after all, is the subject-matter of a play? It is not mere outward action; it is also thought and will culminating in action, and this latter element is, to the judicious spectator, 'much the noblest' part of Drama, and indeed, with Tchekhof, the greater part; <u>for his plays, rightly understood, are more than half soliloquy; the characters seem to converse, but in reality sit side by side and think aloud</u>." George Calderon, *Two Plays by Tchekhof: the Seagull, the Cherry Orchard* (TJ underlining) [Calderon was the first to translate into English and direct a full-length play by Chekhov; *The Seagull*, at Glasgow in 1909] "What we are left with is a sort of choral arrangement, with the characters revealing more and more of themselves not so much in what they say as in their peculiar tone and manner of saying it. And in their speech, they often seem to be responding not to one another but to some inner question or uncertainty or argument. They address each other at oblique angles." Tobias Wolf, introduction to *Anton Chekhov, Five Plays*, translated by Maria Brodskaya, Stanford University Press, California.

"The play's action actually unfolds through silence and, aside from the poem-tirades which are separate, the dialogues exist, as in music, only to make the silence resound." Jean-Louis Barrault

"Our inner life moves in monologues from morning to night, and even our dreams are still monologues of the soul. They are not spoken aloud, that is all; that is the outward difference over which our petty little modern code of aesthetics makes so much ado." R. Von Gottschall, *Zur Kritik des modernen Dramas*, 1900, P. 117.

Ironically Stanislavsky considered such "soliloquizing" unnatural. But in real life people are always giving speeches, thinking out loud, indulging in nostalgic reveries, seemingly oblivious to their immediate listeners, who may not hear or in any event don't respond or are so wrapped up in themselves that they couldn't care less; but these "speeches" are not necessarily revelations but just as often elaborate "covers" or even subterfuges for their most secret thoughts, secret even to themselves.

Stanislavsky had initiated in the early 1900s, an acting device called "the objective" [or "problem"; Hapgood popularized the term "objective"; Jean Benedetti translates it as "task".]: a style of intensive interaction with a partner which was meant to overcome the practice of directly addressing the audience and ignoring one's on-stage partner, which was habitual in the Russian Imperial theaters. It was only after Stanislavsky's death that Nemirovich attempted to discard what came to be regarded as cliché, the "exaggerated and distorted use of the device of 'the objective'" only to be replaced by what he called the "super objective" with a fully sustained "subtext".

Speaking of Chekhov's characters Maurice Valency observes: "Sometimes the speeches make the effect of an interrupted reverie, as if they are the external signs of an inward dialogue, the details of which are only partially suggested."

Gillman has an insight into these seemingly clumsy expositions which aren't merely expositions at all, but true soliloquys: "Information in Chekhov, moreover, is almost never the product of a situation that seems urgently to call for it, and very seldom comes as a direct result of the interrogations or proddings common to realistic plays… Instead, a remarkable number of pieces of information that technically qualify as exposition seem to come out of nowhere, in the middle of a monologue, thrown into other people's conversation, dropping out of the sky. Casual and low-key mostly or, if not, encircled by lyricism, they don't feel tactical but incidental; they have a way of calling attention to things beyond themselves. And they keep to themselves, these facts, or stay in related clusters, almost never forming chains of

progressive scene-setting. Nor do they have about them that peculiar air of apology we sometimes detect in conventional exposition: you have to know this, so forgive me as I go about telling it to you… It's we [the audience] who are being addressed, but not so much with cold facts as with the life and consciousness from which they emanate." Gillman p. 212 As Valency tells us, it is a very complex story that is revealed to us: "… told in snatches first by Anya, then by Lyubov Andreyevna herself. Nobody dwells on it. It is known to all the characters, and they have no desire to hear it again from anyone. It is an exposition without the slightest urgency." Valency. Magarshack: "… their inner life bursts through the outer shell of their everyday appearance and overflows into a torrent of words. It is this spontaneous and almost palpable transmutation into speech of hidden thoughts and deeply buried emotions that is perhaps the most subtle expression of dramatic action in a Chekhov play."
[32] (khoroshiy ona chelovek [Трудился она человек]. legkiy, prostoy chelovek) [легкий, простой человек], Easy, simple person.

[33] In a latter version, the boy's age is fifteen. Chekhov saw Ranevskaya as an "old woman" [by old woman he meant a woman in her forties. Chekhov refers to Knipper playing the "old woman in *The Sea Gull*"; Arkadina is forty-three] In December 1902, calling his heroine "the old woman," Chekhov was assigning the part to the actress Anna Azagarova (not employed by the Moscow Arts Theater), who was in her forties. (To Olga Knipper April 11,1903). "I find it quite impossible to write a play here [Yalta] - no end of visitors.... Will you have an actress for the part of the elderly woman in *The Cherry Orchard*? If not, there won't be any play." (To Olga Knipper April 15, 1903). "I have no desire to write for your [The Moscow Art Theater] theatre, chiefly because you have no old woman. They will be

making you play the part of the old-woman, though there is another part for you, and besides, you have already been acting an old woman in *The Seagull*." To Vera Kommisarzhevskaya January 27, 1903: "the central role in the play is that of an old woman." He reduced her age when the Moscow Art Theater decided that Olga Knipper, his wife, would play the part. I am not at all convinced by James Loehlin that Chekhov "altered his original conception so that she [Knipper] could play it." Even after the play was written Chekhov continued to refer to Ranevskaia as "the old woman." "She's not dressed luxuriously, but with great taste. She's intelligent, very kind and absent-minded. She's nice to everybody and always has a smile on her face." Chekhov to Knipper 1903 "As reconceived by Chekhov for his wife, Ranevskaya was a woman of great beauty, vitality, and style." James N. Loehlin, *Chekhov The Cherry Orchard*, CAMBRIDGE UNIVERSITY PRESS
Cambridge, New York, Melbourne, 2006. But there is no evidence that he changed anything substantial in the text, except the stated ages. She is essentially still a libidinous, if beautiful, old woman.

[34] Rayfield thinks that vypivshi [Випивши] for drunk is a peculiarly peasant term bursting Lopakhin's pretentions.

[35] Muzhik: male Russian peasant, a powerful word which can be full of affection, or derogatory. Here, I believe, it is derogatory but full of beneficent condescension.

[36] But will it heal before his wedding day; and will there be a wedding day? And is it Ranevskaya herself who keeps the wound unhealed?

[37] "It also gives the first hint of Lopakhin's inner weakness or tenderness: Is he so fixated by adolescent gratitude to Ranevskaia that he will never fulfill Varia's expectations?" Rayfield has the question backwards; though he may have been fixated on

Ranevskaia, it is Varya that will not fulfill Lopakhin's expectations.

[38] This was a down to earth saying more common among the peasants than the aristocracy.

[39] "(the speech is reminiscent of the servant Jean's analogous memory in Strindberg's *Miss Julie*)" James Loehlin. P. 13. Similar but definitely not analogous.

[40] It should be noted that Chekhov himself liked to sport yellow high-buttoned shoes and probably considered it the height of fashion and not at all foppish or nouveau riche; or else he was poking very gentle fun at himself. Lazarevsky [the poet] wrote in a letter: "Chekhov sat behind Knipper and peered out from there. He was dressed, unlike Gorky, very fastidiously. Gold cuff links, yellow shoes, a jacket, coat, all most elegant." "Lopakhin's white waistcoat signals gentrification, while his yellow shoes (yellow in Chekhov always suggests detestation and decay) signal vulgarity. Rayfield P. 51 Rayfield could not be more wrong. "Duniasha's mix of her mistress's cast-off dresses and a servant's apron is equally discordant." Where on earth does Rayfield get this from; Stanislavsky, but certainly, certainly not from Chekhov.

[41] Literally, "with a pig's snout in White-Bread Street," a street where fine baked goods were sold.

[42] "Lopakhin must not be played as a loudmouth, that isn't the invariable sign of a merchant. He's a suave man" (Chekhov to Olga Knipper, October 30, 1903). "Lopakhin is a merchant, true; but a very decent person in every respect; he must behave with perfect decorum, <u>like an educated man</u> with no petty ways or tricks… In casting an actor in the part, you must remember that Varya, a serious and religious young girl, is in love with Lopakhin: she wouldn't be in love with some little money grubber…" (Chekhov to Stanislavsky, October 30, 1903). TJ underlining. "Lopakhin— a white waistcoat and yellow high-

button shoes; walks swinging his arms, a broad stride, thinks while walking, walks a straight line. Hair not short, and therefore often tosses back his head, while in thought he combs his beard, back to front, i.e., from his neck toward his mouth" (Chekhov to Nemirovich-Danchenko, November 2, 1903).

"The merchant ought to be played by Const. Serg. [Stanislavsky]. This is not a merchant in the vulgar sense of the word, one must understand" (Chekhov to O. Knipper, Oct. 28, 1903).

"It must be explained to the unaware non-Russian reader that among Russian educated class the word merchant, as well as anything associated with trade or commerce, until the last decade of the 20th century used to have a vulgar ring. Clearly, Chekhov intended to break with the stereotype. His appeal at times sounds like a cry of desperation." Savely Senderovich

Savely Sanderovich: "Let us now summarize what Chekhov said about Lopakhin: 1. He is the central figure in the play. 2. The success of the play depends on the performance of this character. 3. He is not at all a merchant in the stereotypical sense. 4. He is a soft-spoken, intelligent, well-mannered man, he acts as an educated man."

"The Lopakhin role is central one indeed. If it is not played successfully, the whole play would fail" (Chekhov to Knipper, Oct. 30, 1903).

[43] We are not told which book he is reading. Many an intelligent man has fallen asleep reading a dull, stupid book.

[44] As usual, Stanislavsky, always intent on ruining Chekhov's subtlety, has Lopakhin toss the book onto the nearest chair.

[45] Dunyasha doesn't answer him; it's as if he were talking to himself or thinking out loud or indulging in sentimental perhaps delusional reverie not really expecting a reaction or response; *nor does it reveal the true depths of his own feeling* but it does reveal the conflict within him.

⁴⁶ The dogs can't sleep, expecting the masters; Anya didn't sleep during her train trip home; Lopakhin falls asleep when he doesn't want to; Pishchik falls asleep almost in the middle of a sentence, inappropriately but conveniently.

⁴⁷ I think that Chekhov is wickedly suggesting that most of the characters are just like dogs waiting for the masters to return.

⁴⁸ Rayfield seems to think that Danyasha is speaking a "bastard language", with the peasant chuiut, chto khoziaeva edut ("they can sense that the mistress is coming"). Khoziaeva is plural for masters, proprietors or bosses; mistress doesn't do it. Khoziaeva is a powerful word. Before and during the revolution, Lenin had called on the toiling masses to overthrow their masters (khoziaeva). Chuiut might better be translated as know, guess or suppose.

⁴⁹ But then Lopakhin doesn't know "his place" either. Does anyone in this play know their place? Does Lopakhin resent that Dunyasha speaks to him intimately as if he were her equal, that she doesn't completely recognize the transition he has made, a transition that is unconvincing? Is he reprimanding her?

⁵⁰ I think Rayfield goes off the deep end by exaggerating what Chekhov only suggested: "… [I]n telling off Duniasha he lapses into the tyrannical, curt pomposity traditionally associated with Russia's merchant classes, at least in their theatrical images: Tak nel'zia. Nado sebia pomnit' ('Not the way, is it? You want to remember who you are')." Rayfield P. 52. Referring to this scene Chekhov asserts that "Lopakhin, in fact, maintains his position like a gentleman."

⁵¹ Perhaps a parody of the self-made man as represented by Lopakhin; but doesn't Epihodov sincerely wish to emulate Lopakhin? Chekhov first envisaged the character as plump and elderly, but revised this to fit one of his favorite actors, Ivan Moskvin, who was young and lean. Epikhodov's auto-

didacticism, reading serious books to improve himself, may have originated when Chekhov suggested to one of his attendants in Yalta that he go in for self-improvement; so, he bought a red tie, and began to study French. Although formally educated in medicine Chekhov was himself an autodidact when it came to arts, literature and almost everything else.

[52] What a perfect emblem for the up and coming man who seeks to improve himself but can't quite bring it off and embarrasses and brings attention to himself in the attempt.

[53] "Stanislavsky reinforces the farcical entry of Epikhodov with so much business that it is puzzling as to why Chekhov should ever have accused the Moscow Arts Theater of not reading the text, of making a tragedy out of it. Epikhodov was to drop the flowers because he was also trying to manage a hat and shake Duniasha's hand. He then wipes his nose with a handkerchief 'as if playing a violin.'" Rayfield P. 53. I think this farcical low-down slapstick proves exactly what Chekhov claimed, that Stanislavsky never read his play or rather read it with such a total disregard of Checkhov's intention that he staged it to spite Chekhov.

[54] Has he brought the bouquet for Dunyasha but loses his nerve after dropping it, fabricating an excuse, giving her an order to cover his embarrassment? Is his embarrassment sharpened by the presence of Lopakhin? After all she is a servant girl, lower in social standing than Epikhodov; she will reject him for Yasha, an ignorant, pretentious footman. They both assume an "authority" over Dunyasha in the presence of each other. If this is farce it is farce with a soul.

[55] A dark, nonalcoholic or very mildly alcoholic fermented brew made from black rye bread or sometimes beets.

[56] Immediately changing his intimate tone to one of command. Dunyasha resumes her uneasy pose as a subservient servant. In a

letter Chekhov in describing Lopakhin: "Dunya and Epihodoff stand in Lopakhin's presence; they do not sit. Lopakhin, in fact, maintains his position like a gentleman. He addresses the servants "thou" and they "you" him."

[57] The same temperature as at the end.

[58] This is the outside temperature. There is no indication that they have failed to stoke the fires as in the final act.

[59] Prisovokupit [Присовокупит] "to communicate"; possibly suggesting sovokupit "to copulate".

[60] Is it possible that Lopakhin sees himself in Epikhodov, that Epikhodov is attempting to ingratiate and seek the advice of someone he genuinely admires and seeks to emulate? Epikhodov, perhaps touchingly, is dressing up in his new boots just as Lopakhin dresses up with his yellow high-buttoned shoes. Even emulation can be trying to endure especially from someone who, by not pulling it off, distressingly reminds Lopakhin of himself. But then these characters parody each other; even Yasha can be seen as a parody of Lopakhin's "social climbing".

[61] There may be a studied rudeness in this. Could he be jealous? Dunyasha does confide in him; the only other person she tells is Anya who is similarly unimpressed.

[62] Literally, Dvadtsat-dva neschastye, [Двадцать-два Несчасте] Twenty-Two Misfortunes. Neschastye is a recurrent word throughout the play meaning unhappiness, misfortune, trouble, bad luck, affliction, adversity and disaster.

Too many adapters and translators miss the importance of maintaining a consistency of translation for these words and translate it differently each time.

This nickname is also rendered as: Endless Misfortune (David Mamet), There Goes Trouble (Curt Columbus), Double Trouble (Schmidt), Catastrophe Corner (Tom Stoppard), Master Disaster, (Andrei Belgrader).

The characters continually blame their own faults on this external fate, on "misfortune", instead of blaming themselves. It is the word that Ranevskaya uses to blame her own (self-inflicted) (neschastye) "misfortune". Fiers also uses the word to refer to the emancipation of the serfs in 1861.

[63] Still the little boy, uncertain, in his way still subservient to the old masters, seeking their approval or at the very least their recognition. In a real sense Ranevskaya doesn't recognize Lopakhin.

[64] "No, I never wanted to suggest that Ranevskaya is chastened. The only thing that can chasten [Rayfield translates 'settle down'] a woman like that is death . . . It isn't hard to play Ranevskaya; you only need from the beginning to take the right tone; you need to come up with a smile and a way of laughing, you have to know how to dress". (Chekhov to Olga Knipper, October 25, 1903). Unsubdued, indefatigable, unhumbled but also unchanged, unrepentant and unredeemed. But there is no gloomy sense of heavy sin, here, nor need of redemption in the traditional sense, certainly not in the Christian sense.

But certainly, Chekhov seems to "admire" this un-discourageability, this indefatigability, this failure to wither under the blows of "fate" which fate is often the result of our own stupidity; this stubborn refusal to accept defeat; to lie down and die even after being shot. As Frayne points out: "'this ability to endure' had already been identified by Nina at the end of *The Seagull* as <u>the most important quality in life.</u> In *Uncle Vanya* Sonya takes it up as her watchword - 'Endure, uncle! Endure!'" (TJ underlining) The mistranslation of this single, crucial word in Nina's speech, by influential hacks: "What matters is not fame ... but knowing how to be patient", instead of "knowing how to endure" distorts the meaning of the entire play.

"Their mood is comprised of a capacity to resist resignation… Such strength as that and a sense, privileged in Chekhov, **that time as a condition, with its remorseless wearing away of our substance, may be tactically outfaced, made provisionally to relent, before it once again resumes our diminution**." Gilman p. 201. TJ underlining and bold. David Magarshack asserts that Uncle Vanya's principal theme "is not frustration, but courage and hope"; hope may be an inappropriate word for what is courageous endurance, the absolute refusal to give up. Alexander Blok wrote: "Some devilish vitality helps us burn but never burn out." It was Hemingway who made it a personal code and would often end his letters with "Il faut d'abord durer", variously translated as: above all one must endure; a strange or not so strange motto for a man who finally decided he could not endure. As another author said of his own people, who may have been not so different: of their need "to keep going despite everything." "Chekhov is struck not so much by the inexorable nature of terrible events as by their survivability, by their way of slipping out of the mind, once they have occurred, and of disappearing in the endless wash of further events. But the cheerfulness is deeply poignant. The worst has happened, and it is a bad worst. The Gaevs' happiness has been irretrievably lost, as both brother and sister for one moment realize before they leave the house… A few months' work at the bank for Gaev; a few months with her hopeless lover in Paris for Ranevskaya. Then resolution and love and the last of the money will all run out. They will have neither home nor occupation; nothing. There is something absurd about their prospects, though, because the Gaevs remain too feckless to understand them…" Michael Frayne. TJ underlining.
This is not only endurance of the spirit that Chekhov seemed to grudgingly admire but also an endurance born partially of obliviousness, and even imperturbable arrogance, of a class (or

an entire people, the Russian people) that refuses to accept its own defeat; or perhaps, refusing to perceive the direness of the situation correctly.

[65] And who heralds in these illustrious personages, but the Fool himself, in top hat and livery no less, the regalia of thralldom; comic, grotesque, surreal, pitiful and utterly fantastic?

[66] This seems to indicate that this is not the direct route to where they are going, but rather an alternative route and that the room has been closed up for some time. "This room ('a forgotten inner sanctum') has been opened up for a purpose. One could even say that here is the underlying 'plot' of the entire first act— everyone dealing with this room, and the memories and ghosts it evokes." Richard Pevear (Translator and Introduction) with Richard Nelson (Translator), Larissa Volokhonsky (Translator) *The Cherry Orchard by Anton Chekhov* (TCG Classic Russian Drama Series) Theatre Communications Group, August 3, 2015

[67] A head scarf was normally associated with peasant dress.

[68] "Anya [is] a bobtailed, uninteresting role." (Chekhov to Nemirovich-Danchenko, October 30, 1903). "Anya can be played by anybody you like, even by an altogether unknown actress, only she must be young and look like a little girl, and talk in a young, ringing voice. This is not one of the major roles. Varya is a more important role… Varya does not resemble Sonya and Natasha; she is a figure in a black dress, a little nun, a little silly, a crybaby, etc., etc." (Chekhov to Nemirovich-Danchenko, November 2, 1903). "Anya is first and foremost a child, who is merry all the way through, who knows nothing of life, and does not cry once, except in Act II, and even then, she only has tears in her eyes" (Letter to Olga Knipper October 21, 1903)

[69] or "Pass through here" (Proidemte zdes')

[70] [radostno skvoz' slezy] joyfully through tears. Richard Peace points out: "… one of Dostoyevsky's minor comic characters, Dr.

Gertsenshtube in *The Brothers Karamazov*, asserts that Russians very frequently laugh where one ought to weep. There is perhaps something typically Russian in the concept: 'laughter through tears'" Richard Arthur Peace, *Chekhov: A Study of the Four Major Plays*, 1983 p. 119

[71] Chekhov absolutely insisted that skvoz' slyezy - literally "through tears" or "on the verge of tears" did not mean that they were crying. The stage direction "through tears" occurs thirteen times in *The Cherry Orchard*.
Letter of Chekhov to Nemirovich-Danchenko "I am afraid that Anya might have a tearful tone of voice (you for some reason find her similar to Irina) . . . Not once in my text does Anya weep, and nowhere does she speak in a tearful voice. In the second act she has tears in her eyes, but her tone of voice is cheerful and lively. Why in your telegram do you talk about there being a lot of people weeping in the play? Where are they? The only one is Varya, but that's because Varya is a crybaby by nature, and her tears are not supposed to elicit a feeling of gloom in the audience. In my text it often says 'on the verge of tears', but that indicates merely the characters' mood, not tears."
However, I think Chekhov protests too much. As Michael Frayne points out: "According to the stage-directions, Gaev is 'wiping away his tears' in Act Three. Ranyevskaya, at the end of the act, is 'weeping bitterly'. Both of them, at the end of the last act, 'sob quietly'". In spite of Chekhov's protestations, there's a lot of crying going on.

[72] How significant that her very first exclamation is

[73] "'The nursery.' Stanislavsky intensified the pause before the mass entry by having two servants, Efimiushka and Polia (merely mentioned by Varia in Chekhov's text), creeping across the stage then hiding and watching." Stanislavsky is always adding irrelevant and unnecessary characters; the final ball is a veritable

mob scene of characters Chekhov never intended to appear. As revealed in his correspondence Chekhov worked so very hard to pare down the number of actual characters on stage. I would go so far as to say that it is this paucity of characters on stage but invoked by the characters that lends such an almost surreal magic to the play.

[74] (i teper'ya kak malen'kaya [И Тепир'я как Ален'кайа])

[75] Ty vse takaia zhe [Ты все Такаиа же], "The same as always", perhaps

[76] Or as Ronald Meyer mocks the two sides of unchangeablity in the play: "You're the same reliable drab efficient drudge you always were." Ronald Meyer, *The Cherry Orchard in the Twenty-First Century: New Adaptations and Versions* from *Chekhov For The 21st Century* edited by Carol Appollonio and Angela Brintunger, Slavica , Bloominton, Indiana,
The subtlety of Chekhov suggests so much; but that's just it; it only suggests.

[77] A tactless and cruel comment.

[78] "Liuba's second 'tactless comment' is immediately perceivable to an audience. She says that she has recognised Dunyasha, and by implication this suggests that she has failed to recognise Lopakhin." Geoffrey Borny, *Interpreting Chekhov*, Chapter Title: *The Cherry Orchard: Complete Synthesis of Vision and Form,* ANU Press. (2006) P. 237.

[79] In one of Chekhov's early notes: "she fed her dog on real caviar"; indicating her assumption of decadent aristocratic prodigality.

[80] "Charlotta is a major role… Charlotta speaks correct, not broken, Russian, but occasionally she pronounces the soft ending of a word hard, and she confuses the masculine and feminine gender of adjectives" (To Nemirovich-Danchenko, November 2, 1903). (to Olga Knipper November 9, 1903). Charlotta in one

scene wears pants, slings a long gun over her shoulder, performs as a magician, a traditionally male role and above all she is funny.

"Tell the actress that she must be funny in the part of Charlotta. That is the most important thing." (to Olga Knipper November 2, 1903) "You must remember that Charlotta's part is a very important one." "Muratova, who played Charlotta, asks Anton Pavlovich, might she wear a green necktie. "'You may but it's not necessary,' Chekhov answers" (L. M. Leonidov, "Past and Present," Moscow Art Theatre Yearbook for 1944, vol. 1 1946). ("Two words about Uncle Vanya's wonderful neckties— Chekhov made special mention of them to actors. For Uncle Vanya, as we shall see, they were an unavailing attempt to uproot himself from the humdrum" Naum Berkovsky, [*Chekhov, Story Writer and Dramatist* from A Norton Critical Edition, *Anton Chekhov's Selected Plays,* Laurence Senelick, ed., W. W. Norton & Company New York • London]

(We should also remember Chekhov employee in Yalta who bought himself a red tie and studied French to seek self-improvement, to step up in the world.) Chekhov himself was known for his beautiful neck-ties.

Charlotta was supposedly suggested by an eccentric English governess Chekhov met while staying on Stanislavsky's estate; at least according to Stanislavsky: "This acrobatic Miss Prism would leap up on Chekhov's shoulders and salute passersbys by taking off his hat and forcing him to bow." (Stanislavsy's *My Life in Art*). Harvey Pitcher finds this claim exaggerated. Gillman makes a gross error when he says of Charlotta: "her hired companion for the trip to Paris." She has obviously been in the employ of the Gaevs for quite some time and naturally stays on after the return from Paris. The fact that a governess is no longer needed and Anya doesn't seem to want much tutoring is telling in itself; just as Epikhodov doesn't do much "clerking", if he ever did. One critic suggests that Charlotta was all the Gaevs could afford; but I doubt this; she is beautifully, elegantly attired, sits at table with Ranevskaya, has her own little dog, <u>will not perform her magic on command</u>; "I will not. I wish to sleep"; a line worthy of Garbo; and not once does she interact with Anya, her supposed charge, except to make Anya magically appear and disappear in Act Three. The 1903 original version has Charlotta performing a silly imaginary fiancé knocking trick which in my mind would have spoiled our perception of Charlotta.

[81] "Pishchik is a real Russian, an old man, debilitated by gout, old age, and over-indulgence, stout, dressed in a tight, long-waisted frockcoat . . . boots without heels" (Chekhov to Nemirovich-Danchenko, November 2, 1903).

[82] Anya ignores this seemingly heartfelt expression of affection prattling on instead about her own travails.

[83] There may be an assertion of authority here; that Anya may object to Dunyasha's failure to respect her superior position. This unwanted intimacy transgresses, but then again, she is very tired. Fatigue will often unveil a truth.

[84] The seven-day period before Easter, which includes Good Friday, when Christ was crucified and died and Easter Sunday when adherents believe He rose from the dead.

[85] "…he is living in the bathhouse, that spidery wooden construction so redolent of evil in Russian literature." Rayfield P. 54 Although considered a magic place with its own resident spirit, it wasn't regarded as evil; no belt, icon or cross was allowed in it. It was not considered a suitable place to live permanently; even spending a night was considered undesirable.

[86] Rayfield seems to think that her owning a watch is to remind us of her "bourgeois pretensions".

[87] Varya dresses more like a nun or a servant than a lady, which may reveal her actual station. She is never treated like Ranevskaya's biological daughter, never enters into direct discussions with the "family" about the sale of the cherry orchard; never once even mentions the cherry orchard as such and is never given any money; not even the measly hundred rubles which would liberate her to go on her longed for pilgrimage. The fact that she receives none of the great aunt's money and is abandoned to become a housekeeper on another estate reveals the truth of her former position. Revealingly she always addresses her mother and uncle by the polite form of 'you' (vy) whereas the true daughter Anya addresses them in the familiar form ty, (thou); ty is used in addressing members of one's family, close friends and children.

In America keys hanging from a belt are the sign of a janitor or custodian. Varya is characterized in Chekhov's own stage directions by her keys, klyuchi [Ключи] which suggests the Russian word for housekeeper klyuchnitsa [Ключнитса]. Maxim Gorky, who after Chekhov's death succeeded him as the primary playwright for the Moscow Art Theater, regarded Ranevskaya and Gaev as egotistical and parasitical, an opinion that reflected his Marxist convictions; but what he said of Varya rings true: she "…works unstintingly for the benefit of these idlers." In the case of Varya her "forced" labor doesn't require serfdom, she is imprisoned by far more sophisticated psychological means; she is bound by the chains of a familial fiction which is maintained only so long as Ranevskaia and Anya require her services. There is no evidence that Varya and Anya will maintain any bond after the sale; not one word. Nor does Anya show any concern for her former governess, who would have been abandoned except for Lopakhin.

[88] Notice how <u>both</u> servants (Varya and Dunyasha) hop to it when the command comes down. One servant telling another servant. It's as if Varya purposely breaks Dunyasha's illusion of ladyhood, although or because Dunyasha dresses like the lady and Varya like the servant.

[89] It seems that Anya is immune to the charms of Charlotta's magic, which may be her problem, a failure of imagination; not so the old Russian Pishchik who is entranced, as are some of the others; a man who knows magic when he sees it. We must always remind ourselves that Chekhov saw Charlotta as equal to Lopakhin in importance; as the two most important roles. (To Olga Knipper September 29, 1903). "The play is now finished, but I am copying it out slowly because I have to correct and reconsider all leaving it for later. . . Oh, if only you'd play the governess in my play! <u>It is the best part</u>. <u>I don't like the others</u>." TJ underlining.

[90] When Chekhov came to Moscow from Yalta in 1903 to stay at the "new flat" that Knipper had rented, walking up the five floors was "martyrdom" for him. (It may only have been a five story walk-up but it still took Chekhov a "good half-hour" to climb it). There are those who think that Knipper was getting some bizarre revenge; Knipper to Chekhov: "Don't fear the stairs. There's nowhere to hurry to, you can rest on the landings …" "… rest on the landings" was she serious? Are we to assume that there were no first or second floor apartments in all of Moscow?

[91] Chekhov himself loved coffee and suffered greatly when his final doctor, Taube, forbade him to drink it, while instead prescribing morphine, opium, and heroin, a perfect combination. This love of coffee represents a betrayal of Ranevskaya's heritage: coffee instead of tea, Roman Catholic instead of Russian Orthodox. In Russian literature of the period western values are often represented as false, pretentious, and spiritually

bankrupt. Russian culture by contrast is exalted as honest and morally pure. Chekhov plays off these contrasts even though he doesn't entirely buy into it.

[92] Although "cheerless" might be accurate, the silly, overused, comparatively modern word "depressing" seems appropriate to the shallow Anya.

[93] A town on the French Riviera, near Monte Carlo, very close to the border with Italy and in many ways more Italian than French; it is nicknamed perle de la France ("Pearl of France").

[94] Although a literal translation of footman, lackey is perhaps too pejorative a term in today's English.

[95] This is puzzling. Since his mother lives in the local village or countryside and he was presumably brought from Russia to France he is obviously not new.

[96] Mike Poulton's translation has Anya saying: "Nothing I could say would persuade her to leave him behind" to which his Varya replies "Yes, he'll need watching." which implies a sexual relationship between Ranevskaya and Yasha. But this turns the play into melodrama; while the suggestion is there, it is just that, a suggestion.

[97] Even Varya can't seem to get the specific date straight, August 22nd, a date which Lopakhin repeats over and over. Why can't the others get that magic number to stick in their brains?

[98] In production Lopakhin can moo like a cow or bleat like a sheep; the Russian word can have either meaning. Nick Worrall: "whether the girls are to be seen as 'silly cows' or 'lambs to the slaughter' might be a valid interpretive quibble." "As for Lopakhin, his moo is at the same time a reflection of his easy position vis-a-vis the household and a rather clumsy attempt to display it." Gillman p. 218. He has an "easy position" toward Varya, not the household in general.

⁹⁹ How are we to interpret this seemingly garish, goofy behavior? Is this an existential comment about these silly "girls" with their childish, useless, preoccupation, whining about a problem they are incompetent to solve by themselves. David Magarshack argues that Lopakhin is teasing them for their frantic worrying over a problem for which he has the simple solution, "dachas". "Overhearing the two girls talking, he could not contain his excitement any longer: it was he, he alone, who knew how the estate could be saved! This gesture of utter contempt for the inexperience of the two silly girls must be made absolutely clear to the audience." Magarshack p. 199

¹⁰⁰ "One of the clichéd ways of solving problems in nineteenth century well-made plays was to marry off the indigent hero or heroine to a wealthy partner. In this case the scène-à-faire would be the proposal scene which would bring about the reversal in the fortune of the hero or heroine, and this would then lead to the happy ending. <u>Chekhov keeps teasing his audience with this possible wish-fulfilment ending.</u>" Borny P. 239 TJ underlining.

¹⁰¹ nekogda (no time)

¹⁰² From Chekhov's 1903 original manuscript; good cut.

¹⁰³ Yet another reminder of Ranevskaya's profligate ways.

¹⁰⁴ How easily she reverts to being a young child.

¹⁰⁵ This has been translated "go about my business on the estate" which implies, perhaps inaccurately, a much greater authority than just that of housekeeper. Her actual scope of authority is not made clear and may not have been clearly delineated by Gaev and Ranevskaya, given their incompetency. If her authority is broader, then she has been a total failure; that such a vast estate cannot even be made minimally profitable. Valency simply gets it wrong when he says the trees are old and will not bear. The trees still bear every other year, so Lopakhin tells us. Growing cherries and marketing them is not some arcane magic, some sorcerer's

secret; there are books on the subject even in 1903; certainly experts can be hired. Are we to believe that people have stopped eating cherries? How ironically appropriate that dopey Varya should admire the singing of the starlings, the plague of any competent cherry orchard manager.

[106] or "I could then be at peace" (ia by togda byla pokoinoi).

[107] What bliss. Is Lopakhin at all compatible with such a person? However, in fairness to Varya becoming a bogomolets, or pilgrim, was a not an uncommon pastime in pre-Revolutionary Russia, particularly among the homeless, rootless, outcast and disenfranchised. They would trek from shrine to shrine, sometimes in groups, staying at monasteries and living off alms like sanctioned beggars. Varya's vision of such a life is romanticized. Its seamy side is seen in Nikolay Leskov's, *The Enchanted Pilgrim*. (the young Chekhov praised Leskov calling him "a mixture of an elegant Frenchman and a defrocked priest") The character of Luka in Gorky's 1902 play *The Lower Depths* is telling, as is Chekhov's own *Along the Highway*. However, many regarded such a pilgrimage as a touring vacation. (Remember *The Canterbury Tales*) In the summer of 1873, the Chekhov children were, to their relief and happiness, left behind by their father Pavel and mother Evgenia who went on a pilgrimage around Russia, to visit the great monasteries and Holy Relics.

[108] According to Stark Young: "The cucumber in Eastern and semi-Eastern countries is eaten as apples are with us, or peaches. If the effect causes the wrong amusement in the audience, I should advise the actor to say instead: 'You little peach!' The effect is the thing to be sought here." I prefer to stick with cucumber which Charlotta munches on and which were consumed by the half barrel by an illustrious personage from the past.

[109] Donald Rayfield [*Anton Chekhov: A Life March*, 1998 Faber & Faber (November 7, 2013)]: "*The Cherry Orchard* smashes even more props than *Three Sisters*, Dunyasha's saucer is only the first symbol of a crashing world."

[110] Again, we are reminded of the seemingly awkward way in which Chekhov fills us in on necessary background; but these characters are always seeming to talk to themselves, thinking out loud, reminiscing.

[111] Nedotyopa was not a Russian word when Chekhov used it; it was Ukrainian for an incompetent, a mental defective, moron. Chekhov may have remembered hearing it in his childhood; his paternal grandmother Efrosinia was Ukrainian; Chekhov claimed to have spoken Ukrainian in his infancy. The word does not appear in Russian dictionaries until 1938, and then Chekhov is cited as its originator. George Calderon perceived the etymology to derive from ne, not, and dotyapat, to finish chopping, (or half-chopped)
Other English translations render it as: "sillybilly" "booby" "good-for-nothing," "rogue," "duffer," "job-lot," "lummox," "silly young cuckoo," "silly old nothing," "muddler," "silly galoot," "numbskull," "young flibbertigibbet", "bungler" "dimwit" "blunderhead". The critic Batyushkov considered the whole play to be a variation on the theme of "nedotyopery," each of the characters representing a different expression of a botched, wasted life. "In Chekhov's opinion, a civilization crumbles when people become 'nedotyopa,' that is, so confused, careless, insensitive and gullible that they lose sight of what they have achieved as a civilization." Anna L. Linden

[112] The post-chaise was a fast, four-wheeled, closed carriage, containing one seat for two or three passengers drawn by two or four horses for traveling post in the 18th and early 19th centuries.

[113] From Chekhov's 1903 original manuscript; a good cut.

[114]Sharovary: this is not medieval Boyar attire, nor are they "pantaloons" which makes them sound foppish, nor are they really "Turkish". Rather they are Ukrainian trousers tucked into the boots in an affectation of Ukrainian Cossack garb fashionable among this region's aristocracy. Richard Peace thinks these "breeches … link him with the comic heroes of Gogol's Ukrainian tales." Although clownish there is the <u>residual</u> quality of the old boyar warrior about Pishchik. It is ironic that this attire once associated with heroic warriors, the Cossacks, had degenerated into an affectation of a decadent class and thus clownish. The Cossacks were decidedly not peasants and certainly not comic but rather romanticized free warriors. Sharovary may have originally appeared with Persian horsemen, to allow more freedom of movement while riding horseback. The presence of wide trousers in the territory of Ukraine may have originated with the ancient Scythians, a culture which were later absorbed into Slavic culture. Exposure to <u>similar</u> Turkish modes of dress would have occurred in battles on the Ukrainian steppes. The presence of sharovary among the Ukrainian Cossacks of Zaporozhe is noted by German ambassador Erich Lassota in the 16th century. A full description of Cossack dress, including the sharovary, can be found in the 1651 *Description of Ukraine* by French-born cartographer and military engineer Guillaume Le Vasseur de Beauplan.

[115] "Gaev uses phantom billiards as a displacement activity, to hide embarrassment or distress, reenacting tricky shots to exorcise tricky social moments. Stanislavsky reduced the billiards feints to mere clowning." Rayfield P. 56. I think Rayfield is right; Gaev shoots balls when he is nervous or in a difficult social situation; when he is frightened and doesn't know what to say or do. With his low comedy Stanislavsky drains the deep existential humor inherent in Gaev's compulsive game.

[116] Obsessed by the game of billiards, Gaev uses its jargon throughout the play. He plays a version called carom billiards with three balls; a cue sticks hits the balls on a cloth-covered table with raised and cushioned sides. More familiar in the United States is the version called pocket billiards (or pool). In pre-Revolutionary Russia, billiards was also played with five balls, one of them yellow. A doublette occurs when a player's ball hits the cushion, rebounds, and sinks the other player's ball. George Calderon observed that Gaev "always plays a declaration game at billiards, no flukes allowed." Chekhov asked the actor he wanted to play Gaev to learn the terminology and use the proper phrases since he himself had forgotten them.

[117] The colloquial "Kogo" (literally, "Whom?") instead of "chego" ("What's that?"). The strangely affected locution of a confused aristocrat? [or] At moments of embarrassment? he [Gaev] frequently asks: 'whom?' (kogo?) instead of 'what?' (chto?)

[118] "Kogo?" (what, but also who)

[119] Lopakhin repeats, Время, говорю, идет "Vremia, govoriu, idet" (Time, I say, is passing); "vremia idet" is also translated as "time flies" or time goes by. Ronald Hingley's fancifully translates it as "time marches on". "Gaev's [Которые] 'kogo?' however, awakens the sleeping metaphor, "vremia idet"; it anthropomorphizes "vremia," turning "time" into a kind creature on the march, or an incarnation of "horror" (uzhas [Ужас])…" From *What Time Is It? Where Are We Going*? a chapter in *Chekhov's The Cherry Orchard: The Story of a Verb* in *Close Encounters, Essays on Russian Literature*, Robert Louis Jackson, Academic Studies Press. (2013)

[120] Referring to Lopakhin; but he could be referring to Yasha who may have drenched himself in the latest fashionable French perfume so strongly that the smell lingers. Gaev is peculiarly

attuned to the scents associated with certain personages. According to Rayfield: "Chekhov endows Gaev not just with his medical lore but with his fastidious sensitivity to vulgar smells" Rayfield P. 98

Translating patchouli as "cheap perfume" might not be accurate. During the 18th and 19th century, silk traders from China traveling to the Middle East packed their silk cloth with dried patchouli leaves to prevent moths from laying their eggs on the cloth. Some historians have speculated that this association with opulent Eastern goods is why patchouli was considered by Europeans of that era to be a luxurious scent. It is said that patchouli was used in the linen chests of Queen Victoria. There may be some class confusion with patchouli in 1903 with the lower classes considering it upper class while the upper class associated it with the bounding lower class. "But note that Stanislavsky identified Ranevskaia as the source of the smell: in his notes for act 3 he asserted, 'Ranevskaia has the Parisian habit of powdering herself and making sure she is looking her best frequently. She also abuses perfume, always having a bottle of it on her.'" Rayfield P. 57

[121] Nenaglyadnaya ditsyusya moya, [Ненаглядная дитсюся моя] literally; a word combination found in fairy tales; or simply "my beloved child".

[122] It is significant that she does not embrace or kiss cheeks Russian fashion with either of them nor does she say a word to them as she departs abruptly. She hardly acknowledges Lopakhin at all through the entire play.

[123] Is Ranevskaya apologizing for Anya's seeming rudeness?

[124] "You're still the same". This is a refrain throughout the play. Everyone is just the same. No one learns. No one grows or appreciably changes. No one repents or is redeemed.

Richard Gilman, [*CHEKHOV'S PLAYS An Opening into Eternity* Yale University Press February 1, 1996] however, rightly sees something more subtle and profound; speaking of all four plays: "At the end a surprising number of them will move on, going out of the picture, but whether they go or stay, most of them will bear the marks of encounter, interchange, or simple propinquity, and they will have been altered in some essential aspect of self-awareness, which for the most part will be left to us to intuit." So much of the power of this play is because so much is left for us to intuit.

[125] She overrules Varya. There is never any doubt who's in charge here. (You're still the same . . . *as rude as ever*.) My addition in italics TJ

[126] Too many productions miss Ranevskaya's sharp edge. With Charlotte Rampling, in director Michael Cacoyannis 1999 production, we get the feeling of a woman who must have her way; who will be in charge even if it leads to her own destruction. Stephen Holden, reviewing this production for the New York Times, speaking of Rampling's Ranevskaia: "A deeply paradoxical woman, she is one step away from being what we would call a control freak, yet she still ultimately loses control." Rampling's interpretation is closer to Chekhov's original conception of Ranevskaia as "incorrigible and indomitable". Knipper sentimentalized her, hyped "her love of homeland and played down her attraction to the lover in Paris. Since the actress pitied her character so did the public." Senelick P. 70. Rayfield's claim that Chekhov had control of his wife's, Knipper's interpretation is plain wrong: "Only over the part of Ranevskaia, played by his wife, did Chekhov have full control: while she had a mind of her own and could be obtuse, her interpretation is probably authorial." Rayfield P. 41.

¹²⁷ Coffee is an odd European affectation for a traditional Russian tea drinker. But then, Chekhov loved coffee.

¹²⁸ moy starichok or "dear old friend", "dear little old man", "my old man".

¹²⁹ Ironic; she declares her love for Russia but must have her coffee, a very un-Russian habit.

¹³⁰ A clumsy, insensitive thing to say, if you think about it; glad he is alive so that she can have the pleasure of seeing him (the ultimate narcissism). "…Ranevskaya's greeting to him implies a piece of furniture like 'my dear little table.'" A Norton Critical Edition, *Anton Chekhov's Selected Plays*, Laurence Senelick, ed., W. W. Norton & Company New York, London

¹³¹ All of the characters are hard of hearing; they are so wrapped up in themselves they are deaf to each other.

¹³² Or, if you wish, "What a pain in the ass" (Donaghy translation)

¹³³ Lyrics to a folk song; whose next line reads: "lost my heart head over heels".

¹³⁴ Rayfield, however, claims that it comes from a letter to Chekhov's from his brother Alexander in 1903.

¹³⁵ Kulak, literally a fist, but figuratively a tight-fisted, ruthless but prosperous peasant or small merchant trader.

¹³⁶ "vsyo ravno" [Всё равно], "still", "it's all the same", "it doesn't matter".

¹³⁷ Lopakhin romanticizes Ranevskaya. Except for the incident when she allows him into the nursery to wash the blood off his face when he was a boy, which he has blown all out of proportion, we are given no other instances, if there are any other instances, of the "once did so much for me". Gillman's: "… we can speculate that she may have helped him get started in business." p. 221 This is pure imaginative conjecture on Gillman's part and spoils the play. Part of the deep irony is that

such a down to earth, shrewd and practical businessman like Lopakhin should remain under the sway of a woman seemingly unworthy of his devotion. Is he in some strange way as guilty as Fiers of being in thrall to the old masters or at least master? (Can we dare to call this Stockholm syndrome where the least kindness of your imprisoner is exaggerated and fixated upon?)

[138] As Peace points out the word Lopakhin uses here is not 'sister' but rodnoy (Lyublyu vas kak rodnuyu [Люблю вас как родную] . . . bol'she chem rodnuyu) — i.e. 'I love you as kith and kin . . . more than kith and kin'. I've translated kith and kin, which had become a cliché in English by the 1300s with another cliché: "flesh and blood"; or my own, my native self.

[139] Ranevskaya doesn't respond to this seemingly heartfelt speech but then the characters so seldom respond to each other and when they do the results are often unpleasant. Is she oblivious or indifferent or just deaf like Fiers? Or does she perhaps believe that this intimate speech equating her with Lopakhin's own flesh and blood is impertinent and even offensive, though she would never say so.

"The fact that Lopakhin can venture even this tentative overture to the daughter of his father's master is indicative of the collapse of the old social barriers - just as her failure even to register it shows how rooted she still is within her own class." Edward Braun, *The Director & The Stage: From Naturalism to Grotowski*, Methuen Drama, May 13, 1986

"Lyubov Andreyevna completely ignores this declaration of affection and kinship. Instead she proclaims her restlessness and almost immediately exhibits her affection for an inanimate object, using the very same kinship-like term of endearment — rodnoy. 'My dear little bookcase' (shkafik moy rodnoy). She kisses it, then addresses her table." Richard Peace p. 139

[140] This may not be quite as absurd as it seems. This room, the nursery, may have been locked up and unused since Ranevskaya went away or maybe longer.

[141] Nanny

[142] Ranevskaia seems quite indifferent to the servants who were supposedly close to her. Drinking the coffee before responding is especially cold.

[143] "This atavistic gesture speaks eloquently of his nostalgia for being nursed (sucking of the candy being a substitute for breastfeeding) and his resistance to being weaned away from the maternal breast" Svetlana Evdokimova

[144] This may be addressed to Lopakhin. Is there a possible relationship here? We should remember that Dashenka reads Nietzsche; this is in tune with the self-improvement that Lopakhin strives for. Although Ranevskaya would never even consider marrying off her <u>real</u> daughter, Anya, to Lopakhin, Pishchik, her fellow aristocrat, may have no such reservations about marrying off his own daughter. Effusive with his flattery, he genuinely admires Lopakhin, more so than any other character. But typically, no one answers him when he conveys Dashenka's regards and no one returns their regard to her nor do they courteously ask after her, nor does she appear at the final ball which is short of women. (Stanislavsky actually has Dashenka show up at what should be a ghostly ball; but then Stanislavsky screwed up everything.)

[145] Chekhov's original manuscript read: "To stop your estate running at a loss you must rise at four o'clock in the morning each and every day and work the whole day through. But for you people, of course, this is impossible, I can see that." Chekhov did well to exclude it because Chekhov did not entirely believe it and it cheapens the play. "The cry 'Work! for we must work!' is heard throughout the last plays. In almost every case the

character is speaking out of desperation, not conviction; to claim that the orchard is being lost because the family's ancestors scorned work is both silly and false." Richard Gillman, Chekhov, Anton. Plays: "Ivanov", "The Seagull", "Uncle Vanya", "Three Sisters" Translated with Notes by PETER CARSON, with an Introduction by RICHARD GILMAN (Penguin Classics). Not silly or false but certainly not the whole story or even the central issue.

[146] nekogda razgovarivat (no time to talk)

[147] No, I'm going off now; "uedu seichas," or I am going off this hour. There's no time

[148] Or "have a tranquil sleep" (spite spokoino).

[149] Twenty-five thousand a year income: Maxim Gorky's play *Summerfolk* examines just such a colony of dachas and its summer population. The first draft was finished a month after *The Cherry Orchard* opened on 20 January 1904. Did Gorky intend his play as a comment on Chekhov's?

[150] Literally "tithing" [Десятину]

[151] Tom Stoppard hits us over the head with "deep enough for swimming" when Chekhov says only that the river is deep and Stoppard further adds the stage direction *"a miss-step; he recovers from almost instantly"* One critic calls this insertion brilliant but I think it clumsily intrudes upon Chekhov's subtle suggestion of how purposefully and completely Grisha is forgotten.

[152] The mania for old classic houses didn't exist at the time and Lopakhin shouldn't be regarded as a vulgarian for tearing down a treasure. In a letter to Stanislavsky November 3, 1903 regarding the Ranevskaya manor house: "It is a very large and very old house. Holiday makers do not rent such a house. As a rule, such houses are pulled down and the material is used for the building of dachas . . . People buying such a house usually think that it is

much cheaper and easier to build a smaller house than to convert the old house."

[153] vyrubit' [Вирубит]

[154] Vo vsei gubernii [Во веселись губернии] the most fun in the provence.

[155] Chekhov's play emphasizes, at least indirectly, the idea of a Russian "paradise lost," depicting the "Fall" of the old nobility from their Edenic existence in the Garden of Cherries. In several earlier short stories, Chekhov had ironically compared this estate world of the nobility with the Garden of Eden and introduced motifs of the Fall; this irony continues in *The Cherry Orchard*, where the "paradise" of one class was built upon the blood, sweat and floggings of another.

[156] Lopakhin says that the estate spreads over 2,500 acres, and the cherry orchard is supposed to cover most of it. There were never any cherry orchards of this size in Russia or anywhere in the world at that time. And the fact that an orchard of this size which, by the estimate of Donald Rayfield, would produce more than four million pounds of cherries each crop, even if harvested every second year, could not profit Ranevskaia is an absurdity, a profound absurdity of wasted wealth. "A cherry orchard that could glut the world with cherries and yet cannot earn its owners a living symbolizes a decrepit world, a decrepit Russia for which ordered destruction is the only alternative to disordered ruination." Rayfield. However, if it had any possibility of economic viability wouldn't Lopakhin exploit that; he goes in for farming; remember the poppies returned him a neat profit; but perhaps harvesting the trees would yield him the greater profit and free the land for leasing dachas. Chekhov chose to call the orchard "Vishnyovy sad" (accentuated on the second syllable, "a cherry orchard"). This kind of orchard gives no profit, "it does nothing but preserve within itself and its snow-white blossoms,

the poetry of the life of the masters of olden times" (My Life in Art). Stanislavsky

[157] The first intelligent thing Fiers says and Gaev tells him to shut up. Why doesn't anyone work at making the orchard productive? It is doubly ironic that old Fiers poses the solution to their problems, preparing and selling cherries; the orchard is still productive, producing a crop every second year. This isn't some arcane lost art; certainly, an expert might be hired or Epikhodov, the autodidact, could be instructed to learn the cherry business.

[158] "… the recipe for which has been 'forgotten', Firs tells us. It's a fateful word, testifying to the erosions of time, which in one way or another is always at least a partial subject of Chekhov's plays." Richard Gilman, *Chekhov, Anton. Plays: "Ivanov", "The Seagull", "Uncle Vanya", "Three Sisters"* (Penguin Classics). Penguin Books Ltd. TJ underlining.

[159] They've all forgotten how to prepare the cherries and yet she eats crocodiles, if only in jest.

[160] Dachniki [Дачники]

[161] More than one critic has pointed out this third ring of the keys as the ring of doom. They will ring again when Varya flings them to the floor and again when Lopakhin picks them up, the consummation of the rite of anathema.

[162] "The consummate mastery of *The Cherry Orchard* is revealed in an authorial shorthand that is both impressionistic and theatrical. The pull on Ranevskaya to return to Paris takes shape in the telegram prop: in Act One, she tears up the telegrams; by Act Three, she has preserved them in her handbag; in Act Four, the lodestones draw her back." Laurence Senelick

[163] "Gayev's bookcase speech can be played as a natural effusion of his loquacious and sentimental spirit, or as a deliberate attempt to distract Ranevskaya from her thoughts of Paris; if it is the latter, it gives his character a little more weight at this point in the

play." Loehlin p. 16. TJ underlining. But it may not be to save her feelings but rather to save all the Gaevs from her money guttering lover in Paris.

[164] This also suggests that the room was closed off and only recently opened. So rather than the irrational ranting of a muddled mind they are an attempt to come to terms with memories long buried, embodied in this long-locked room.

[165] plodotvoritel'naya rabota [Пудокворител'на работа]

[166] obshchestvennoye samosoznaniye [Обшчественное Самосознаниие]: not social awareness; honor, identity, self-consciousness.

[167] Chekhov is mocking the Russian obsession with commemorating such anniversaries. He utterly detested such jubilees.

[168] This "you haven't changed a bit" or "you're the same as ever" repeats itself with variations throughout the play.

[169] Is this her "fix"; is Yasha her enabler? Is it an accident that the traditional old Russia, reduced to clownishness, intercepts this transaction?

[170] Does he share the magician's art with Charlotta, her sleight of hand? Or is he revealing the ineffectiveness of what are no more than placebos, to which Ranevskaya is addicted; her sugar pill fix like her brother's sugar candy fix?

[171] No "excellencies" come to visit anymore.

[172] "Slender, tightly corseted with a lorgnette"; elegantly European; what a contrast to the nun-like Varya with the keys at her belt.

[173] "… Charlotta making a strange and inconsequential pass across the stage." Loehlin p. 16. And there is something strange, but only seemingly inconsequential, about this pass across the stage like a disconnected spirit trying to slip away, presaging the "ghost" of Lyubov's mother which Lyubov sees momentarily. It

also portends the only seemingly inconsequential "pass" of Epikhodov in Act Two leading to "There goes Epikhodov" twice repeated which I am at a loss to explain why I find so profound yet comical.

[174] Is she suggesting that his "advance" has a romantic edge to it? One critic called this a mock-courtship of Charlotta.

[175] Out of luck or "out of fortune" <u>seems</u> to acknowledge the romantic, sexual aspect to his interest. One can fully understand Chekhov regarding Charlotta as one of two most important characters and wanting his wife to play the part. Lopakhin seems to be charmed by Charlotta's magic. Chekhov was particularly displeased and complained bitterly about the actor, Muratova, who Stanislavsky chose to play Charlotta. "Charlotta is a question mark. Muratova might be good, but not funny. It's a role for Mme. Knipper. When other actresses were suggested for Charlotta, Chekhov balked…"

[176] She will not perform her magic on demand; she is emphatic in her refusal; not for Lopakhin, not for Ranevskaia. "I will not. I wish to sleep"; a line worthy of Garbo; sleep, something which eludes so many of these characters. She exits without any of the Russian polite niceties. Sitting at table with Ranevskaya she shares with Yasha certain "immunities". Charlotta's adamant refusal to perform on command is a crucial and I would say perfect change from Chekhov's original 1903 manuscript. Throughout the play we have servants and peasants assuming a power over their "masters" and former masters who become as children. These masters have lost whatever magic they once possessed and cannot command or control the "inheritors" of that magic.

[177] Instead of Do svidaniya, "Be seeing you," Lopakhin facetiously says "Do svidantsiya."

[178] How appropriate that he exchange this old Russian custom with this old, "old Russian".

[179] He does not kiss Varya on the cheeks, he graciously extends his hand to Fiers and even to Yasha, which he would not do if Yasha was the beast so often melodramatically depicted. Yasha is somewhat of a prude, even warning Dunyasha of the moral dangers of a woman falling in love.

[180] Magarshack translates this as "oaf".

[181] French "boyfriend"

[182] Translated variously: "well then" "But why not."

[183] This sounds like scant praise. Does she seriously want this union to take place?

[184] In Chekhov's first manuscript later revised: "He's a good man. [after which we get] By the way, how much do we owe him?
Gaev: For the second mortgage, just a trifle — about forty thousand."
A necessary cut. Stanislavsky and company were wrong about so much but with some of these cuts I sometimes think the hand of God was operating.

[185] Once again, we have this association between Lopakhin and Dashenka. It's as if Pishchik is about to reveal something and then bites his tongue. There may be a good reason why we never see Dashenka and nobody asks after her; she is perhaps Varya's rival in love of Lopakhin.

[186] This falling asleep may not be a result of clownishness but rather a defense mechanism, a technique to avoid saying what he seems about to say. This traditional old Russia has no trouble sleeping.

[187] By 1903, almost one-half of all private land in Russia (excluding peasant land) was mortgaged, forcing the landed

aristocracy to sell their estates and join the professional or commercial classes, as Gaev does at the end of this play.

[188] Starlings, while wonderful mimics, are not true "songbirds." Extremely clever and companionable, they are a plague for anyone attempting to run a profitable cherry orchard; they devour cherries. Traditional operating orchards had their own means of controlling these birds and were unlikely to admire their "singing", as the inept, ignorant steward Varya does.
As a boy Chekhov trapped starlings in order to sell them and would never forget the tormented cries of the wounded starlings. Donald Rayfield, *Anton Chekhov: A Life,* Faber & Faber, Henry Holt & Co, 1st American edition, March 1998.

[189] Svetlana Evdokimova compares this passage to a passage from Lev Tolstoy, who unlike Chekhov romanticized childhood, the pastoral peasantry and simpleness. "Like Tolstoy's narrator, Ranevskaya endows the image of childhood with explicitly Edenic attributes: happiness, purity, and, of course, angels, and then contrasts the bliss of childhood to the heavy burden of post-lapsarian and post-puerile adult life. Chekhov's allusion to Tolstoy, however, serves to subvert rather than to exalt Ranevskaya's nostalgic evocation of her childhood." Svetlana Evdokimova.
But in contradistinction Lopakhin also reminisces about his childhood which except for the vision of the young, slender and kind Ranevskaya, was a time of beatings.
"The theme of childhood (irretrievably lost) or parents (dead or forgotten) is also repeated in various ways by Charlotta, Yasha, Pishchik, Trofimov, and Firs. The ancient Firs, like a living historical calendar, every so often returns from what is to what 'used to be,' what was done 'at one time,' 'previously.'… The perspective from present to past is opened up by almost every character, though to varying depths." Kataev P. 276

[190] я иду с ним на дно; I go with him to the bottom. "'If only one could take off this heavy stone from my breast and shoulders, if only I could forget my past.' Later in Act III she will be more precise about the nature of this stone — it is her lover in Paris from whom she has parted: 'I love, love . . . this stone round my neck. I am going down to the bottom with it, but I love this stone, and cannot live without it.' The fact that the image here is one of drowning (ya idu s nim na dno) suggests yet another identification for this 'stone' of the past — the grief and guilt associated with the drowning of her young son; a punishment, she feels, for having taken up with a lover." Richard Peace p. 121

[191] Obviously, she isn't even listening to herself. She wants to remember, to wallow in nostalgia, and at the same time laments her inability to forget.

[192] It's as if he regards the auction sale as an unstoppable inevitability, an act of fate which renders them powerless.

[193] Is this a loose allusion to Hamlet's father's ghost, come also to warn them?

[194] "I'm worried about the second act's lack of action and a certain sketchy quality in Trofimov, the student. After all, time and again Trofimov is being sent into exile, time and again he is being expelled from the university, but how can you express something like that?" (Chekhov to Olga Knipper, October 19, 1903). One of the reasons he couldn't express it was because of state censorship.

"Chekhov had the same difficulty with Trofimov in *The Cherry Orchard* - how to explain that someone had been expelled from university for his political activities. It was impossible to get a direct reference to this past the censor…" Michael Frayne

[195] University students were obliged to wear uniforms as were their professors; so were members of the civil service and government officials.

[196] Talk about ghosts and who shows up?

[197] These people are forever blaming misfortune, the will of God instead of taking responsibility. Little boys just don't drown; someone should have been watching; one of them is to blame.

[198] Ranevskaya repeatedly comments about how everyone she has not seen for some time has grown old or is just the same; or both; Chekhov repeatedly described the part as that of an "old woman" yet no one ever mentions that she has grown old which her formidable presence would prevent; as if she imagines that she is immune from ageing.

[199] Kataev stresses the theme of bewilderment and incomprehension: "In Act I it is carried by Ranevskaya's questions. What is death for? Why do we grow old? Why does everything disappear without a trace? Why is everything forgotten that used to be?"

[200] Oblezlyj barin [Облезлиж барин] translated a myriad number of ways including "used up old gentleman", "scruffy gent", "moldy gentleman", "moth-eaten gent".

[201] Or "eternal student". Students with radical ideas such as Trofimov were often expelled or more often suspended from school by the Tsarist government. Orlando Figes [*A People's Tragedy; The Russian Revolution 1891-1924*, London, 1996]: "The universities had been the organizational centre of opposition to the tsarist regime since the 1860s. In the Russian language the words 'student' and 'revolutionary' were almost synonymous." As already quoted, (Chekhov's letter to Olga Knipper, October 1903): "After all, time and again Trofimov is being sent into exile, time and again he is being expelled from the university, but how can you express something like that?" [without being censored]. Under Alexander III, political reaction to reforms set in, the police and censorship became extremely repressive. Real political reform became impossible, so liberal intellectuals

devoted themselves to local improvements in the villages and Tolstoyan passive resistance. The social and political impotence which resulted <u>may</u> have contributed to the indolent aimlessness we see in Chekhov's characters.

[202] Echoing Varya's threat that she's going to "give it to" Lopakhin, while shaking her fist.

[203] The "reek of the hen house" or "chicken coop" or chicken is a euphemism; Gaev would not use the term "pussy" openly; but Yasha knew exactly what Gaev meant. Chekhov was famous for his private allusions, his manipulation of polysemy and sous-entendu. Speaking of Gaev: "Above all, he speaks a language of duality, of double-entendre under any pretext." Savely Senderovich

[204] So many melodramatic versions of this play depict Yasha as a beast; but what evidence do we really have. No doubt he is callous, stupid, insensitive but we sentimentalize his mother; maybe she's looking for money; maybe she beat him when he was a child but more likely reminds him and everyone else of his humble roots. He, like Dunyasha, Varya and Charlotta was adopted; brought to the big house by the masters to better serve them. Yasha, like Gaev, is a prude, who lectures Dunyasha about the perils for a woman of falling in love; he's careful to warn Dunyasha to pretend that she has gone to the river to bathe so that the masters, and they are still the masters, don't suspect that there might be a liaison between them. (But then there is also the possibility that he is protecting his relationship with Ranevskaya, which might demand exclusivity.) But perhaps Ranevskaya likes the innocent company of good-looking young men or someone close to the age her dead son would now be.

[205] A city at the confluence of the Volga and the Kotorosl Rivers, 160 mi northeast of Moscow. Yaroslavl is said to have been founded in 1010 as an outpost of the Principality of Rostov

Veliky, and was first mentioned in 1071. Capital of an independent Principality of Yaroslavl from 1218, it was incorporated into the Grand Duchy of Moscow in 1463.

[206] Magarshack translates this as "howl which gives a very different picture to Varya's weepiness

[207] vyshla za nedvoiyanind [Вышла за недвоийанинд]

[208] Slut is a perfectly valid translation (so is depraved) which is usually rendered "wanton woman" which sounds ridiculous and out of date in today's English; "loose woman" is equally old fashioned. Poulton is taken to task for using the word slut; but this is one case in which I agree perfectly with him. But we should never forget that it is Gaev, who seems peculiarly unsexed, that calls her a slut; and decidedly not Chekhov. Nor does Chekhov call her lover in Paris a gigolo, as some critics have. Chekhov presents the case and refrains from overt judgment. Ranevskaya has nursed her lover when he was sick and must run back to Paris because he is sick again, is alone and needs her; not exactly the actions of a "slut".

"Russia in the 1900s was more akin to Paris or Vienna than to London or Boston: the fact that a widow had a lover and that her family knew about it would not exclude her from society or destroy her self-esteem. Memoirs of foreigners in Russia (such as Gustave Lanson, tutor to Alexander III) confirm that the Russian gentry were the most broadminded in Europe; the behavior of Chekhov's sister, or of their women friends such as the writer Shchepkina-Kupernik, the actress Iavorskaia, or the schoolteacher Lika Mizinova, was far more libertine than Ranevskaia's. To see a condemnation of Ranevskaia's sexuality, rather than of Gaev's puritanism, is to misread text and mores." Rayfield p. 62. However, I think Rayfield goes overboard; even Olga Knipper, Chekhov's wife, an actor and no prude was appalled at the sexual libertinism of Chekhov's sister Maria.

[209] Chekhov admired the writings of Leopold Sacher-Masoch whose sick fantasies often portray a world of ascendant females, often libidinous older females who torment their male underlings. Sacher-Masoch play Unsere Sklaven (Our Slaves) was very popular in Russia in the late 1870s.

Chekhov repeatedly describes the part of Ranevskaya as that of an old woman; and although he technically reduces her age to accommodate his wife playing the part, he changes nothing else; she is still an old woman even if played by a younger one. Chekhov to Knipper: "The central female role is an old woman who lives entirely in the past and has nothing in the present." Does she really have anyone? She abandoned Anya long ago and her lover in Paris is at best problematical. Yasha seems to be no more than decoration and "serves" in no traditional sense, and is exempt from restraint; a nightmare parody (a common type in the theater of the time) of the servant bounding out of his class for suspect reasons; getting away with continually insulting Gaev the putative master of the house. Chekhov suggests, <u>and only vaguely suggests,</u> that this is Ranevskaya's "boy toy" who impudently sits at table with his mistress; or that Ranevskaya might be described by the modern term "cougar"? There are sexual overtones to Ranevskaia's tormenting, her cat and mouse teasing of both Trofimov and Lopakhin. Or as Rayfield puts it, her feelings for them "are tinged with impropriety." In Chekhov's earlier notebooks, he saw Ranevskaya as "a liberal old woman" who "dresses up as a young girl"; how typical of the modern cougar who dresses inappropriately and cavorts like a girl. We have Gaev's own words; she's a slut; (the term "wanton woman" sounds patently ridiculous in modern English and although once powerful has lost its edge) she exudes it in her every movement (or however you translate it); she is possessed of a vulgarity which betrays her class and makes a mockery of her offence at the vulgarity of dachas and the dacha people, which vulgarity could prove her salvation; so she could continue to indulge her more deep seated vulgarity. [Brother and sister haven't seen each other for five years, speak badly of each other and will part at play's end. There is little permanence to their bond which is characterized by gushing sentimental affection.] But as I have said, it is Gaev that calls her a slut, not Chekhov. Nor does Chekhov call her lover in Paris a gigolo as some critics have. Chekhov presents the case and refrains from overt judgment. Ranevskaya has nursed her lover when he was sick and must run back to Paris because he is sick again, is alone and needs her; not exactly the actions of a "slut". Vladimir Korolenko, who knew Chekhov, overstated the case, turning the play into melodrama, when he described Ranevskaya, as an "aristocratic slut, of no use to anyone, who departs with impunity to join her Paris gigolo." Lopakhin may have just seen *Hamlet* whose own mother is lectured by her son for lacking the sexual restraint supposedly befitting a woman her age.

One Czech staging (director Otomar Krejca Düsseldorf 1976?) has Yasha massaging Ranevskaya's thigh beneath her skirt and Dunyasha obviously quite pregnant in the last act. A recent staging at the Young Vic portrays Yasha, not only as a pitiless seducer but also a brutal sadist, who deliberately condemns Fiers to his death by having him locked in the house. Both these productions turn this extremely subtle play into gross, ridiculous melodrama.

[210] There is a possibility and only a possibility that Gaev knows that Anya is within hearing distance; his pretense allows him a leeway in expressing opinions he would never openly express to Anya. This is the Gaev family estate; how has Ranevskaya, who married a mere lawyer, a profligate drunk, not a nobleman, managed to usurp Gaev's position of primacy? It is Ranevskaya

that Lopakhin tries to persuade. It is Ranevskaya that Gaev allows to run off with the money sent by their great aunt, the Countess; the money sent in trust for Anya who Gaev is powerless to protect. She not only steals from Gaev but she steals from her own daughter, before abandoning her.

[211] We are never told for certain whether she has requested a loan from Lopakhin to pay off the interest or whether he has refused her. There is indication in the play that he is funding Ranevskaya's day to day expenses.

[212] Aleksei Sergeevich Kiseliov on whose estate, Babkino, Chekhov rented a dacha for three summers influenced the character of Gaev, who wrote to Chekhov in 1886: "Well, Chekhonte, tell me what to do. I've thought of one thing—I've set my authoress to work writing a tearful letter to her aunt in Penza, saying, 'Save me, my husband and children.'… Perhaps she'll take pity and send not just enough to pay the 500 rubles but to buy us all some sweets. What can I tell you about myself? I'm getting fat, I eat and drink very well, sleep even better."

[213] Ironically, he proves it.

[214] During the 1880s under Tsar Alexander III, social reformers tried but were unable to effect significant changes, only minimally improving living conditions among the peasants. "Intellectually it was largely a cowed and demoralized generation, so that for Gaev to suggest that he has suffered for his convictions as a 'man of the eighties' must strike a Russian audience as ludicrous." Richard Peace p. 130

"For although Gaev really is, in one way, the 'superfluous man of the eighties' so solemnly imputed to Chekhov as his characteristic 'type', the fact that he himself perceives his relation to that type liberates him, comically, from it." Hahn p.14

[215] We have no evidence in the play itself that Gaev has any interest in the peasant; all we have are his empty words.

[216] A less formal rendering of Andreyevich
[217] "Stanislavsky uses the story's imagery to build up a final impression of the South as the curtain falls. His instructions were, 'The shepherd plays, you can hear horses snorting, cows mooing, sheep bleating and flocks of geese screeching. Birds are twittering. The sun rises and blinds the spectators.' Rayfield P. 63
[218] John Tulloch [*Chekhov: A Structuralist Study,* Barnes & Noble Imports, January 1981]: "(The Shepherd's reed pipe) …the mournful sound responds to the nursery's proper tone… It is a sound which evokes the enclosed nostalgia of the nursery, embalms the dialogue of fragile innocence and fatalistic experience, and speaks of man's inability to comprehend the world beyond the nursery walls"

"In effect, just before the onset of one of the most momentous social transitions in modern history, Chekhov renovated stylized elements of an old pastoral mode for his own distinctly modern purposes: to define the yearning for lost innocence that is so central to Lyubov's individual psychology, and to indicate by ironic disjunctions from the pastoral ideal the state of a culture in which innocence and energy have long since been lost." Hahn p. 21. "… (for Chekhov) poetics, innocence, childhood, simplicity, idealized landscape, and the golden age were routinely associated with the pastoral. That Chekhov intentionally introduces some pastoral allusions to his play is obvious from his references to shepherds. The fact that shepherds are not actually depicted in *The Cherry Orchard*, but merely alluded to, that is, remain in the background, indicates that Chekhov wanted to depict pastoral life as one that inevitably recedes into the past." Svetlana Evdokimova. "Assuming that Andrew Durkin is correct in distinguishing three primary modes of pastoral perception within the Russian nineteenth century tradition -spatial pastoral, social or political pastoral, and psychological pastoral, one could say that *The Cherry Orchard* launches a powerful attack on all aspects of the Russian pastoral: the pastoral view of nature, the pastoral idealization of the peasants and of the country estates, and the pastoral of childhood. The harmony of pastoral-- of nature, of the gentry estates, and of childhood is threatened by continuous intrusions from the outside world, be they the mysterious sounds of a breaking string, a row of telegraph poles and a faint outline of a large city against the idyllic landscape, the reality of debts, or death. The image of the nursery, or literally 'children's room' (detskaia), I suggest, is an ultimate symbol of childhood as pastoral. It is this symbol that Chekhov uses in this play to present childishness as a malaise of contemporary Russian society." Svetlana Evdokimova. Detskaia, Детская

[219] Poidiom [Поидиом] "Off we go" or "Let's go".

[220] This seems to come out of nowhere and is not continued elsewhere in the play. "So, at the end of Act One, when Trofimov, alone, says tenderly, 'My sunshine. My springtime,' isn't he referring to the eleven-year-old Anya, to this nursery, to the lost child, and to his own lost youth? Instead of the beginnings of a love affair that never evolves in the play, perhaps these last two words are the cri de coeur of a man wracked with a guilt evoked by all the associations he has with this room." Richard Pevear. I find this analysis convincing.

[221] "Stanislavskii and Nemirovich-Danchenko forced Chekhov to rewrite Act II in order to show boredom and dissatisfaction with life. Stanislavskii and Nemirovich-Danchenko omitted the opening scene in Act II, between Ania and Trofimov. Adding Charlotta, the governess, on the same bench with Iasha and Duniasha (with Epikhodov standing nearby) ruined the love triangle pantomime. According to the new stage directions, all four characters are very pensive. The mood has changed from comical to absurd, even depressing." Anna Linden. I think

Linden is wrong and although Stanislavskii and Nemirovich-Danchenko were wrong about many things in their interpretation of *The Cherry Orchard* I believe that in making these changes to Act Two, including the deletion of the poisonous scene between Fiers and Charlotta, they were absolutely right, magically right. Almost as right as Ezra Pound was in editing Eliot's *Waste Land*. Chekhov's original is so off-key in Act Two that without these changes it would not be regarded today as the consummate masterpiece, which it is. The fact that both the Marx (early June, 1904) and Gorki (May 25, 1904) versions published, contained the changes made by the Moscow Art Theater indicates that Chekhov accepted these changes. Although Gorki may have had ulterior motives to incorporate these changes, Marx had no reason to violate Chekhov's wishes. Marx, who bought the rights to and republished almost the entire Chekhov canon, was not in the habit of tampering with Chekhov's work. If we are to believe Stanislavsky, which in this case I do, Chekhov was persuaded to make the changes: " … when we dared to suggest to Anton Pavlovich that a whole scene be shortened, the whole end of the Second Act of *The Cherry Orchard*, he became very sad and so pale that we were ourselves frightened at the pain we had caused. But after thinking for several minutes, he managed to control himself and said: 'All right, shorten it.'" This revised copy was submitted to the censor; the same one published by Marx and Gorky which has remained the standard text for virtually all productions and for virtually all translations over more than a century.

[222] Little chapel or "chasovenka" [Часовенка] (the root of the word is "chas" for "hour"): a small wooden building adorned with icons where pilgrims could pray, read psalms or verses and observe the canonical hours (sluzhit' chasy). But it is abandoned, forgotten, the "hours" unobserved.

[223] Perhaps Chekhov had in mind to remind us of Victor Vasnetsov's painting, *The Knight at the Crossroads*, 1878, depicting Ilya Murometz, a folk hero of Kievan Rus, a bogatyr. (akin to a knight-errant) Chekhov's estate at Yalta had five paintings by his friend Isaak Levitan.

[224] Stanislavski wanted to stage the second act in a graveyard. Chekhov objected: "There is no cemetery; there was one a very long time ago. Two or three headstones lying in disorder—that is all that remains." Chekhov was very precise about stage décor. "What Chekhov wished to evoke was probably the awesome inhuman loneliness evoked by the prehistoric tumuli of his stories, and this would explain his insistence here on the precision of the décor." W. Gareth Jones, *Chekhov's Undercurrent of Time,* The Modern Language Review, Vol. 64, No. 1 (Jan., 1969), pp. 111-121 Modern Humanities Research Association. But it should be remembered that Chekhov: "was drawn to cemeteries and liked to visit them on his own. That way he could wander about undisturbed, trying to read the inscriptions on tottering headstones and then imagining the fates of those lying underneath. The fruit of cherry trees spattering the slabs with red spots made him think of drops of blood." Philip Callow, *Chekhov: The Hidden Ground,* Ivan R. Dee.

[225] It is important to be reminded that this is the Gaev family estate. Ranevskaya married a mere lawyer, a drunk, who helped dissipate the Gaev wealth. The question: why is Ranevskaya the master of the estate rather than Gaev? And there is no doubt than Gaev is subordinate to his sister. The fact that he calls his sister a slut, that her every move exudes it may be suggestive of deeper resentments.

[226] "By removing the characters in *The Cherry Orchard* from the memory laden atmosphere of the nursery (where children should feel at home), Chekhov strips them of their habitual defenses. In

Act Two, the characters meet on a road, one of those indeterminate locations halfway between the railway station and the house, but, symbolically, halfway between past and future, birth and death, being and nothingness. Something here impels them to deliver their innermost thoughts in monologues: Charlotta complains of her lack of identity, Yepikhodov declares his suicidal urges, Ranevskaya describes her 'sinful' past, Gaev addresses the sunset, Trofimov speechifies on what's wrong with society, and Lopakhin paints his hopes for Russia. As if hypnotized by the sound of their voices reverberating in the wilderness, they deliver quintessences of themselves." Senelick, Preface to *The Cherry Orchard*, A Norton Critical Edition, *Anton Chekhov's Selected Plays*, Laurence Senelick, W. W. Norton & Company, New York, London p.319 TJ underlining. Many critics seems to feel this scene takes place outside the bounds of the estate; although it is outside the orchard Chekhov gives us no indication that it is not on the estate grounds. It is in light of this that the passerby becomes all the more ominous; he trespasses with impunity as if the Gaevs had surrendered their absolute ownership and opened their estate to anybody who wished to cross it. The ever-present night watchman, so ubiquitous in Chekhov other plays and stories, seems to be nonexistent. Even the old peasants have been subletting the premises setting up a kind of vagrant hostel: "In the old servants' hall as you know, where only the old servants live, Yefimusha, Polya, Evstigney, and Karp, too. They started letting some crooks and beggars in for the night there—and I didn't say anything about it." In Chekhov's notes for Act Four, which were never implemented in the play, Lopakhin seems to attempt to reestablish a claim to ownership that the Gaevs had, in fact, abandoned. He posts signs: "unauthorized entry forbidden," "do not trample on the flowers."

[227] Ephikodov's revolver, as well as Charlotta's rifle (or shotgun), satirizes nineteenth-century theater tradition's reliance on "the gun"; Chekhov himself boldly warned that if you introduce a gun in a play it better go-off by the final act. What he presumably meant is that there must be no irrelevant details introduced. These fire arms may not go-off but they aren't irrelevant. We might ask ourselves, what character needs shooting and who would the shooter be, in this play without heroes or villains. As Maurice Valency observes: "…it is quite unnecessary to shoot Gaev. He is ineffectual, but no longer dangerous. He has retired gracefully from the fray, and taken refuge in a dream."
Chekhov no doubt came to believe that this early dictum was obsolete and even juvenile; especially in his final play he introduces numerous "guns" that lie all over the place but that don't go-off; he introduces "teasers" and dangles intriguing loose threads that he never completely ties or rather that he leads us to believe that it may be possible for us to tie them for ourselves. Chekhov's seemingly inconsequential dialogues, non sequiturs, and the inconsequentialities of everyday life are the crux of his seemingly undramatic "drama". "… everyday life is not the background, the backdrop to the scene; it lies at the very heart of the plot, is interwoven with it." Alexander Chudakov, *Dr Chekhov: a biographical essay (29 January 1860-15 July 1904)* in Allain, Paul and Gottlieb, Vera editors of *The Cambridge Companion to Chekhov*, Cambridge University Press, 2000 P. 8. "After all, in real life, people don't spend every moment in shooting one another, hanging themselves, or making declarations of love. They do not spend all their time saying clever things. They are more occupied with eating, drinking, flirting, and saying stupidities. These are the things which ought to be shown on the stage. A play should be written in which people arrive, depart, have dinner, talk about the weather, and

play cards. Life must be exactly as it is and people as they are. . . . Let everything on the stage be just as complicated, and at the same time just as simple, as in life. People eat their dinner, just eat their dinner, and all the time their happiness is taking form, or their lives are being destroyed." Anton Chekhov. Also quoted by Ronald Hingley, *Chekhov: A Biographical and Critical Study*, New York: Barnes & Noble, 1966, P. 233. But Chekhov does not give us a facsimile, rather he creates an intensely focused, distilled illusion of everyday life, a relentless dream of life, otherwise he would bore us to death and there would be no "theater". "Chekhov does not depict ordinary everyday life… <u>He seizes on high points, festive occasions, often moments that are almost tempestuous. His everyday life is concentrated; his everyday situations are seen in their oddity, their singularity, and their uniqueness.</u>" Otomar Krejca, *Chekhov's Plays*. TJ underlining. The view that Chekhov reproduced "life as it is" is simple nonsense. Chekhov was a consummate artist; he creates only the illusion of everyday life. "That the theatre should attempt to present a picture of the world as it really is never occurred to the theoreticians or practitioners of pre-modern drama. The theatre was an art — and art was artifice." Martin Esslin 'Chekhov and the Modern Drama' in Clyman, T. W., ed., *A Chekhov Companion,* Greenwood Press, Westport, 1985, p. 136. The preceding words could have been written by Chekhov himself. "… writers whom we call eternal, or simply good and who intoxicate us have one very important characteristic in common: they move in a certain direction … <u>they have a goal … because every line is permeated, as with sap, by the consciousness of a purpose, you are aware not only of life as it is, but of life as it ought to be.</u>" Anton Chekhov, Letter to Suvorin, November 25, 1892, in Yarmolinsky, P. 226.

Philip Hensher, speaking of Chekhov: "Only an artificer of the highest skill could have produced so seamless an illusion of reality." The Atlantic January, 2002

J. L. Styan: "… every detail fits, not just by a progressive illumination of a character's roots or the ramifications of a social situation, as in any good naturalistic play, but by its contribution to an embracing structure of comi-tragic ambiguity." But they fit as if into a puzzle in which the author has purposely denied us some of the essential pieces.

James Agate [September 1877 – 6 June 1947 English diarist and an influential theater critic. The Manchester Guardian (1907–14) and a drama critic for The Saturday Review (1921–23), and The Sunday Times (1923–47)] while declaring *The Cherry Orchard* "one of the great plays of the world" specified that it was "a comedy of guesswork"; presumably meaning that the audience needed to do the guessing.

These seemingly irrelevancies have puzzled critics. Schmidt sees evidence of the Symbolist Technique, particularly Maeterlinck: "…his [Chekhov's]dialogue is often like Maeterlinck's, [Maurice Polydore Marie Bernard Maeterlinck (called Comte Maeterlinck), August 29, 1862 – May 2, 1949) a Belgian playwright, poet, and essayist, Flemish but wrote in French; awarded the Nobel Prize in Literature in 1911 "in appreciation of his many-sided literary activities, and especially of his dramatic works, which are distinguished by a wealth of imagination and by a poetic fancy, which reveals, sometimes in the guise of a fairy tale, a deep inspiration, while in a mysterious way they appeal to the readers' own feelings and stimulate their imaginations"] consisting of mutually incomprehensible pieces of dialogue, phrases repeated and repeated until they become mere sound effect, lacking sense." Quoted by Paul Schmidt, Introduction in *The Plays of Anton Chekhov, A New Translation,* Harper Collins Publishers,

1997. But Chekhov's repetitions aren't mere side effects, nor are they incomprehensible; rather they are pregnant with hidden meaning. I think Rayfield misunderstands Chekhov's essentially poetic repetition when he says: "Chekhov's full-length plays, whether subtitled "comedy" or "drama," deal with human beings doomed to repeat themselves because they are unable to grapple verbally with their predicament." Rayfield P. 106. In real life we all repeat ourselves using the same words and locutions over and over and over; it is in writing that we are supposed to avoid repetition and use synonyms with the same meaning in an artificial attempt at variety and originality; it is the multiplicity of translations of the exact same repeated word that ruins Chekhov in the rash attempt to be more wide-ranging.

"Repeated phrasings and bouncing echoes are the secret handshake, the musical through-line and rhythm within the plays, making the characters part of one another's world, inextricably linked in ways unbeknownst to themselves." Tobias Wolf
Nothing is irrelevant or unnecessary in Chekhov whether a phrase or detail. Chekhov's contemporary N. K. Mikhailovsky [November 27, 1842- February 10, 1904, a Russian literary critic, sociologist, writer on public affairs, and one of the theoreticians of the Narodniki movement], took note of these strange, incidental details that only <u>seem</u> to clog up the text. N. K. Mikhailovsky, *'Literature and Life', Russkoe bogatstvo 6,* 1897 and *Literaturno-kriticheskie stat'i,* Moscow,1957

Over a hundred years later, A. P. Chudakov pronounced these incidentals as key features of Chekhov's style, stating that Chekhov inserted details functionally irrelevant in the narrative but: "…pointing to the broad open context of the surrounding world; in order to <u>reject the positivist</u> view of the world as rationally and neatly organized system." A. P. Chudakov,

Chekhov's Poetics, transl. by E. J. Cruise and D. Dragt, Ann Arbor, Mich., 1983.

However, Savely Senderovich thought that Chudakov's was one of the "crudest misconceptions". According to Senderovich: "[these seemingly irrelevant details] point beyond the immediate context of his narrative or drama, however, not to the open surrounding world but, on the contrary, to the depth of his own world, toward a second context masterfully constructed beyond the one which takes place in the foreground. What looks incidental in Chekhov is incidental only on the surface but actually is an invitation to step into the region of deeper meaning. Seemingly incidental details are super determined in regard to the motives of the surface events. Chekhov's incidental is the most non-incidental that can be in a work of literary art." I don't think these two views (Senderovich vs. Chudakov) are necessarily mutually exclusive. These numerous details not only reflect an inner life that we must intuit but also a much larger world which necessarily impinges upon the world of the orchard in ways that are only hinted at and must also be intuited by the audience.

But Stanislavsky totally misunderstood the primary importance of Chekhov's only seemingly "irrelevant" details. And so, he mimicked Chekhov as a dumb beast does who impersonates human speech he does not understand and in the process produces disrupting gibberish. Stanislavski never outgrew his habit of entombing the fundamental vision of Chekhov's plays in 'a heap of useless details'. It was Meyerhold who pinpointed the vulnerability of Chekhov's plays to be exploited in this mindless fashion. As S. Balukhaty observed:

> "In Meyerhold's opinion the use of images which are impressionistically scattered onto a canvas makes up the basic characteristic of Chekhov's dramatic style; it

provides the director with material suitable for filling out the characters into bright, defined figures (types). Hence, the characteristic enthusiasm of directors <u>for details which distract from the picture as a whole.</u>"

"At bottom, this quotidian incoherence, both concrete and funny as well, constitutes the true frontlines of human combat, to wit, the combat for control of everyday life, and not control of great crisis situations. These great catastrophes occur only occasionally. They too can lead to death, but to tell the truth, daily life gets us there much more inevitably". Peter Stein, *My Chekhov,* from A Norton Critical Edition, *Anton Chekhov's Selected Plays*, W. W. Norton & Company New York, London, p. 639

"In Chekhov the terrible thing is that the quotidian surface of life is itself a kind of tragedy." Eric Bentley P. 231.

In the Symbolist journal *Balances* in 1904, Andrey Bely said: "They walk, drink, talk rubbish, while we behold the spiritual poverty transpicuous within them. <u>They talk like men confined in prison, but we have learnt something about them that they themselves have not noticed in themselves.</u> <u>In the minutiae by which they live, a certain secret cipher is revealed to us—and the minutiae cease to be minutiae.</u> The banality of their life is in some way neutralized. <u>Something grandiose is revealed throughout in its minutiae.</u> Isn't this called seeing through banality?... The minutiae of life will appear ever more clearly to be the guides to Eternity... [Chekhov] draws back the folds of life, and what at a distance appeared to be shadowy folds turns out to be an <u>aperture into Eternity</u>." Andrey Bely (Boris Nikolaevich Bugaev), *The Cherry Orchard,* Vsevolod Meyerhold, Perepiska (Moscow: Iskusstvo, 1976), 45, and "Teatr (k istorii tekhnike)," in Teatr: kniga o novom teatre St. Petersburg: Shipovnik, 1908. TJ underlining.

"The structure of each play is tight. Lines that appear tangential, even incongruous, are in fact inward-referring and congruent." Richard Peace p.156

Richard Gilman: "The artificiality of conventional dramaturgical design, whose effect is to seal off stage-life as hermetic, in a mode of the exemplary or inimitable, has been replaced by an openwork structure which resists climax, definition, or resolution, rejecting the dragooned shapeliness of a narrative frame for the display of heightened emotions, important truths. The truth distilled in these plays, modest, lowly, oblique is rooted in the recognizable rhythms of our lives, with nothing set off by obvious 'construction,' nothing inflated beyond its familiar size, yet with everything transfigured by an imagination whose chief instrumentality is its penetration into the strangeness of the familiar." Gilman, Richard, *Chekhov's Plays: An Opening into Eternity,* Yale University Press; February 1, 1996

"Those critics who complain of stasis, that nothing happens aren't paying attention. There is a rich world outside which impinges upon the only seemingly isolated world of the cherry orchard. The auction itself, the outside force of the bank, evidences this. There is no doubt this world is dense, alive, active, 'teeming' which intrudes upon and even to some extent inhabits the world of the orchard (some like unwanted presences, like the ghosts of the past which also haunt it)." Jean-Louis Barrault, *Why the Cherry Orchard?* in A Norton Critical Edition, *Anton Chekhov's Selected Plays*, edited by Laurence Senelick. Senelick: "… 'the action' of the play is measured by the outside pressures on the estate…If there is a norm here, it exists offstage, in town, at the bank, in the restaurant; in Mentone and Paris, where Ranevskaya's lover entreats her return; or in Yaroslavl, where Great Aunt frowns on the family's conduct. Chekhov peoples this unseen world with what Vladimir Nabokov might call 'homunculi.' Besides the lover and Auntie, there are Ranevskaya's alcoholic husband and drowned son; Pishchik's daughter and the Englishmen who find clay on his land; rich Deriganov, who might buy the estate; the Ragulins, who hire Varya; the famous Jewish orchestra; Gaev's deceased parents and servants; the staff eating beans in the kitchen; and a host of others—indicating that the cherry orchard is a desert island in a teeming sea of life… In *The Cherry Orchard*, the <u>plethora of invisible beings fortifies the sense of the estate's vulnerability, transience, and isolation.</u>" Laurence Senelick, (TJ underlining) Or perhaps the impossibility of isolation or the isolation of enchantment.

"What Chekhov accomplished, in a kind of miraculous progression through those four last plays, was gradually to cut away the melodramatic moments of the 'plot,' or shift them offstage, leaving finally only his characters' helpless, unheeding responses to those moments." Paul Schmidt, *The Plays of Anton Chekhov, A New Translation,* Harper Collins Publishers, 1997

"…The Cherry Orchard depends upon a theme external to the play which is developed entirely through exposition and allusion…Since the author puts on the stage only the consequences of the primary action, the play makes the effect of a chess game played by invisible hands, and the characters seem to move without any will of their own, like characters in a dream." Maurice Valency, *The Breaking String* p.268

"In the course of the play there are passing references to well over thirty characters who never appear on-stage, including Lopakhin's brutal peasant father, Anya's aristocratic great-aunt in Yaroslavl, the rich merchant Deriganov, Charlotte's fairground artiste parents, Ranevskaya's late lawyer husband, Trofimov's chemist father, and many others." Petrov, 50 i 500 vserossiiskoe teatralnoe obschchestvo, pp. 415-24.

[228] (To Olga Knipper September 25, 1903). "I can't help thinking that there's something new in my play however boring it may be. There is not a single shot in the whole of the play, incidentally." "In The Cherry Orchard, Chekhov struck his final blow at nineteenth-century theatrics. There is no shot fired, either on or off the stage. In Act II, Charlotta has a rifle and Epihodov a pistol, but these weapons are now handled by comedians purely for the joke. Even the amorous pairing of characters common to the earlier plays has been turned entirely into comedy: the 'love scenes' between Varya and Lopahin are illuminatingly stillborn; between Anya and Trofimov they remain pathetically ludicrous; and between Yasha and Dunyasha they border on farce." J. L. Styan

[229] "Papers", the "internal passport," or identity documents carried when traveling through the Russian empire.

[230] Knipper was 35 and Muratova 29 in 1904 suggesting that Chekhov intended a young woman to play Charlotta; and a very attractive woman.

[231] Russian annual fairs featured circus acts, dancing bears, trained horses, magicians, puppet shows and dramatic presentations.

[232] A double summersault sometimes on a high wire called the leap of death. In the original, Italian, salto mortale (jump of death, a full somersault, a dangerous or critical undertaking.)

[233] Charlotta is a skewed simulacrum of Varya who was also taken in by a kind lady. But Varya has no tricks nor any magic, nor was she taught German, nor did Ranevskaya have her educated in any serious way, nor does she show any evidence of an education; and it is finally Charlotta, who has no shyness about seeking a position, who comes under the care of the new master of the cherry orchard, Lopakhin. In one early letter to Knipper in

October of 1903 Chekhov wrote: "Varya is rather crude and rather stupid, but very good-natured."
Chekhov originally wanted his wife to play Charlotta. In his correspondence to Knipper he affectionately calls his wife a German, dear German lady and little German

[235] "Man is compelled to play a role in life that is not his own and that he therefore cannot understand- right up to the characters in *The Cherry Orchard* remarking 'who I am, what I'm for no one knows', this type of nonunderstanding of life will be one of Chekhov's most constant situations." Vladimir Kataev.

[236] "It is part of the comic convention that the sorrows of which Charlotta speaks are itemized rather than felt, partly balanced by, and partly deflected into, her cucumber-eating. The expressions of melancholy are stylized. But the fact that feelings are formalized in this arrangement does nothing to discount the fact that they are there." Hahn p. 27
Cucumbers (ogurets) were often eaten in this manner much as we would eat an apple; there is nothing particularly comic about it.

[237] Although there is a great deal of hugging and gushing and empty talk about family, none of the characters really hear each other. Only Charlotta has the sense to realize that she has no one to talk to. The same can be said of all the characters. But it is especially true of Chekhov himself.
In 1926 Mirsky said: "No writer excels [as Chekhov does] in conveying the mutual unsurpassable isolation of human beings and the impossibility of understanding each other."

[238] "As the context shows us, the 'someone' she is longing to talk to at this moment is Yepikhodov. The clerk, however, fails to register Charlotte's subtextual appeal because he is longing to talk to Dunyasha." Borny P. 251. This is absolute total nonsense. "Women must be crazy for you. Brrr!" expressed by Charlotta

with withering irony after Epikhodov exposes himself, or rather his gun; and has nothing to do with any perceived rejection.

[239] A popular soulful Russian ballad.

[240] "Chekhov specified only the opening lines of Epikhodov's song 'What should I care for life's clamor, / What for my friend or my foe, / Had I a passion requited, /Warming my heart with its glow'—but they are the beginning of a 'cruel romance' well known in the 1900s, and the audience, like Duniasha and the other listeners onstage, would suppose it to be the confession of a man convicted for the murder of the woman he loved. It contributes to the caricature of Epikhodov as a would-be murderous psychopath." Rayfield P. 66

[241] Charlotta's "Uzhasno poyut éti lyudi" [Ужасно поют Éти люди] as "How awful these people sing" misses her idiosyncratic syntax which might be translated: "It's awful the way these people break into song without the least encouragement."

[242] He shows his weapon but doesn't shoot it; exhibiting but impotent. It is notable that nobody shoots anything in this play. What is Charlotta's rifle for? Hunting? What does she shoot, if anything? Her weapon is bigger than Epikhodov's.

[243] I think she's right; he is intelligent as so many ridiculous intellectuals (or "clever" people) are. Magarshack is wrong when he describes him as, "a conceited half-wit who imagines himself a highly educated person because he possesses the bovine patience to wade through 'learned' books he has not the brain to understand". This is a caricature unworthy of Chekhov. Lopakhin, an astute businessman, would not hire a half-wit. It is Borny who has some insight into this complex character: "Yepikhodov, with his pretensions to learning and his absurd manner of speaking, is not simply the one-dimensional character who appears in the text. That is merely his objective manifestation; how he appears to others. His subjective inner life

is far from farcical. He is, in fact, so unhappy with himself and his maladroitness that he seriously contemplates committing suicide, and it is for this reason that he carries a gun." Borny P.235.

This is an intelligent man who is so socially clumsy and inept that he cannot even win the affections of a stupid chambermaid, Dunyasha, who prefers a shallow, ignorant valet.

Borny: "Yepikhodov's pain is hidden from other characters partly because he tries to hide it … Yepikhodov, apart from allowing himself a sigh that wells up from the subtext of his inner life, covers his own anguish by discussing trivialities." Borny P. 235.
After Chekhov's death Ivan Moskvin, who Chekhov had approved of for the part of Epikhodov, larded on even more excessive and tasteless stage "business"; and yet through this Hugh Walpole managed to perceive the spirit confined within this buffoonish shell. Concerning Moskin's Epikhodov, connecting it with Knipper and Stanislavsky in Act Three of *The Three Sisters*, which puts the audience "in the presence of an art that is so supreme, so apart from the art of any other country or any other period, that you have no other terms of comparison with which to estimate it."

[244] English historian Henry Thomas Buckle (1821–62) gives prominence to the ordinary man in his depiction of events. Maybe that's why Epikhodov quotes him, suggesting that there is more to Epikhodov that his withering self-mockery would lead us to expect. Deep down there is a cockroach in every glass; we're just too busy to notice. Buckle proposed that skepticism was the servant of progress and that religion retards the advance of civilization. His materialist approach was admired by progressive Russians in the 1870s and Chekhov had read him as a student. By the end of the century Buckle's ideas were old-fashioned already,

suggesting that Epikhodov's efforts at self-education are anachronistic and irrelevant, the pitfall of the autodidact.

[245] "She doesn't respond, and so he continues his would-be courtship of the girl with what must be one of the most inappropriate and, consequently, pathetically funny small-talk lines that one could make to someone as feather-brained as Dunyasha." Borny P. 252.

[246] Literally, talmochka [талмочка], or little talma, or shawl, a smaller version of the garment Nina wears in the last act of The Seagull. "… Nina's mysterious enveloping 'talma' in The Seagull has dwindled into Dunyasha's talmochka, a fancy term for a shawl." Senelick, A Norton Critical Edition, *Anton Chekhov's Selected Plays,* edited by Laurence Senelick, p. 317

[247] Fully four characters have been adopted out of their humble or peasant roots. Varya and Charlotta, both adopted by kind Ladies, one educated, one seemingly not; only Charlotta, slender, tightly corseted in her white dress, lorgnette, (an upper class affectation usually used as adornment or jewelry rather than to enhance the vision) and pet dog on a leash, assumes the privileges of her adopted position; sitting at table with Ranevskaia, refusing to do tricks on command. Yasha and Dunyasha both have roots in the neighboring peasant village. It is only Varya who assumes none of the trappings and pretentions of acquired class.

[248] This echoes Lopakhin's warning in Act One to Dunyasha that she doesn't know her place, doesn't act appropriately.

[249] There was a railway boom in Russia in the 1890s which gave new potential value to the lands along its routes.

[250] The train which could be their salvation, giving value to their land for dachas, instead becomes a means of indulging their vulgar extravagance; restaurants with tablecloths that stink of soap.

[251] According to Stanislavsky: "Epikhodov has trodden on whatever Ranevskaia has lost"

[252] The practice of Yasha picking up the coins and putting them in his own pocket started with the original Moscow Art Theater's staging. Again, Stanislavsky pounding home the point with his own big clumsy hammer.

[253] Before the reign of Tsar Alexander III, during the 1870s, a period when the intelligentsia formed the Narodniki [Народники], or Populists, who preached a socialist doctrine which tried to educate the peasants. They were severely repressed in 1877–1878. "Decadents" was a derogatory term for certain so-called Symbolist writers.

[254] Obviously Yasha has a special dispensation, no doubt connected to the services he performs.

[255] "common, vulgar, banal" (poshlost Пошлость); to translate this as "sordid" misses the power of the word. Vladimir Nabokov proposed rendering the Russian word пошлость as it is, transliterated but untranslated: "… poshlost is not only the obviously trashy but also the falsely important, the falsely beautiful, the falsely clever, the falsely attractive. By describing something as 'poshlost', we pass not only an aesthetic but also a moral judgment. Everything that is true, honest, beautiful cannot be described as poshlost." Poshlost has to do with triviality, vulgarity, a lack of spirituality, and sexual wantoness. Poshlost is a pretense to having an elevated taste when it is entirely lacking; the snobbery of the tasteless, the corrupt. The word perfectly describes Ranevskaya herself. Chekhov treats her gently, but more than anything she is vulgar; she exudes it; it drips from every fiber of her being. I think Valency misses the profound irony of the most vulgar of characters disdaining dachas as too vulgar to even consider. "But by character and background she is precluded from acting like a merchant in this crisis. The psychic

impotence and the economic bankruptcy of her class at this period of history are aspects of the same illness.... With regard to her estate, she has a deep sense of noblesse oblige, and prefers to lose it honorably rather than to degrade it as she herself has been degraded." Valency *The Breaking String* p. 270

[256] "Is she trying to make light of her genuine need for him as the only practical man of business in her sphere? Is she exploiting, consciously or unconsciously, his more- than-flesh-and-blood devotion to her? How deeply is she frightened, and of what?" Loehlin p.21 Or perhaps she shows how shallow she is, unable to exist without company, perhaps too frightened to be alone with her own thoughts, her haunting memories. Chekhov described an early conception of Ranevskaia as an old woman dressing like a girl and craving "company".

[257] It is as if Lopakhin is blind to Ranevskaya's "sins", as if he's under some kind of a spell.

[258] Like the child he is, he eats out his substance in sugar candy and his time in frivolous games.

[260] Or: Does it still exist? A very good question. We never do see it, that is the audience doesn't.

[261] Chekhov uses the word vecherok [Вечерок], a comical diminutive of vecher, literally "an evening", but here meaning an evening's entertainment, "a party".

[262] The question is, why doesn't he hear the music, the orchestra? Are they imagining its music? Chekhov gives no direction that it should be heard by the audience and in Stanislavski's first production the audience couldn't hear the music either. There is an ominous quality to the forever unseen Jewish orchestra. There are so many ghosts haunting this play. Lopakhin finally takes command of it in the Third Act when we can be somewhat more certain that it does exist. He tries to take command of it only after

he buys the Orchard, as if they are connected, as if possession gives him the right to its music. What right has he to take over the party; he didn't organize it; it's not his party; though Ranevskaia cannot pay for it; pathetic though it is; although not half so pathetic and grotesque as Stanislavsky made it out to be.
[263] One critic finds evidence that the play that Lopakhin has seen is *Hamlet*, which would explain a lot. Funny? Well, certainly it has the aura of the absurd. The "hero" brings down death and destruction on everything he touches; destroys his patrimony, has his boyhood friends murdered, destroys the woman he loves and through his incompetence ushers to power the son of his father's enemy. Another thing that Chekhov shares with Shakespeare is an almost universal misinterpretation by his admirers; they are both turned into melodrama. Both authors stand back, refuse to preach, refuse to overtly reveal their moral judgments and strike a godlike balance subjecting their creations to a withering irony. Lopakhin's skewed quotes of *Hamlet* are quite literate.
[264] Ranevskaya in this moment of clarity does not exempt herself, as one critic proposed, putting words in her mouth: "I haven't led a drab life!" It makes sense only if she includes everyone, the audience also. "When Lyubov tells Lopakhin that rather than going to plays, people should look at their own lives to 'see how drab [dull] they are,' it feels like a taunt aimed at the audience. A mean one." Soloski, [Review of Lev Dodin's Maly Drama Theater production at the BAM in *The New York Times* Feb 18, 2016 *'The Cherry Orchard,' the Myopia of an Aristocratic Family*] It is definitely a taunt. Chekhov's anger, if we can use so strong a word, extends to his own audience, an audience which often had no idea what he was getting at. In many ways he despised this audience which misunderstood him, admiring him for the wrong reasons. And there is no doubt of his growing fame: "From 1899 onwards, articles and reviews of his works

appeared in the Russian press almost every day (up to 300 articles a year)." Chudakov p. 12. "If we look at readers' and critics' responses to Chekhov's writings, we come to the conclusion that he is the most misunderstood writer in Russian literature - misunderstood and at the same time highly successful, broadly popular… Chekhov was a good judge of his audience and took pleasure in playing a sadistic? - joke on his audience which remained unaware of his joking on his own account… He was profoundly unhappy with being famous without being understood." Senderevich P. 24. "No contemporary playwright has been more widely misinterpreted; none has been more often wrongly directed and performed." Gillman, Chekhov, Anton. Plays: "Ivanov", "The Seagull", "Uncle Vanya", "Three Sisters" Translated with Notes by PETER CARSON, With an Introduction by RICHARD GILMAN (Penguin Classics). Penguin Books Ltd., 2002. When Charlotta says she has no one to talk to it is Chekhov speaking of himself. "I don't think that an artist should bother about his audience. His best audience is the person he sees in his shaving mirror every morning. I think that the audience and artist imagines, when he imagines that kind of thing, is a room filled with people wearing his own mask" Vladimir Nabokov, *Strong Opinions*, New York, Vantage International, 1973, p. 18. "In front of that dreary, gray crowd of helpless people there passed a great, wise, and observant man; he looked at all these dreary inhabitants of his country, and, with a sad smile, with a tone of gentle but deep reproach, with anguish in his face and in his heart, in a beautiful and sincere voice, he said to them: 'You live badly, my friends. It is shameful to live like that.'" Maxim Gorky, *Anton Chekhov: Fragments of Recollections,* B. W. Huebsch, 1921. We have to be very careful not to take what Gorky, a shameless flatterer, said, at face value. But I think the "rather than going to plays" was also Chekhov talking to himself, about the futility, not only of watching plays but of writing them as well; that he doubted the efficacy of literature itself, especially his own, which he fully realized were misunderstood.

[265] Even Ranevskaya has moments of lucidity and self-knowledge; and this is the ultimate irony: that the most feckless and inept of the characters should get to the core of the play. Chekhov writes to his friend Serebrov: "You say you wept watching my plays . . . You are not alone. However, I wrote them not to this end. It was [Stanislavsky] who made them tearful. I wanted something different . . . I wanted only to say to people: <u>look at yourself, look how poor and dull is your way of life</u>!" Chekhov wrote in his notebook: "Man will become better when we have shown him to himself as he is".

[266] Chekhov like so many great writers had questionable handwriting but joked "the main thing in life is good handwriting." Rayfield, Donald, *Anton Chekhov: A Life*, Faber & Faber.

[267] (ona u menya iz prostykh [Она у меня из простых]) This is all we are ever told about Varya's origins; Ranevskaya condescendingly believes that two former peasants would make a fine match. They talk repeatedly about marrying Anya off to a rich man (no doubt an old rich man would be just dandy) but never once consider Lopakhin. It is as if Anya is out of bounds for him; they never once interact (except when she offers him her hand almost rudely in the opening act; rudely when one considers all the hugging and Russian cheek kissing; (Lopakhin does moo at the two "sisters" but this seems mostly aimed at Varya) and at the end when Anya requests that he delay chopping down the cherry trees until after they, the former masters, have left.)

[268] Does she have any idea how condescending this sounds? Marry Varya, she's a peasant just like you and works just like you.

[269] Also translated "They were making plans to marry me off long before your daddy even saw the light." I don't know. Does colloquial American really fit?

[270] In 1861 Alexander II signed the emancipation act abolishing the landlord's right to own serfs or "souls" as they were called.

[271] "In the great Volga famine of 1890-92, with the peasantry abandoned to the clutches of debt and tax collectors, epidemic disease and crime led many thinkers—liberal or socialist—to agree with Firs that the emancipation had worsened, not improved, the peasantry's condition." Rayfield p. 70. It should be noted that it would take an army of serfs to harvest and process 2500 acres of cherries. So instead of marshaling hired labor the Gaevs, unable to adapt, have simply abandoned the orchard, perhaps.

[272] Stanislavsky turned this scene into gross low comedy; since he misunderstood Chekhov's innate existential humor, he substituted his own crass slapstick: "A kissing scene. They do not smack but slobber. They moo, wheeze, catch their breath and laugh… It ends of course with tickling and fighting… Ranevskaia begins to defend herself with hay and towards the end slings it at them. They almost overdo it." Almost, you say. The megalomaniacal Stanislavsky marred the masterpiece of a giant whose height he could not hope to glimpse. His fondness was for excremental excess, attempting to give "corroborative detail" and to impart verisimilitude. "… by this time, he regarded himself not as the playwright's interpreter but as a collaborator, filling in the unspoken with subtext…" Senelick, Laurence, *The Chekhov Theatre: A Century of the Plays in Performance*, Cambridge University Press, 1997, p. 74

[273] When he gets angry with Lopakhin, Trofimov switches to the informal "you" when addressing him, in this way regarding him as no more than a peasant or servant. However, Harvey Pitcher believes that their use of the familiar second-person pronoun suggests an underlying affection or even friendship.

[274] A possible reference to Maxim Gorky's "Proud man" in the play *The Lower Depths* (1902). "Man is truth… He is the be-all and the end-all. Nothing exists but man, all the rest is the work of his hands and his brain…"

[275] These people do a lot of talking, even when not "on stage" and get to the bottom of nothing.

[276] vsio ravno umriosh' Всё равно Умриош ' "It makes no difference you still die" or no matter what you do, you die.

[277] Also mistranslated "free and easy with the servants" According to Stark Young: "What Chekhov really says is that they are careless about using the 'thou' with the servants."

[278] Literally, "they address the servant girl with the familiar form of 'you,'" as Lopakhin does Dunyasha. Trofimov's demands token respect for the servant class but cannot foresee doing away with it completely.

[279] Does Trofimov realize he is talking about himself?

[280] Translating this as "workers" is a mistake; that word is too charged with political meaning.

[281] The line beginning "Anyone can see" and ending "moral squalor" was deleted by Chekhov at the direction of the state censor Vasili Vereshchagin in November of 1903, and restored only in 1917. It was replaced by a line reading, "the vast majority of us, ninety-nine percent, live like savages, at the least provocation swearing and punching one another in the mouth, eating nauseating food, sleeping in mud and foul air." Not exactly the original Chekhov.

[282] Public day care centers.

[283] Sometimes translated as Asiatic barbarism, Aziatchina, a pre-Revolutionary term of abuse, a slur referring to negative qualities in the Russian character such as laziness and inefficiency identifying Russians with the vast Asiatic hordes and the large Asiatic land mass which makes up so much of Russia. Early in World War I a Professor Munsterberg declared with obvious intent to damn that "culturally Russia is Asia." Such anti-Slav critics have found all Russian art, all the Russian writers, tainted with this Orientalism. However, it would be wiser for the Russians to turn the tables and take it as a compliment.

[284] Chekhov had used this term similarly in *The Bride* by Sasha, a Trofimov like character: "…our self-love and conceit are European, but our development and actions are Asiatic"

[285] Letter of Chekhov to I. I. Orlov: "I have no faith in our intelligentsia, hypocritical, false, hysterical, ill-bred, lazy;
I have no faith in them even when they suffer and complain, for their oppressors come from the same womb as they … whatever comes to pass, science keeps advancing, social-consciousness increases … And all this is being done … despite the intelligentsia en masse."

Yet another perfect and necessary change from Chekhov's original manuscript:

> After Anya (Dreamily.) There goes Epikhodov ...
> Varya: How come he's still living with us? He only eats and drinks tea all day long ...
> Lopakhin: And makes plans to shoot himself.
> Lyubov Andreevna: But I love Epikhodov. When he talks about his misfortunes, it's so funny. Don't fire him, Varya.
> Varya: There's no other way, Mamma dear. We have to fire him, the good-for-nothing.

[287] "The scene is now set for one of the most extraordinary moments in all of Chekhov's drama. Yepikhodov strolls along the back of the stage playing his guitar, and the meditative tone is set by one of Chekhov's quasi-musical repetitions: 'RANEVSKAYA. (Pensively.) There goes Yepikhodov ... ANYA: (likewise) There goes Yepikhodov ...'" LOEHLIN, JAMES N. CHEKHOV, *The Cherry Orchard,* University of Texas at Austin

[288] These lines were added during rehearsal, either by Chekhov or at least with his approval.

[289] It certainly has; for him and all that he represents. "With the setting sun, in deliberate contrast to the sunrise of Act I, Chekhov prepares imaginatively for the demise of the landed class in this play and for the loss of everything which that class has contributed, positively, to the culture." Hahn p. 27

[290] "This scene marks the very zenith of Chekhov's art. Gaev has been presented as an old windbag, a foolish man given to inappropriate oratory, an aging dandy who has taken refuge from life in an imaginary game of billiards. But the moment is magical, and quite unexpectedly this empty vessel is inspired. In his apostrophe to nature is said all that can be said of the mystery of life, and in this moment Gaev gives voice to what all those present must feel in their hearts. It is the essential theme of the play. But the young people find his words unbearable, and they force him to be silent. It is at this point that we hear the sound of the breaking string in the sky... And so, even though at this moment Gaev speaks with the tongues of men and of angels, though the whole of the heavenly choir is ranged behind him, and all the universe crowds forward to listen, these people who are nearest to him will not listen, cannot listen. To them he seems an utter fool, the relic of a bygone age. His frustration brings about a moment of inexpressible sadness. A string breaks in the sky."

Maurice Valency, *The Breaking String: The Plays of Anton Chekhov,* New York, Oxford University Press. But Valency is not alone in granting Gaev some level of dignity. The Chekhov Art Theatre introduced a production by Estonian Adolph Shapiro in 2004 to commemorate the 100th anniversary of the play's premiere. In it Gayev was played by Sergei Dreiden "as a relatively serious man: a cranky philosopher like Astrov rather than an overgrown child or snobbish aristocrat.... he mostly came across as a thoughtful if rather quirky observer, not unlike Chekhov himself. When his nieces hushed him at the end of the play, preventing him from making a farewell speech to the house, the scene conveyed their shallowness rather than his volubility; he seemed to have earned the right to speak." Loehlin p. 212
There is profound irony in the fact that Ranevskaya, Gaev, Lopakhin and Trofimov, in spite of their shortcomings or because of them, have their fleeting moments of insight, profundity and even self-knowledge. Dopey Varya seems to be immune to any insight at all. Anya only manages to parrot Trofimov.
Most critics, unlike Valency, however, are entirely unmoved by Gaev's speech: "…he falsifies this perception with his embarrassing apostrophe to Nature." Barricelli p. 107. Actually, it's not a bad little speech, poignant, not embarrassing. But the most poignant part is that they tell him to be quiet and won't listen, just as Fiers is told to be quiet when he talks about the old days when they sold cherries by the wagonload; selling cherries, dried, juice or preserves would have solved all their problems.

[292] Rayfield calls this: "a pastiche of Turgenev at his most saccharine."

[293] According to Batyushkov, Chekhov thought this sound was critical; that Stanislavsky, not yet having read the play, asked him about its sound effects. "In one of the acts I have an offstage

sound, a complicated kind of sound which cannot be described in a few words, but it is very important that this sound be exactly the way I want it...." Is the sound really that important? Stanislavsky asked. Chekhov looked at him sternly and said, 'It is.' Eventually in production "Stanislavsky used three piano strings of different weights, strung from the flies behind the scenes, with a rumble of thunder on a drum to set the sound in relief." Loehlin p. 24.

For Maurice Valency the breaking string is the symbol of Chekhov's theater, expressing both its ideology and mood; reflecting the historical moment when there snapped "the golden string that connected man with his father on earth and his father in heaven, the age-old bond that tied the present to the past.... The symbol is broad; it would be folly to try to assign it a more precise meaning than the author chose to give it... [But] its quality is not equivocal. Whatever sadness remains unexpressed in *The Cherry Orchard*, this sound expresses."

Magarshack: "The dying, melancholy sound of a broken string of a musical instrument... is all Chekhov needed to convey his own attitude to the 'dreary' lives of his characters... With the years this sound acquired a nostalgic ring, and it is this sad, nostalgic feeling Chekhov wanted to convey by it. It is a sort of requiem for the 'unhappy and disjointed' lives of his characters." Magarshack emphasized how the force of this moment depends on Chekhov's stilling his characters into a state of 'suspended animation': " a trance-like frame of mind which is somehow induced by the spectacle of Epihodov silhouetted against the setting sun and signaled first by Lyubov's and Anya's dreamily repeating 'There goes Epihodov'..." Hahn p. 28

"It is the sound of social transition, of the passing away of a particular class, as the wheels of a society begin to turn. As the string snaps in the sky over characters momentarily silent and

stilled, the historical process that will absorb them is almost palpable. There is a strong premonition of the defeat of the play's major characters - of all, that is, except Lopahin" Hahn p. 17
"The sound of the snapping string feels like the triumph of some impersonal process over these characters' lives. It is like a forewarning of the judgment of history on their lifelessness and decadence. And as soon as that sound is heard in the play, a whole series of changes occurs. A wayfarer enters, begging and then ridiculing Varya's money; Lopahin taunts her openly about the general presumption that they will marry, which he has never quite done before; and Trofimov decisively wins Anya's loyalty." Hahn p. 29
"The noise of the breaking string is associated in Chekhov's work with the death of nature, industrialization, the crippling of human beings; this threat from an underground world to the frivolous gentry on the surface conveys some of the numinous horror of the Morlochs in H. G. Wells's *The Time Machine*." Rayfield p. 74.
James N. Loehlin, [*Chekhov: The Cherry Orchard (Plays in Production)* Cambridge University Press; (October 2, 2006)]: "The eerie sound effect of a breaking string that concludes the play represents not only a social and political rupture, but an aesthetic one" that the naturalism of the nineteenth century was being supplanted by the theatrical experimentation of the early twentieth century.
This so-called "naturalism" aspired without succeeding to a comprehensive recreation of life on the stage in all its social intricacy and material solidity. The myriad sound effects introduced by Stanislavsky and the obtrusive scenery were just as hokey as the melodrama it pledged to replace. For all of Stanislavski's empty talk about naturalism there was a flamboyance and excessive theatricality in the old sense that infected the Moscow Art Theater productions; it wallowed in a

particular melodrama all its own. And yet the one sound that Chekhov insisted upon they couldn't seem to get right.

In a letter to his wife Olga Knipper, Chekhov wrote: "Tell Nemirovich that the sound in the second and fourth acts of *The Cherry Orchard* must be shorter and must be felt as coming from afar. How petty it all is. They cannot cope with a trifle, a sound, although it is described so clearly in the play."

"To our way of thinking, the two counterpoising soundings, symmetrically placed, are central to the play: to its structure and symbolism and therefore to its innermost meaning. More than a psychological device for the audience, the double sounding is a substantive and structural device embedded deep in its heart..." Jean-Pierre Barricelli, *Counterpoint of The Snapping String: Chekhov's The Cherry Orchard,* New York University Press, 1981

J. L. Styan: "To interpret that sound is to interpret the play... The string suggests time in its most inscrutable mood; it is the passing of one order of life, with what seems like irreparable loss; but it is also the mark of change, ushering in the new order, both hopeful and frightening, because it is unimaginable."

F. Fergusson refers to it as a "sharp, almost warning signal," Aleksandr Revyakin suggests that it has "an especially large, realistico-symbolic meaning" and "announces a coming catastrophe."

In Eastern Slavic folklore, a player may leave his instrument behind as a "life token," an extension of himself, and if during his absence a string breaks, this is considered an evil portent. The chord that snaps involves the idea of a separable soul. One may come upon several such examples of a breaking string: "If a string of an instrument breaks for no special reason, then there will soon be a wedding, or, according to a more widespread superstition, one must expect a death."

In 1882 Turgenev published *The Nymphs*, based on a legend told by Plutarch at the beginning of Christian hegemony. The poet enraptured by the beauty of nature, decides to shout out, not 'Great Pan is dead', but instead 'Great Pan is risen' and is rewarded by cries of joy and laughter and into the clearing rushes Diana, the goddess, with her nymphs and dryads but their elation quickly turns to horror for: 'on the horizon, of the fields there burned like a fiery ball the belfry of a Christian church'. Then the uneven, long sigh, <u>like the vibrating of a breaking string</u>". The nymphs have disappeared and the poet is left disserted and utterly downcast. In this poem the sound represents the severing and destruction of the natural, joyful, fertile pagan by the sterile, guilt ridden, suffering obsessed Christian, the old order by the new; (as if the cord which tied us to the real heaven, snapped, leaving us deserted, to kneel before a dead tortured mortal man.) Swinburne captured the essence of this feeling in *Hymn to Proserpine*, 1866: "Thou hast conquered, O pale Galilean *(apocryphal dying words of the Roman Emperor Julian);* the world has grown grey from thy breath; we have drunken of things Lethean, and fed on the fullness of death." I am only suggesting that Chekhov is equating the destruction of the rich, fertile, potent, joyful paganism with the sterile, suffering obsessed, blood-soaked Christianity with a similar destruction of the edenesque, pastoral, joyful, old order in Russia.

Many critics sees a similarity with the sound evoked in Chekhov's short story *Happiness* (Schast'ye) "mysteriously happening between the narrator's evocation of the images of the barrows and the Milky Way." W. Gareth Jones
"The moment [of the breaking string] is framed by those pauses that evoke the gaps in existence that Bely claimed were horrifying, and that Beckett was to characterize as the transitional zone in which being made itself heard." Laurence Senelick, A

Norton Critical Edition, *Anton Chekhov's Selected Plays*, W. W. Norton & Company, New York, London   p. 320

In Mamet's interpretation the sound disappears, at least for the audience. Perhaps at the suggestion of Giorgio Strehler [*Notes on the Cherry Orchard,* from A Norton Critical Edition, *Anton Chekhov's Selected Plays*, Laurence Senelick, editor, W. W. Norton & Company New York]: "The characters react to a sound they hear or perhaps imagine. Better nothing, courageously. And why not? Why couldn't this sonic symbol be something the characters hear in the twilight—'they' hear it, and we, the audience looking on, do not? ..."

[294] But on the practical level Lopakhin might be right, that it is a breaking mine bucket cable, making it no less pregnant with meaning; the orchard is set, presumably, in the southern Ukraine which is undermined with catacombs of abandoned coal shafts of the Don Basin.

David Magarshack reports that Chekhov had heard the sound as a child, in a little hamlet in the Donets Basin, where he used to spend the summer: "It was there that he first heard the mysterious sound, which seemed to be coming from the sky, but which was caused by the fall of a bucket in some distant coal mine" *Chekhov the Dramatist* p.286).

"But in addition to this real-life antecedent there was also a literary one: the sound that the boys hear in Turgenev's story 'Bezhin Meadow.' 'Everything went silent. Suddenly, far away, a sound was heard, drawn-out, ringing, and almost like a moan, one of those unintelligible nocturnal sounds that sometimes emerge in the midst of deep silence, increase in volume, hang in the air, and in the end float slowly off, as if dying away.' The parallel is reinforced by the similar situation in which the unintelligible sound is heard, and by the moods it evokes among the characters in both story and play: one shivers and is scared, another becomes reflective, a third reacts calmly and rationally." Kataev P. 287. But I think Philip Hensher is more on target: "Plenty of productions have tried to turn that into a symbol, but it is rather more than that: it is a convulsive acknowledgment that there are things in the world, and in these lives, that neither the artist nor the audience can understand."

[295] In folk tales the screeching of an owl was a bad omen; for the ancient Egyptian it signified death, night and cold.

[296] Under the terms of the Emancipation Act field peasants were allotted land but had to pay back the government in annual installments, in order to indemnify the former landowners. House serfs, on the other hand, were allotted no land. Both these stipulations caused hardship and resulting turmoil among the newly "freed".

[297] ".... a tramp enters and creates a welcome diversion by his begging." Or so says Andrey Bely p. 580. The mysterious sound does in fact introduce him and he may be connected with it in some way, but the passerby is not a welcomed diversion. "The Vagrant is also in his way the 'sound of a breaking string.'" Anatoly Efros p. 649. Peace calls the passerby a "portent of dispossession". Perhaps this is what lies in the future for Gaev and only Varya recognizes it. "The shabby stranger can be seen as a premonition of the possible future awaiting Gaev himself." Peace p. 145. The passerby is educated and guilty of the same over-blown rhetoric as Gaev. "The straight forward and properly dialogic input of the Passerby is his reciting lines of the populist poet Nekrasov and the decadent poet Nadson in such a way as to reveal their manner of expression: their high-blown rhetoric something which Chekhov couldn't hear without a smile." Savely Senderovich. "... the original verses by Nadson and Nekrasov from which [the passerby] quotes half-remembered snatches have a rebellious ring to them that echo Trofimov's radical

sentiments..." Edward Braun. "In performance, this character can range from a comic stage drunk to a spectral herald of doom." Loehlin, James, p. 25 According to Rayfield the passerby suggests "the newly insolent and insubordinate lower classes." For a change Stanislavsky gets it right: "Let the audience suspect something ominous in this figure or let them understand that it is unpleasant to meet such a gentleman at night in the woods."

[298] Gaev is unaccountably courteous to this shabby gentleman.

[299] As Michael Frayn points out: at the turn of the century in Russia the word for passerby "prokhozhy [Прохожий]", a Siberian usage that Chekhov might have picked up on his trip to Sakhalin, implied someone tramping the countryside to escape from prison or exile in Siberia; but whether Chekhov intended this particular sense is questionable. In a short time, most of these characters will be displaced, in exile. Trofimov will be double exiled; exiled even from his exile as a student.

[300] These lines are from Populist poems written in the 1870s. The passerby quotes from a popular poem of 1881 by Semyon Yakovlevich Nadson (1862– 1887) and from Nekrasov's "Reflections at the Main Gate" (1858). The laments are supposed to come from barge haulers along the Volga.

[301] In Russian, Lopakhin's remark is awkwardly phrased perhaps purposely. In any event he is reprimanding the "passerby" harshly, taking charge of a perhaps dangerous situation. But this can be seen as the old aristocrat being patient and kind while the former peasant is abrupt and rude.

[302] In the original MAT production Lopakhin physically pushes the Passerby back and Fiers threatens him with his stick. A contemporary critic, Yuly Aikhenvald, applauded the "chance nameless passerby with a tree-limb in his hand; he appears to the spectators for only a moment with unsure steps, with verses of

Nadson and Nekrasov on his drunken lips, - but his face flashed before us a complete drama, a whole life, wasted, bitter, pitiful."

[303] There is no real generosity in Ranevskaya's extravagant liberality; like giving ruble tips to the waiters and allowing herself to be fleeced by the lover who jilts her. She gives no money to Varya; the servants eat peas porridge and she "steals" the money the great aunt has sent "in trust" for the sake of Anya.

[304] Prosvatali [Просватали]: to make or arrange a match, like a matchmaker.

[305] Given the circumstances this seems flippantly cruel. One might ask: does Ranevskaya really want this union to occur?

[306] "Later, after giving money to the vagrant, Lyubov Andreyevna asks Lopakhin for a further loan. Then, virtually in the next breath, she tells Varya that she has arranged her marriage, and congratulates her. Varya is in tears at her lack of tact; it is as though she is being given away for money." Richard Peace p. 150

[307] "Varya, who is often likened to a nun, is placed in an extremely awkward position by her mother's remark. She sees her mother 'sponge' yet more money from Lopakhin. For her to happily go along with Liuba's announcement could only make it appear that she is also after Lopakhin's money." Borny P. 241.

[308] Okhmeliya, from okhmelyat, to get drunk, instead of Ophelia. (perhaps) One translator tries to capture what he perceives as vulgarity in a coarse play on Ophelia, "I'll feel ya, get thee to a nunnery" I think this unnecessarily demeans Lopakhin.

[309] "Lopakhin, who had shown his anger at the Passer-By for frightening Varya, is clearly out of his depth in the face of Varya's distress at her mother's tactless announcement about their marriage. <u>In his embarrassment,</u> he could hardly have chosen a less felicitous quotation than the garbled line from

Hamlet about a 'nunnery'." I see more offence than embarrassment, at Ranevskaya's unbelievably crude remark.

[310] Slight but purposeful misquotation from Hamlet Act III Scene I when Hamlet scolds and thus spurns Ophelia. Lopakhin knows exactly what he's quoting and knows Shakespeare's play. Does Lopakhin feel let down by Varya? She never once speaks up for his dacha proposal. But then does she have any real sway with Ranevskaya?

[311] In Tom Stoppard's rendition it becomes: "Get thee to a scullery" and "In thy orisons be all your sinks remembered." I think this brings home too ponderously what is only suggested, that Varya is no more than a lowly "housekeeper", an exploited servant.

[312] As if billiards was his "fix".

[313] Curt Columbus [*Chekhov: The Four Major Plays: Seagull, Uncle Vanya, Three Sisters, Cherry Orchard* (October 7, 2004) Ivan R. Dee] and Van Itallie change orisons to horizons to indicate the playful misquoting.

[314] Lopakhin is playfully misquoting Hamlet, "Nymph, in thy orisons, be all my sins remember'd" (Act III, scene 1).

[315] It is significant that August 22nd is the only numerical date mentioned, as opposed to references to the church calendar and natural seasons, during *The Cherry Orchard*; it is a play in which this sense of time is so pervasive that, in Styan's words, it "compels the audience to watch the clock and the calendar." "Time as place, place as time, Proustian, Einsteinian, a pact among the tenses, the scene of an appointment for which we're always too early or too late." Gillman, *Chekhov, Anton. Plays: "Ivanov", "The Seagull", "Uncle Vanya", "Three Sisters"* (Penguin Classics), Penguin Books Ltd.

It is extremely important to preserve Epihodov's nickname in translation associated with the number 22, to preserve this sense of associative absurdity.

[316] "Passerby" sounds clumsy but "bum", "hobo", "vagrant", "homeless person" or "vagabond" doesn't do it.

[317] This almost exactly echoes a revolutionary ode by Pleshcheyev, the writer friend of Chekhov: "On, on, with neither fear nor doubting/To great and valorous feats, my friends . . ./And like a guiding star on high/Let blaze for us the sacred truth …"
"This was the sort of rhetoric which made Chekhov smile. There can be no question that in inflating Trofimov to this point, he meant to make him out an ass, though likeable…" Valency, *The Breaking String* p. 274

[318] "How beautifully you talk" not how beautiful your ideas are. Without Anya knowing it her words reveal the irony: just talk, beautiful words nothing more.

[319] In the context of this speech: "'All Russia is our garden', with a wooded setting, a romantic moon rising, a balmy evening, a convenient bench and a young man and woman, the audience expects a love scene in the old tradition and Trofimov himself talks of love. But Chekhov has his anti-romantic surprises in store. The young couple may embody hope for the future, but this is not the pair upon whom to place much trust, either to rebuild upon the ruins of the orchard or to make love." J. L. Styan

[320] "The verb, which Trofimov uses to indicate 'degeneration' — pererodit' is based on the root rod (the concept celebrated by Gaev in his speech to the bookcase). The first meaning of rod is 'birth', 'breed' but it also means 'kith' as well as 'kind'. The adjective derived from it: rodnoy, denotes close blood relationship; so that Gaev is the 'blood brother', rodnoy brat, of Lyubov Andreyevna. More loosely, however, the adjective can

be used as a term of endearment indicating that someone is regarded as 'close', or 'dear'. By using the verb pererodit' Trofimov is asserting that a complete change of 'kind' has come about in the nation as a whole, through the owning of 'living souls'. 'Soul' is the legal term for a serf. It is a term which contains a great irony, in as much as serfdom treated living human souls as though they were inanimate objects — mere chattels." Richard Peace p. 138

[321] So, there are two debts to settle with both in their own way settled at the auction.

[322] The line beginning "They owned living souls" and ending "darken your doorway" was deleted by Chekhov to accommodate the censor and restored only in 1917. It was replaced with this line: "Oh, it's dreadful, your orchard is terrifying. At evening or at night when you walk through the orchard, the old bark on the trees begins to glow and it seems as if the cherry trees are dreaming of what went on one or two hundred years ago, and painful nightmares make them droop. Why talk about it?"

[323] Trofimov talks about work without working, much; Lopakhin works.

[324] According to Richard Peace: "This is undoubtedly the most important speech in the play." p. 137 "By the end of Trofimov's sermons we should have remembered how in Chekhov the future *as a subject* is always ghostly, bodiless, and most often compensatory for a present felt to be oppressive, and <u>that work is never a solution.</u> The future as liberation, work as atonement: these are in no sense themes of *The Cherry Orchard* but notions expressed *within the play,* chiefly by Trofimov, <u>who no more speaks for Chekhov than did Tuzenbach or Vershinin</u> in their play." Gillman p. 227 TJ underlining.

[325] Trofimov is more of a despoiler of the cherry orchard than Lopakhin; he woos the landowner herself (Anya) from any

allegiance to the orchard or its value, her birthright, which he turns into a sterile burden of guilt, [the new order, the Christian hegemony]. (It is, perhaps, Lopakhin the grower of beautiful poppies who will see the orchard's rebirth into fertile dacha plots.) Anya who looks just like her mother when her mother was young; like her mother succumbs to the blandishments of a man; she is seduced, with the added irony that her seducer is impotent, with nothing but flowery empty words. "Indeed, his portrait of the family comes largely from theory, congealed bias, for the exploitation he charges them with is a thing of the past, for which they surely have no responsibility, and his indictment totally ignores Liubov's generosity, Varya's industriousness and probity, and even Anya's innocence. And when he extols work, were entitled—and meant—to ask, 'What have *you* ever done?'"

[326] I thought Varya had the keys; it is Varya who throws the keys on the floor after she hears that Lopakhin has bought the orchard and it is Lopakhin who picks them up and jingles them like holy bells. In the end it is Lopakhin who has the real keys and locks up the place, unintentionally confining the very innocent victim that Ranevskaya, Gaev and Anya should be atoning to, the living, lingering memory of all those imprisoned souls.

[327] Without responding or commenting about what he's saying she repeats the same phrase she used before without being aware of the apparent irony. He's intoxicated by his own highfalutin words about creating a future and Anya by the mistaken romance of the words themselves disconnected from any reality.

[328] "… ironically, she emphasizes the manner and not the matter of his speech…" J. L. Styan

[329] (schast'ye [Счста'е]) happiness, fortune, luck; (neschast'ye [несчаст'е]) unhappiness, bad luck or misfortune as in twenty-two

³³⁰ Vladimir Nabokov explained Chekhov's appeal: "What really attracted the Russian reader was that in Chekhov's heroes he recognized the Russian idealist . . . a man who combined the deepest human decency of which man is capable with an almost ridiculous inability to put his ideals and principles into action; a man devoted to moral beauty, the welfare of his people, the welfare of the universe, but unable in his private life to do anything useful; frittering away his provincial existence in a haze of utopian dreams; knowing exactly what is good, what is worthwhile living for, but at the same time sinking lower and lower in the mud of a humdrum existence, unhappy in love, hopelessly inefficient in everything—a good man who cannot make good." (Nabokov, Vladimir, *Lectures on Russian Literature*, London, 1981, p. 253.). Guter Mensch aber schlechter Musikant: "a good man but poor musician."

³³¹ As if a prop for his melodramatic speechifying. Certainly, Chekhov meant a stageprop moon rising to get a gentle laugh.

³³² Yes, the footsteps of Varya. If this line doesn't get a laugh the production is all wrong.

³³³ Yes, the river, the bringer of death. She's hoping for love or at least romance while Trofimov has in mind more impotent speeches.

³³⁴ "Anya's mother had left the estate, in order never to see again the river where her little son had drowned. Anya ends Act II with a gesture of defiance, not only escaping from Varya, but more importantly exorcising spectres of the past: 'Let us go to the river. It's nice [i.e. 'good'*] there.'" Peace p. 144

³³⁵ Varya is calling out the answer to Trofimov without realizing it "Anya" and which he is too blind and self-intoxicated to see.

³³⁶ It is truly a miracle that the play survived Stanislavsky's obtuseness; this description from his prompt book:

"A complete failure of a ball. Not many people. Despite all efforts, they couldn't find more people. It was all they could do to get the station master and post master. A soldier (the son of a civil servant) in coarse soldier's clothing (uniform), a shop assistant wearing a jacket and red tie, a young boy (son of the old woman), dancing with the tall thin priest's daughter, even Duniasha has been recruited. Half the dancers don't know the steps of the quadrille, let alone the grande ronde.... The audience looking at those dancing is even sparser. They are sitting around in the doorway, backs to the spectators. You can see the priest's wife, and old officer and his wife, an old woman in black. Iasha is leaning on the doorframe looking at the dancers. ... In the billiard room Epikhodov and the neighbour's manager, a benevolent old German with an imperial beard and a pipe, are playing a game. The noise of billiard balls goes on almost all evening. Silence reigns all evening. You'd think everyone was there for a requiem mass. When the dances stop, they all freeze on chairs along the wall. They sit and fan themselves. The moment anyone shows a sign of animation—running past or talking loudly—everyone is embarrassed, and the guilty person, ashamed of the disorder he has provoked, becomes even more embarrassed and silent. . . The food on the table is sparse.... Fresh nuts, apples, soda water. The soda water has been drunk and there are no new bottles. When the dancing is over, the Jewish musicians smoke in the hall, as do the smokers among the guests."

[337] It is essential to note that this scene takes place outside the ballroom; we are never allowed to enter; to join the party; to see the famous orchestra. "And the ballroom-where celebration

occurs, where motion is felt, where joy is ours for the taking-is just outside our reach. We remain outside looking in, without celebration, movement, or joy." Columbus, Curt, *Chekhov: The Four Major Plays: Seagull, Uncle Vanya, Three Sisters, Cherry Orchard*, Ivan R. Dee, October 7, 2004

[338] There is an ominous quality to the forever unseen orchestra. There are so many ghosts haunting this play. Lopakhin takes command of it in this Third Act when we can be somewhat more certain that it does exist. He tries to take command of it after he buys the Orchard as if that gives him the right to its music. What right has he to take over the party; he didn't organize it; it's not his party; pathetic though it is; although not half so pathetic and grotesque as Stanislavsky made it out to be.

[339] "After the outdoor setting of Act II, this indoor scene is burdened with the accessories of a past age, oppressing the non-aristocratic present with their disproportionate formality and weight. The dance, designed to promote high spirits, can only manage a forced gaiety, beneath which lie frustration and a flickering aggression." Hahn p. 30

[340] Calderon and Loehlin both quote Meyerhold who calls it a "danse macabre representative of the entire play… as in a nightmare… a tedious latter-day dance, with no life, no grace, no vigour in it, not even any desire of the flesh; and they do not realise that the very ground on which they are dancing is passing away from under their feet." Meyerhold quoted by George Calderon, *Two plays by Tchekhof : the Seagull, the Cherry Orchard*. But Meyerhold said something a little different in a letter to Chekhov: "… all of the 'dancing' people are unconcerned and do not sense the harm. The tempo of the act was too slow in the Art Theater. They wanted to convey boredom, which is a mistake. One must picture unconcern. There's a difference. Unconcern is more active. Then the tragedy of the Act

becomes more concentrated." Meyerhold to Chekhov, Translated by Nora Beeson, The Tulane Drama Review, The MIT Press, Vol. 9, No. 1 Autumn, 1964, pp. 24-25. Andrey Bely saw it as "a crystallization of Chekhov's devices: in the foreground room a domestic drama is taking place, while at the back, candle-lit, the masks of terror are dancing rapturously."

J. L. Styan likens the staging to an Elizabethan theatre, where different parts of the stage platform were used for distinct scenes within the one scene: "In the drawing-room itself we shall be loaded with the anxieties of the present, while the action in the more formal ballroom beyond represents a parody of the gay past." J. L. Styan. While Ranevskaya is agonizing over the auction outcome, upstage, "In the ballroom a figure in grey top hat and check trousers waves its arms and leaps about." "This clownish figure, the governess Charlotta, can become <u>a kind of presiding deity</u> for the act, as she performs magic tricks, ventriloquizes, and leads the atmosphere of grotesque gaiety." Loehlin P. 27. TJ underlining. "The juxtaposition of public festivity and private anguish was a staple of party scenes throughout Russian dramatic literature, as Laurence Senelick points out, citing Griboyedovs *Woe from Wit*, Pushkin's *Feast in Plaguetime*, and Lermontov's *Masquerade*." Senelick quoted by Loehlin P. 27

But, wouldn't it be far more effective and ironic and Chekhovian to stage it as if they all knew these silly dance steps perfectly and accurately mimicked the "excellencies" they have displaced and had a grand good time or at least the pathetic perfect pretense of one. This final "ball" is sad enough with its inappropriate timing, and inappropriate guests without the need to pummel us with its pathetic and supposedly macabre or grotesque aspects. The party should be portrayed as lively, not dull; hilarious not tedious; the orchestra good, not bad and Charlotta's tricks utterly convincing;

she's magic. The wonder is that Chekhov did not summon the strength to literally murder the man who ruined his play, a ruin which continues to haunt Chekhov's masterpiece more than a hundred years later. The following are Stanislavski production notes: "The ball is a complete failure. There are few people. Despite all efforts, it has not been possible to get more people to come … A soldier (the son of one of the servants) in a coarse military uniform (ordinary not ceremonial), a steward in a jacket and red tie, a young boy (the old woman's son) who is dancing with the tall thin daughter of the priests wife, and even Dunyasha – all are allowed to come to the ball. Half of the dancers don't know the figures to the quadrille, never mind the grand rond." Stanislavski's description of Charlotta's performance is too painfully grotesque to even recount: she dresses up in Gaev's clothes.

[341] "The presence of such figures is in itself significant — they represent the modern world of rapid communication: the railway (newly built) and the telegraph (Lyubov Andreyevna is constantly being summoned back by telegram to her lover in Paris). Thus, Lyubov Andreyevna's ball not only acknowledges social change, it invites the new forces which are disrupting the old way of life." Richard Peace p. 128

[342] They are dancing the quadrille and Pishchik is calling out the steps in French.

[343] A jacket that is fitted at the waist and extends to the knees sometimes called tails.

[344] "To one of his chariot steeds named Incitatus… besides a stable all-built of marble stone for him, and a manger made of ivory, over and above his caparison also and harness of purple… he allowed a house and family of servants, yea, and household stuff to furnish the same… It is reported, moreover, that he meant

to prefer him into a consulship" (Suetonius, History of Twelve Caesars, trans. Philemon Holland [1606]).

[345] Frederich Nietzsche 1844-1900 wrote *Beyond Good and Evil*, not exactly condoning counterfeiting.

[346] Nietzsche proposes a new morality for his supermen and a revolt against the conventional constraints of Western civilization in his Morgenröthe. Gedanken über die moralischen Vorurtheile (Dawns. Reflections on Moral Prejudices, 1881). Chekhov stated in a letter (February 25, 1895): "I should like to meet a philosopher like Nietzsche somewhere on a train or a steamer, and spend the whole night talking to him. I don't think his philosophy will last very long, though. It's more sensational than persuasive."

[347] Dashenka reads Nietzsche and is a constant presence in the play. The character who is never appears. In fact, her name, suspiciously, is never even mentioned by any other character. We might reasonably question whether she still exists, or ever did, except in Pishchick's mind. He says her name so often, almost as if to conjure her into existence. There is a shortage of woman at the "ball", but still no Dashenka. Of course, Stanislavsky, particularly deaf and dumb to Chekhov's magic, inexplicably introduces Dashenka, this mysterious presence, at the final ball along with a whole host of dreary guests: a soldier (the son of one of the servants) in a coarse military uniform (ordinary not ceremonial), a steward in a jacket and red tie, a young boy (the old woman's son) who is dancing with the tall thin daughter of the priests wife. There is a vaguely suggested "relationship" between Dashenka and Lopakhin and that is perhaps the reason she is never alluded to or asked after, except by her father. Perhaps, as the self-deceived Varya's "rival" her name could not even be spoken by the others as if mentioning her would summon her into actuality; and certainly, under no circumstances, could

she be invited to the final ball or if invited would refuse to come. As many critics have noted *The Cherry Orchard* is haunted by ghosts who inhabit it and impinge upon it; having any of them show up live and in person breaks the spell.

[348] A sword dance from the Caucasus popularized by Glinka and by Rubinstein in his opera *The Demon*. The Lezginka, also known as the Lezgi dance or Lezgian dance is a national dance of the Lezgins, also common among peoples in the Caucasus region. Azeris, Nogais, Chechens, Ossetians, Circassians, Karachays, Balkars, Abkhazians, Kabardins, Ingush, Ingilos, Mountain Jews, Georgians, Armenians, Kuban Cossacks, Terek Cossacks, Caucasian Avars, Dargwa, and Kumyks: all have their own version. This is one of the most lively of acrobatic dances. If they dance the Lezginka it is hardly a staid, depressing or somber ball.

[349] Understatement to the point of absurdity.

[350] Jean-Louis Barrault believes that Charlotta's card conjuring is an image of life ("And we assume the deck of cards to be life.") while W. Gareth Jones commenting on Barrault finds her shuffling of the cards and her production of chosen cards as a suggestion of life's mysterious inevitability. Laurence Senelick: "[Charlotta]… a nameless, ambiguously sexed phantasm erupting out of nowhere."

[351] German: "Mr. Pishchik, one, two, three." "The impact of this scene is increased, of course, because Charlotta's conjuror's patter, the inevitability of her 'ein, zwei, drei', reminds us of the auctioneer's patter in another place, and the 'one, two, three' which is to lead to the sale of the estate." W. Gareth Jones P.119

[352] This card "trick", as described, is utterly impossible. I've had a number of magicians review the text and they are in agreement. This isn't sleight of hand, it's real magic.

[353] "There is more pathos in the presentation of Firs and Sharlotta than there is in the portrayal of the other comic characters. In Firs

this stems from his age, but in the case of Sharlotta it is perhaps significant that she of all the characters is the nearest to the professional clown." Richard Peace p. 127

I would contend that Charlotta is the least pathetic because she knows what she is: a purposeful, self-aware clown while the others are unintentional, oblivious clowns.

[354] Trofimov's card, the queen of spades, is "the harbinger of destruction in Russian literature ever since Pushkin's story of that name." Rayfield

[355] In the Russian, Charlotta uses the masculine singular instead of the feminine plural. Chekhov does not tell us she is German; rather she is taken in by a German lady who educates her: "Charlotte speaks not broken but pure Russian; only seldom instead of a soft consonant at a word's end she pronounces a hard one and mixes up the masculine and feminine adjectives." Chekhov to Nemirovich-Danchenko

[356] Charlotta is purposefully using grammar ironically?

[357] "This propensity for aggression infects nearly all the characters, but it is most obvious in Charlotta - that curiously displaced and autonomous person, obscure as to class, mannish, and yet not without a feminine quota of loneliness. Charlotta works with artifice, she is skilled in illusion; and it is by illusion that she distracts attention from the painful fate hanging over the cherry orchard. In her check trousers and grey top hat, and springing into the air to shouts of 'Bravo!', she is an unrealistic figure, belonging, one comes to see, to the stylized tradition of mime. Yet the significance of her tricks is important and intriguing… The rapid succession of one trick after another and Charlotta's triumph in her power of command make this a tour de force of personal assertion which has also an edge of aggression about it. In the circumstances, with Lyubov helplessly awaiting news of what has happened to the estate, Charlotta's

demonstration of her power to will the world as she wants it, and her willing a kind of anarchy, feels to the audience like an act of psychic violence. The violence is cleanly achieved: it is probably not even conscious. But Chekhov makes it impossible for us not to feel that <u>Charlotta in some sense wills her employers' loss of power."</u> Hahn p. 31. TJ underling. Hahn is on to something. Remember Yasha laughing at the impending loss of the cherry orchard.

Charlotta like Trofimov is or was a tutor to these aristocrats and thus exercises a power to "teach" although Anya seems to be immune to Charlotta's magic and the education she might attempt to impart; so, at least with Anya, it is magic Charlotta who is displaced by the impotent Trofimov. It is her dead brother's tutor come back from the haunted past who instead "teaches" her and in a real sense suborns and subjugates her, ripping her from her aristocratic moorings so powerfully represented by the cherry orchard.

Charlotta, so unlike the stereotypical tutor, so unlike the nun-like Varya decked in black: *"Charlotta Ivanovna, dressed in white, very thin and tightly corsetted, with a lorgnette dangling at her waist, walks across the stage"* and with her own little dog. How much more "aristocratic" in trappings than the aristocrats she attempts to teach. She charms the men, Pichtchik especially, but Lopakhin also, who attempts to kiss her hand which she rightly if ironically interprets as an act of sexual forwardness; she understands these people better than they do. He may not be attracted to Varya, but then why would he be. Charlotta has the sultry magical quality of the femme fatale, (more than one critic has mentioned this) an archetype often portrayed as a victim caught in a situation from which she cannot escape and it is Lopakhin who winds up as her protector and perhaps liberator. And if she is impelled to the level of jester or clown, as the best teachers often are, especially those not listened to, she is a magic clown who talks to voices in the ground, who has the power to make Anya and Varya appear out of thin air and make them disappear also, as she in effect does. She is also a merchant or auctioneer selling, not the cherry orchard directly, but the magic robe which can make Anya and Varya appear or disappear. "Everyone in Chekhov resembles Charlotta Ivanovna... with her card tricks, and ventriloquism. Each in his own way attempts a kind of magic, a spiritual mumbo-jumbo, a little number designed to charm or placate or simply elegize reality - the reality of life slipping away, of the dissolving process. They are sad clowns, redeemed only by being fully felt as people, and not the comic icons they are always threatening to become - failed shamans, whose magic does not work though it has cost them everything to perform." Michael Goldman, *The Actor's Freedom: Towards a Theory of Drama*, pp 72-73.

[358] This is a question that might be asked of every character in this play. Do they really love or do they rather indulge themselves in sentimental gushing? Charlotta is a more important character than most productions recognize. She may be the character with the truest self-knowledge. She doesn't know who she is but at least she knows that she doesn't know who she is. We should always remember that Chekhov insisted that Lopakhin and Charlotte were the main characters and should be treated as such; that they be played by the two most important stars of the Moscow Art Theater, Stanislavsky and his, Chekhov's wife, Olga Knipper; who has a German name, was a ventriloquist, performed card tricks and more importantly performed the disappearing baby trick. To have these two important actors, Knipper and Stanislavsky, play Ranevskaya and Gaev warps the production from the very start.

[359] German: "a good man but poor musician." This saying may be more pregnant than it appears: a good man but poor practitioner; what good is goodness if you are ineffectual in bringing goodness about; a quintessential Russian trait, who mean the best but are often powerless or inept to bring it about.

[360] The line is a quote from *Ponce de Leon*, a play by Clemens Brentano.

[361] "With unflinching honesty, Chekhov in *The Cherry Orchard* demonstrates the fatal divergence between a person's good personal qualities and subjectively kind intentions, and the consequences of his social activities." Kataev P. 286.

[362] "…isn't this a charade presenting the magic power of transformation possessed by a dramatic actress? or, perhaps, presenting the absolute power of a playwright over his personages? a power of artistic sleight of hand?" Senderovich. Or is she a marginalized Prospero abandoned by the Gaevs (that is the family name, lest we forget) who are too inept to recognize her power, finally rescued by the man of the future, Lopakhin? In this way Chekhov rescues himself, the entertainer, the clown, the magician, the artist rescued by the astute businessman and landowner. If he had not been a businessman, the artist in Chekhov would not have survived. The same might be said of Shakespeare.

[363] But the "eternal student" should not be confused with the Western sense. According to Michael Frayne: "The Russian phrase, vyechniy studyent… is a variant of vyechniy zhid, literally 'the eternal Jew', but in English the Wandering Jew, who was condemned to wander the earth for all eternity without shelter. Chekhov makes the implication of this clear in the same letter to Knipper in which he admits to his worries about Act Two. His other anxiety, he says, is '… the somewhat unfinished state of the student, Trofimov. The point is that Trofimov is

perpetually being exiled, perpetually being thrown out of the university -and how do you show things like this?' Exiled, of course, for his political activities; and the difficulty of showing things like this being the censor..."

[364] "... Lyubov Andreyevna explains to Varya that no one is forcing her to marry Lopakhin, but the phrase she uses: 'No one's trying to force you' (nikto ne nevolit) semantically evokes the spectre of serfdom (i.e. nevolya). Here, as elsewhere, there is an 'ill-defined attitude to the past', a submerged suggestion of the old ways: the marrying of serfs according to their masters' wishes." Richard Peace p 150

[365] He's growing old but going nowhere; decaying in place, another perpetual child; in his own way as childish as Ranevskaya and Gaev; a case of arrested development, childish even in his declared love, the sexless love of a young boy or eunuch.

[366] Appalled at the social breakdown of which she herself is a prime example.

[367] An extremely evocative word that needs no translation but has been variously translated: "dovie"

[368] Perestradat

[369] It's difficult to make any sense of this. She had to leave the orchard because her son drowned and now she's telling us, "I love this house, and I can't imagine my life without the cherry orchard, and if it must be sold sell me along with it ..."; as if her son's death binds her to the orchard.

[370] This is a cliched, formulaic phrase which offends her.

[371] Trofimov, being above love, is described as a kind of eunuch, sexually immature, trapped like so many of these characters in a permanent childhood; the ineffectual man; and like the eunuch always with the ladies as Lopakhin chides him.

[372] This is one of the times that the characters are actually listening to each other and the effect is brutal with Ranevskaya lashing out with all her previously hidden viciousness.

[373] Negodiai, Негодиаи;

[374] Nichtozhestvo, ничтожество; a nothing

[375] gimnazist vtorogo klassa, гимназист второго класс

[376] Strange as it may outwardly appear Ranevskaya seems to resent that her daughter Anya is being deprived of the love of a real man and wasting her time with this stunted sexless boy.

[377] This is Fiers's untranslatable word, nedotyópa. He uses it when he criticizes Dunyasha and Yasha for their irresponsibility. Lyubov uses it here when she reprimands Trofimov for not acting like a real man; and Chekhov ends the play with Fiers cursing himself with it when he lies down perhaps to die, deserted in the locked empty manor house. The word might be Ukrainian for "incompetent" or slang that Chekhov picked up while working as a doctor in the provinces. Russian dictionaries from the 1930s cite Chekhov as its originator. Translators have interpreted it as: "you old fool," "good for nothing," "sillybilly," "addle pate," "pathetic old fool," "flibbertigibbet", "half-baked bungler" "duffer" "useless lumber" "bungle-arse", "noodle" "simpleton", "ninny" "good for nothing" "booby" "rogue," "duffer," "job-lot," "lummox," "silly young cuckoo," "silly old nothing," "numbskull," "muddler," "silly galoot," "young flibbertigibbet", "bungler" " just green behind the gills". None of these do it justice. Mental defective or moron although politically incorrect these days would be accurate. Checkhov's early conception of Varya gave her the comic? name, Varvara Nedotyopina (Varvara Left-in-the-Lurch): a variation is nedotyopa. This word could be used to describe each of the characters in the play. "Its periodic repetition suggests that Chekhov meant it to sum up all the characters." Senelick, from A Norton Critical Edition, *Anton*

Chekhov's Selected Plays, ed. by Laurence Senelick, W. W. Norton & Company New York, London p 322
"Most of Chekhov's characters expire as Firs does, still in footman's dress, locked in the ornate vacuum, 'as if I'd never lived.'" Sonia Kovitz, *A Fine Day To Hang Oneself: On Chekhov's Plays* p. 198 from Jean Pierre Barricelli, *Chekhov's great plays: a critical anthology*, New York, New York University Press, 1981. Gotham library of the New York University Press.
[378] This ridiculous line is more suitable for a female insulted by her lover.
[379] *The Wanton Woman* a poem by Aleksy Tolstoy 1817-1875, cousin to Lev, known largely for his historical verse dramas. Chekhov did not share the stationmaster's taste in poetry, regarding Aleksy Tolstoy as a mountebank (I'amyati).
The title figure in his moralistic poem is a "wanton woman", (slut) who sees the error of her ways when confronted by a Christ-like figure at a lavish orgy in Judaea. These lines shed a mordant light on the sad group gathered on this inappropriate occasion; the prudish lady-like Trofimov and the "sinner" Ranevskaya, a Seedy Christ in a worn-out uniform and a wanton woman decked out in her incongruous Parisian finery. "The opening lines [of Tolstoy's poem], describing a sumptuous banquet, cast a sardonic reflection on the frumps gathered on this dismal occasion. They also show the earlier interview between the puritanical Trofimov and the self-confessed sinner Ranevskaya to be a parodic confrontation between a Messiah in eyeglasses and a Magdalene in a Parisian ballgown."
Chekhov, Anton. The Complete Plays Laurence Senelick
[380] "She rails bitterly; she stabs seemingly to the heart; what she says is unforgivable; but Trofimov is fundamentally as good-humored as she, and he forgives her readily; he understands.

Gorky, in his autobiography, marvels at the Russian character: people who are at one another's throats one moment, sit down comfortably together to dinner the next. But whether or not this sort of volatility is a national characteristic, it is certainly universally understandable, and a scene of this sort makes an extraordinarily vivid effect. There is nothing in the least abstract about Trofimov. Unlike the characters of tragedy, it is possible for him to fall down a flight of steps, and to survive the fall, completely intact in every aspect of his personality. Indeed, it is by putting his characters through the ordeal of laughter that Chekhov proves their validity" Maurice Valency

[381] dedushka

[382] Not as ridiculous as it sounds. The traditional cure was to soak the wax in water, and then drink the water.

[383] There is the possibility that Yasha is laughing because the orchard has been sold and thus lost to his masters. Ranevskaya suspects as much, explaining her annoyance. Not only does he want to get back to Paris but also expresses a class resentment.

[384] What is implied Rayfield takes as given: "… shocking us with his tactless joy at the prospect of losing the cherry orchard…"

[385] Or "There's nobody left but me to serve the whole house." (odin na ties' dom, [Один на галстуки 'дом]) In the end he is left to serve an empty abandoned house.

[386] A popular Russian ballad of the 1870s belonging to a genre known as the "cruel romance" which incorporated elements of Gypsy music. This is not a folk song but rather a popular, trendy song.

[387] or "And will you know just how my heart beats faster?" (Poimiosh' li ty dushi moei volnenie?)— Поймёшь ' ли ты души Моеі волнение

"Chekhov assigns this song to the arrogant and heartless servant, Borkin, in the first (1887) version of Ivanov, and there, too, it signaled the singer's callousness. It was a woman's song (composed by N. S. Rzhevskaia) and one of the most popular romances in Russia in the 1880s. Literally translated, it goes, 'Will you understand my soul's emotion, the sad grief of fateful thoughts and the shy fear of involuntary doubt and what draws me into the mysterious distance? Will you understand? (four times). Will you understand whom I call for, whom I entreat to understand me fully, how I languish, how much I suffer, how ardently and passionately I love? Will you understand? (four times).' On Iasha's lips the song mocks Duniasha's infatuation and echoes Ranevskaia's passionate speech of a few minutes before: Iasha is not just parodying but parroting his mistress. The song operates here just as it did 17years before in Borkin's mouth, where it makes fun of Ivanov's deplorable search for new happiness and desertion of his loving wife. The servants' vaudeville culture deeply subverts their masters' romantic aspirations. But vaudeville culture lacks permanence: today nobody acting Iasha can rely on his audience knowing Rzhevskaia's song to make Iasha's heartlessness obvious." Rayfield P. 96

[388] "And for a climax of grotesqueness the half-crazy German governess dresses herself in a marionette costume, check trousers and tall hat, and dances a pas seul [solo dance] somewhere in the background amid the applause of the company." George Calderon, *Two plays by Tchekhof: the Seagull, the Cherry Orchard Translated with an Introduction and Notes* Grant Richards Ltd. London, 1912. I don't share Calderon's dark interpretation. This is a scene of hilarious, if absurd, empowerment over the Gaevs, contrasted with Charlotta's impending and foreshadowed abandonment by the Gaevs.

[389] Epikhodov seems to understand what Varya isn't sure of. She has no ultimate authority; she's the glorified, exploited hired help; but because of the charade they don't really have to pay her.

[390] It is important not to be "informed" by previous versions which were cut with Chekhov's approval; they were cut for a reason, a good reason.

[391] Or "superiors" (starshiye [Старшийе])

[392] The stick seems a potent indicator of servitude. Fiers walks with one, Lopakhin was beaten by his father with a stick when he was a child. Varya is working against herself, sabotaging her own chances of happiness.

[393] "In production it is quite common, and, I would argue, quite appropriate, for Lopakhin to cringe in terror when the stick bears down on him. This is, after all, the man who, though he has just bought the cherry orchard, subjectively is still a peasant who was commonly beaten by his father when he was young. It is a conditioned reflex that his behavior reverts to that of his peasant youth, origin and experience." Geoffrey Borny, *Interpreting Chekhov*, Chapter Title: *The Cherry Orchard: Complete Synthesis of Vision and Form Published*, ANU Press. (2006) p. 259. Magarshack also indicates that the blow recalls Lopakhin's childhood beatings: "the stick is the symbol of the serf in Lopakhin."

[394] As Loehlin reminds us Chekhov's stage direction doesn't say that Varya actually strikes Lopakhin. In the original manuscript Chekhov indicates that the blow lands. J. L. Styan: "by just missing him, in the same way that Vanya just misses the professor in Act III of Uncle Vanya, the incident is relieved of its more serious implications and turned into a joke." Stanislavsky's production notes indicate Varya striking him. Loehlin: "Certainly, the episode deflates Lopakhin's entrance, preventing it from being either the triumphant return of the victorious

peasant or the dreaded appearance of the usurper." TJ underlining.

³⁹⁵ Some critics feel that she is addressing Lopakhin rudely, forgetting who he is; treating him like a peasant, which doubles the irony since he is now lord of the manor.

³⁹⁶ Stanislavsky gets it right for a change: "I advise the actor [playing Lopakhin] … to forget for the time being about any joy, on the contrary to express embarrassment and awkwardness as much as possible."

³⁹⁷ Lopakhin is not very drunk and to portray him as such is a mistake. He is giddy with the excitement of owning the cherry orchard.

³⁹⁸ A seafood delicacy from the area of the Black Sea which is connected to the Sea of Azov by the Strait of Kertch. The Cherry Orchard has been lost but Gaev's inappropriately preoccupied with buying herring.

³⁹⁹ Yasha has usurped his game, even.

⁴⁰⁰ RANEVSKAYA: Prodan Vishnyovy Sad? [Продан Вишневый Сад] Was the cherry orchard sold?

    LOPAKHIN: Prodan. [Продан] Sold

    RANEVSKAYA: Kto kupil? [Кто купил] Who bought it.

    LOPAKHIN: Ya kupil. [Я купил] I bought it.

⁴⁰¹"As he picks them up, he remarks, somewhat superfluously, 'She threw away the keys to show she's not in charge here now.' But in truth it is a gesture (or rather 'Gestus') as profound in its social and economic significance as anything that Brecht himself would ever conceive." Edward Braun

⁴⁰² Once again Varya acts as her own worst enemy. Isn't she in fact divorcing herself from the possibility of a union with Lopakhin? Shouldn't his purchase be regarded as a coup; after all, if not Lopakhin then Deriganov would have gotten it. Does she in no way foresee the possibility that she might become the

lady of this house, a house in which she had been no more than a privileged servant; is her position not analogous to Lopakhin's? Does she not see that he might be the means of her own liberation? But she is too blind to see it. Certainly, Lopakhin could have been persuaded by a new bride to spare the main house while harvesting only some of the trees.

[403] In pre-revolutionary Russia, as in the United States, the debtor, that is the Gaevs, would receive any balance once the original debt was paid at auction. Therefore, they would receive the "ninety thousand over and above the debt" that Lopakhin bid. I presume Chekhov knew this; it just didn't fit into the story he wished to tell.

[404] Although Lopakhin certainly reminds us of Chekhov, there were many former peasants or the descendents of peasants who who bought the estates of the nobles in Russia. Chekhov's first editor, Nikolai Leikin, in 1885 bought an aristocrat's estate and bragged, to Chekhov, "Once noble counts owned it, and now it's me, Leikin, the oaf."

[405] I believe the original stage direction may have him tripping here which can be a perfect way of shattering the high drama while maintaining the poignancy. Raul Julia (The Serban Lincoln Center Production of 1977) pulled this off perfectly; the audience moved to tears, broken by their own laughter, which Julia stops by screaming: "Do not laugh at me" rang through the theater and the laughing stopped immediately both from the audience and the characters on the stage. Although, I grant there were "scenes of almost slapstick physicality" in the Serban production which spoiled the overall effect. Senelick also commented on the Serban production: "… understatement was less common than athleticism: Dunyasha performed a striptease and at one point tackled Yasha like a football player." Raul Julia dominated this production with his own star power, much as Stanislavsky was

perhaps intended to do. Although Chekhov gave more than lip service to a collegial approach to acting, he loathed the scene stealing stars of the old Russian Imperial theater, there is no doubt that Lopakhin and Charlotta should dominate. But: "He [Chekhov] understood that essential aspect of the theater (which only Shakespeare and a few others have also understood): that theater exists only when the necessarily personal viewpoint of the narrator is effaced by multiple viewpoints."

[406] It is Lopakhin, more emphatically than any other character, who declares his love for this garden.

[407] Or perhaps better still: "bought an estate more beautiful than anything in the world."

[408] George Calderon states that this is "a cant jocular phrase, a literary tag. Lopakhin is quoting out of some bad play, as usual when he is lively." I don't think that's the case; Chekhov also uses this phrase in his correspondence.

[409] I think he may have made a decision here: if that's the way she wants it to be "that's alright with me." She is stupidly, self-destructively, incapable of identifying with the interests, which could be her own, of the man she loves.

[410] If you are wondering why so many newer productions ruin *The Cherry Orchard* all you have to do is read Stanislavsky's notes; Brian Dennehy as Lopakhin inexplicably dances a jig which stumps us until we read that Stanislavsky has Lopakhin dance "a vulgar polka."

[411] "When Chekhov signed himself 'Landowner A. Chekhov' upon purchasing his Melikhovo estate in 1892, it was with the same mixture of jocularity and pride [as Lopakhin]." J. L. Styan

[412] The 2017 production by Mehmet Ergen using Trevor Griffiths 'new English version' (originally directed by Richard Eyre in 1977) has Lopakhin brutally order the musicians to play, a stark sign of a vindictive ascendency.

[413] This is one of the central points of the play; you can't go back again, to a past that never existed or even to redo an act that happened the morning of the same day.

[414] neskladnaia

[415] neschastlivaia

[416] His jubilation is quickly tempered by his profound and genuine sympathy as here expressed; he is ashamed of his own happiness.

[417] Chekhov's capitalists "…are sensitive, restless people who find their position inappropriate and incomprehensible, and would like but are unable to cast off the burden of their inheritance, power and wealth." Vladimir Kataev

[418] "On a personal level, Lopakhin is trying to reach out to Ranevskaya emotionally, trying very belatedly to bridge the gap between them by looking ahead to a future where this kind of situation could never arise. But the remark is also striking because it is the only occasion in *The Cherry Orchard* where, one of the characters manages very briefly to place himself outside the situation in which they all find themselves." Harvey Pitcher.

[419] "Lopakhin lives by the clock. He is the timekeeper in the play, a friendly, but indefatigable man of action, constantly on the move with his own affairs, but with a plan of salvation for the estate. It is given to him not only to buy the estate and chop down the cherry orchard, but succinctly to express the profound wrench and disjointedness of the present moment; to express in one sentence not only the dislocation, the pain, the suffering that the present represents to everybody including himself, but to define what it is that gives that experience its tragi-comic character… That which is 'neskladnyi'—awkward, without logical sequence or connection, disjointed, disconnected, inharmonious, awkward, disproportional, or irregular, can give rise to 'neschast'e'—unhappiness or misfortune; but that which is 'neskladnyi' is also

the essence of the humorous, the ridiculous, or the absurd."
Jackson p. 133

[420] Pishchik shows great subtlety and understanding here, striking the right note. He has demonstrated an admiration for Lopakhin in the past far exceeding that of the other characters.

[421] It wasn't enough that Chekhov has Lopakhin almost knock over a candlestick. "Anton Pavlovich fearing crudeness wants to tone things down, so the candelabrum almost falls down and breaks, not on stage, but back in the salon." Stanislavsky. Of course, Stanislavsky had no fear of crudeness, he positively wallowed in it.

[422] She seems to have taken speechifying lessons from Trofimov.

[423] Poidiom Поидиом. But now the roles are reversed with Anya consoling Ranevskaia

[424] In the Moscow Art Theatre's original production of *The Cherry Orchard*, according to Chekhov, Stanislavski shamelessly dragged Act Four, stretching it from the twelve minutes that Chekhov intended originally to forty minutes, in an effort, as Magarshack puts it, "to wring the last drop of pathos out of the final scene". But Loehlin thinks "Chekhov is exaggerating; the actual playing time of Act IV is just about the twenty minutes that Lopakhin specifies they have before the departure to the station. So, the act plays in real time, and the concern for catching the train places a real pressure on the scene and its few events: the packing, the farewells, the possible engagement of Varya and Lopakhin, and the final departure of the family from the house." Loehlin p. 33

[425] German and Russian medical etiquette suggests that a doctor at a colleague's deathbed, when all hope was lost, should offer champagne. Champagne was consumed by Chekhov, in a toast with his German doctor, moments before he died.

[426] A statement heavy with irony; true of all the characters.

⁴²⁷ Yasha is distorting a phrase usually applied to welcome arrivals, perhaps purposefully.

⁴²⁸ Of course not, that would be considerate.

⁴²⁹ The new man, the keeper of time and the calendar, always looking at his watch while Ranevskaya can't get one date straight. How many times did he repeat August 22nd?

⁴³⁰ We know exactly how he feels; the whole play is hanging around, doing nothing.

⁴³¹ There is an edge to this remark, as if all of these people are no more than a distraction and interruption from the real work at hand, in the real world; as if the play is an <u>unreal interlude in time and space</u>.

⁴³² Lopakhin uses the informal "you" addressing Trofimov and then Trofimov uses the same informal "you" to address Lopakhin.

⁴³³ Trofimov rather than being the hero of the play, as some like to believe, is repeatedly undercut by comic devices: after a melodramatic, ridiculous exit line, "All is over between us," he falls down the steps, and, despite his claim to be in the vanguard as the creator of a new world, is too absent-minded to find his own galoshes. ["Charlotta plays a conjuring trick with Trofimov's galoshes in the fourth act." Or so wrote Chekhov in a list of original casting notes; how fortunate that he was persuaded to drop this heavy-handed idea. Once again, it was almost as if the hand of God was guiding the editing of this play.]
However, in his private conversations Chekhov often sounded a lot like his idealistic proclaimers: "Once upon a time this place was a wilderness covered with stones and thistles… but I came and cultivated it and made it beautiful" [speaking of his Yalta property to Kuprin [Aleksandr Ivanovich Kuprin (Russian: Алекса́ндр Ива́нович Купри́н) (7 September 1870 25 August 1938 in Leningrad), a Russian writer best known for his novels,

The Duel (1905) and *The Pit*, *Moloch* (1896), *Olesya* (1898), *Junior Captain Rybnikov* (1906), *Emerald* (1907), and *The Garnet Bracelet* (1911),] "In two or three hundred years all the earth will become a garden full of flowers." How similar to the words used by Trofimov and parroted back by the guileless Anya. But Chekhov was prone to subject his own ideals to a withering barrage of self-deprecating irony. He was not taken in by his own high-sounding blather. "In drama you mustn't be afraid of farce, but philosophizing in it is disgusting. Everything goes dead." Chekhov's advice to the writer as reported by that writer, Ilya Yakovlevich Gurlyand. But Chekhov loved to philosophize in private conversation and so do his characters and so do Russians in general. As Thomas Mann put so well: "The question: 'What is to be done?' haunts Chekhov's writings at every turn in a deliberately confused way which even borders on the ludicrous because of the odd, helpless, stilted manner in which his characters indulge in fruitless speculations on the subject of this vital question. The truth about life which this author felt it his bounden duty to proclaim devalues the very ideas and opinions which he has his figures argue and fight about. That truth is by nature ironical." Thomas Mann, *The Stature of Anton Chekhov*, New Republic, May 16, 1955, TJ underlining. We must be careful not to adopt a typically "English" attitude toward these high-sounding philosophical speeches. There was a traditional English distrust of words; real men didn't philosophize; as if words were an excuse for a failure of action. There was a time when English language novels succumbed to terse, laconic, almost telegraphic conversational exchanges that bore no relation to reality, at least not in non-English, English speaking countries. People love to give speeches, to think out loud, to try ideas on for size, to hear the sound of their own voice, to explore their inner psyches or more likely hide their inner psyches in a barrage of words.

Borny seems to understand this: "However, the difference between English and Russian sensibilities creates a cultural divide that is difficult to bridge. English directors, for instance, seem to find it difficult to give due value to the positive ideas expressed by Chekhov's 'philosophers'. The difficulty stems from the fact that these characters tend to express their ideas in lengthy tirades. Such effusions are not easily accepted by English theatre practitioners and audiences brought up to value understatement or who feel that 'politics' or 'religion' are not proper subjects for polite conversation." Borny P. 263. But it is Gottlieb who understands that this is a peculiarly English phenomenon not at all shared by English speakers generally: "The question of 'positive affirmations' is, perhaps a more contentious one: there is a peculiarly English embarrassment at people or characters who 'spout' positively about life or who talk idealistically or hopefully about the future ... hence, perhaps, the difficulty English actors, directors and audiences have with characters like Vershinin or Tuzenbach or Trofimov ... Debate, which sits uneasily on the English stage, is treated as something which emanates from Chekhov's charming idiosyncratic characters, not from the whole social fabric of the plays." Trevor Griffith understood this: "There is something very contained about English, [he should have said the English in England] and when it does express deep emotion, it does so in simple rather than purple ways; in oblique and understated rather than rhetorical language." But it is essential not to try to turn Chekhov into a constricted Englishman. Mike Alfreds is right: "In performing Chekhov, it is important to try to replace our Anglo-Saxon mode of emotional expression by a more extrovert, Slavic one." But while he distrusted the mesmerizing effect of high-flown language, he loved these speeches just as Shakespeare [that most un-English of writers] loved his speeches. Shakespeare gave his best speeches to his most questionable characters, his finest poetry to Macbeth, a mass murderer, a murderer of children. "The satirist, like every other writer, goes to himself for much of his material; pen in hand he sees his own foibles with the sobriety of inspiration." Calderon "Do not believe that Tchekhof the dramatist was gulled by the enthusiasms of that Tchekhof who walked in the garden at Yalta! It is all his sad fun." Calderon

"Chekhov is frequently admired for his sane objectivity and his refusal to preach at his readers, but the serious ideas he presents in many of his short stories (such as those of Gromov in Ward No. 6, of Poleznev in *My Life*, or Ivan Ivanovich in Gooseberries) are made more objective through authorial self-distancing, using the device of humour." Richard Peace p. 122

Chekhov received a letter from a Viktor Baranovsky, a radical student: "I heard ... a call to an active, energetic life of ferment, to bold, fearless struggle—and so to the end of the play I felt intense pleasure. Lopakhin and the student are friends going arm in arm towards that bright star." But one must be especially careful not to confuse the ideas of Chekhov's characters with those of Chekhov himself. In a letter to Suvorin: "If you're served coffee then don't try looking for beer in it. If I present you with a professor's thoughts, then trust me and don't look for Chekhov's thoughts in them…. [ideas] have no value for their content. It's not a question of their content; that's changeable and it's not new. The whole point is the nature of these opinions, their dependence upon external influences and so on. They must be examined like objects, like symptoms, entirely objectively, not attempting either to agree with them or to dispute them. If I described St. Vituses' dance you wouldn't look at it from the point of view of a choreographer, would you? No? Then don't do it with opinions." The Soviet communists loved to make a hero of Trofimov, who couldn't find his galoshes; but other critics see in his character what Chekhov perhaps just hinted at: the roots of a dangerous ideologue. Trofimov is "the prototype for a Stalinist commissar, an ideological fanatic who has lost contact with reality and with all the finer human emotions." Edward Broide. Serban's Trofimov, presages the coming new world, which is hammered home by donning him in a Soviet army overcoat with red lapels. A self-proclaimed communist, Trevor Griffith's version, performed at the Nottingham Playhouse in 1977 has Trofimov proclaim: "Forward, mes amis, meine Kameraden. We're on the march towards the brightest star in all history." But Gorky, the committed communist wasn't taken in by Trofimov's supposed ardor: "The miserable student Trofimov talks prettily about the need to work and spends his time in idleness, entertaining himself with stupid ribbing of Varya, who works tirelessly for the benefit of these drones." Tyrone Guthrie's 1941 production had Trofimov scratching his ass while proclaiming the future of mankind.

There were both communists and critics of communism who found the circumstances of *The Cherry Orchard* ephemeral, irrelevant and uninteresting and the plight of the decadent, narcissistic aristocrats unworthy of consideration or even of satire; much as many modern critics find the plight of Holden Caulfield offensively irrelevant and in its own way equally decadent. While on tour in 1922, from Berlin, Stanislavsky wrote to Nemirovich-Danchenko back in Russia: "Acting the scene where Vershinin says goodbye to Masha in Three Sisters, my mind is confused. After what we have been through, it is quite impossible to be moved because an officer has to leave and his

lady has to stay behind. I am not enjoying Chekhov. On the contrary, I would prefer not to be acting in his plays."
Viacheslav Pietsukh [born November 18, 1946; one of Russia's most published contemporary authors of fiction and essays] has a character hold forth, "Ditherers, bastards, they had a bad life, did they? I'll bet they wore excellent overcoats, knocked back the Worontsoff vodka with caviar, mixed with lovely women, those reptiles philosophized from morning to night for want of anything to do and then they say they have a bad life, you see? You sons of bitches ought to be in the clutches of a planned economy, you should be brought to an Executive Committee's attention—they'd show you what a cherry orchard was!" But perhaps famine, war and pestilence or even the suffocating minutiae of everyday rote existence only distract us from the true perils of human life, which come clear only when we are relieved of these burdens.
However, I believe as Geoffrey Borny does, that "in The Cherry Orchard, it is vital that the character Trofimov should not be played as either 'the heroic visionary Bolshevik' or as 'an emotionally immature student', but as a combination of both." Borny P. 229.
Frayne also strikes this balance which is the essence of Chekhov: "Chekhov plainly takes Trofimov seriously as a man who holds sane and genuine convictions for which he is prepared to suffer. But then to go to the opposite extreme, as was done in Trevor Griffiths' adaptation of the play and to turn him into a 'positive hero' in the Socialist Realist sense, is also an absurdity" I think Raymond Williams is right on target when he says: "… the contradictory character, of the group and its feeling, has to be conveyed in the tone: a kind of nobility, and a kind of farce, have to coexist. (This is not, by the way, a cue for the usual question: are we supposed to laugh or cry at such people and such

situations? That is a servile question: we have to decide our response for ourselves. The point is, always, that the characters and situations can be seen, are written to be seen, in both ways; to decide on one part of the response or the other is to miss what is being said.)" Williams, Raymond, Chapter 7. *The Cherry Orchard: Complete Synthesis of Vision and Form*

[434] They are never going to see each other and this is the one piece of wisdom he wishes to impart, one last dig.

[435] One especially inept translator comes up with: "Don't flap your hands". As a result, Lopakhin is constantly flapping his hands throughout this particular production, flapping ridiculously to emphasize every point.

[436] Lopakhin is a man of broad, enthusiastic, manly gestures. Chekhov describes Lopakhin not uncomplementarily "walks swinging (waving: alternate translation) his arms, a broad stride, thinks while walking, walks a straight line". Trofimov wants to turn him into a prissy imitation of a jaded, constrained aristocrat with his stagnant arms close to his stiff sides.

[437] Lopakhin is a practical dreamer, a "visionary", even, willing to put down his money and his life on his dreams. This was no pipedream. Chekhov was personally aware of the success of just such ventures; Babkino, the estate where he rented a dacha from the aristocratic Kiselevs for three summers was eventually divided into just such dacha lots because of the recent construction of a railroad nearby. In fact, Lopakhin seems to have his finger on the pulse of Russia, in which a country dacha, often little farmsteads, became almost obligatory for the developing middle class.

Chekhov dreamed of being a real estate developer like his creation, Lopakhin. In an October 13, 1888 letter to his brother Alexander: "If our book trade goes well, we'd buy a farm. Save money: for 600 rubles I can buy you a piece of land in such a location that you couldn't have dreamt of. If I buy a farm, I would divide it into plots with the price of each no more than 500-600 rubles. A bearable structure, quite livable, costs also no more than 500-600 rubles depending on the number of rooms. Reckon 100 rubles per room."

In the summer of 1888 Chekhov negotiated to purchase a farm near Poltava; he wrote to his friend, Pleshcheev: "If I indeed succeed in buying, I'd build cottages on the banks of the river Khorol and lay the basis of a literary colony" (August 27, 1888). In 1888 Chekhov took a ten-day tour of the market towns of the northern Ukraine that Gogol had made famous fifty years before. "For three years Anton considered properties, but every deal fell through. The 250-mile tour left Chekhov a lover of all things Ukrainian." Rayfield, Donald. [*Anton Chekhov: A Life,* Faber & Faber.]

But in ironic juxtaposition Chekhov's other great love was planting trees: "Chekhov's other preoccupation, after buying the estate at Melikhovo in 1892, was gardening on a large scale—his journeys to France were typically to plant nurseries, not to attend writers' reunions." Donald Rayfield

"… [His] Yalta garden still survives as an exotic monument to a man whose feeling for trees equaled his feeling for theater." Donald Rayfield

[438] Chekhov had fine sensitive fingers.

[439] These lines did not exist in the first version of the play but were added by Chekhov to support his view of Lopakhin as a decent person. Too many critics emphasize these lines in finding a positive aspect to Lopakhin. Actually, I think they are unnecessary in reaching this positive judgment and a case of Chekhov succumbing to audience misinterpretation. However, there is the added irony: Can we really trust Trofimov's judgement on anything and why would Lopakhin, a man of the

world, want his approval? "And yet Trofimov's literary sensibility is justified for once when he tells Lopakhin…" about his delicate fingers. I can find no literary sensibility in Trofimov.

[440] Is it really possible that Trofimov has actually worked at something rather than just expounding the glories of work? "Here it is right in my pocket." As if he'd lost it, just like his galoshes. This sounds a bit defensive, as if Lopakhin doesn't believe him and he has to show him the money to convince him. I don't think we can in any way conclude that "he makes his living as a translator"

[441] This is the size of the cherry orchard.

[442] Perhaps as beautiful as the Cherry Orchard but productive and profitable. Profit and beauty are not mutually exclusive or so Lopakhin seems to imply.

[443] Suggesting that Lopakhin by generously offering Trofimov a loan of forty thousand rubles is "reverting to mercenary type… and that it is ill-judged, clumsy and downright offensive" as one critic suggested is nonsense.

[444] Yes, but two hundred thousand would be more tempting; he may be a beggar but he's not a piker.

[445] One critic singled out *The Cherry Orchard* central point as "debunking human pretentions to transcendent ideals" which is perhaps too harsh a judgment.

[446] But he can't find his galoshes, falls down the stairs in a silly quarrel and is a virgin. Chekov, a man of many liaisons, was no fan of chastity in men. In Soviet productions Trofimov was played as a revolutionary firebrand. What were they thinking? Lyudmila Parts [*The Chekhovian Intertext: Dialogue with a Classic*, 2nd Edition, Ohio State University Press, April 22, 2008)] demonstrates how Gorky, Lunacharsky and Stalin himself established Chekhov as an influential canonical writer of the early Soviet period. She quotes statistics suggesting that Chekhov

was almost first among writers printed in these early Soviet years and quotes an analysis in a 1926 Soviet textbook: "...a harsh verdict on aristocratic culture." (Vasily Grossman, in his novel *Life and Fate,* has a character say: "Chekhov is allowed here, [in the Soviet Union] because they don't understand him...") Or they purposely misinterpret him to suit their own ends.

Chekhov even foretold the consequences of these "radical liberals": in reproving the editors of "Russkaya Mysl," (a publication Chekhov later published in), a left-wing paper (it was only after 1905 that it became the organ of the more conservative wing of the Constitutional Democratic Party.) Chekhov made a prediction: "Just you wait . . . Under the banner of learning, art and persecuted freedom of thought Russia will one day be ruled by such toads and crocodiles as were unknown even in Spain under the Inquisition...Narrow-mindedness, enormous pretensions, excessive self-importance, a total absence of literary or social conscience: these things will do their work....[and]...will spawn an atmosphere so stifling that every healthy person will be nauseated by literature, while every charlatan and wolf in sheep's clothing will have a stage on which to parade his lies..."

[447] "golubchik" (diminutive of "golub'" or dove), often translated as "my dear," or dovie, both inadequate translations. Some critics believe that Lopakhin is using the word ironically. I used to hear the word in the New York City area all the time and it needs no translation. Mylienkaya (миленькая) and Galubchik (голубчик): dear, darling or sweetheart, or simply very good dear friend, the first is said to a woman and second to a man. I am told they are both obsolete and aren't heard in Russia today. Maybe they died there with the "revolution".

[448] Nu, proshchai, golubchik. Pora ekhat'

[449] We turn up our noses at each other, but life goes on its own way. (My drug pered drugom nos derem, a zhizn' znai sebe prokhodit).

[450] There is no certainty in Lopakhin's words alternately translated "seems to me as though" He seems to acknowledge that his work is a distraction from the fundamental problems of why we exist.

[451] A heavy-handed addition. Does this really need to be said?

[452] Significantly this is the only time Anya addresses Lopakhin directly.

[453] The cherry orchard was sold on August 22nd and it is already October; Lopakhin has waited all this time, lost valuable building and chopping time to allow them to vacate in their own good time.

[454] The title *The Cherry Orchard* was first mentioned to Masha, Chekhov's sister in 1902, shortly after the news came to Chekhov that the cherry trees that Chekhov planted at Melikhovo, his former estate, had been chopped down by Konshin, the purchaser. "This should have been no surprise since Konshin was a timber merchant who was interested only in chopping down and selling Chekhov's forest land. In each of the plays, too, trees are objects and emblems of despoliation. Astrov fights against the ongoing destruction of the local forests. Natasha announces her intention of having the beautiful firs and the maple at the house cut down. And of course, the last sound in The Cherry Orchard is of an 'axe chopping down the ... trees.'" Richard Gilman p. 199

[455] The only time Epikhodov is addressed by his proper name.

[456] Each character shifts the responsibility to someone else.

[457] This line doesn't appear in any of the printed editions; it was improvised in performance by Ivan Moskvin. It got a laugh, and he asked if he could keep it in. "Tell Moskvin he can insert the new lines, and I will put them in myself when I read the corrected

proofs. I give him the most complete carte blanche" (Chekhov to Olga Knipper, March 20, 1904). Chekhov never did insert the line in the proofs; it appears penciled in to the Moscow Art Theatre prompt script.

[458] Also translated "nursing home".

[459] Although too much is read into this failure on Yasha's part, it is instructive that the old peasant woman doesn't dare enter the house but sends word from the old peasant quarters; things haven't changed all that much.

[460] Long Live France; but said with a thick Russian accent which makes it sound absurd.

[461] It is significant that nobody will toast with Lopakhin. Yasha guzzles the same champagne he disparages, so there is not even champagne for Lopakhin to toast his proposal to Varya. A bad sign: no champagne, no proposal. To raise a glass, what a wonderful prop has been stolen, taken out from under Lopakhin. These characters are always undermining and defeating each other in ways small and great.

To have the full glasses sit there untouched as one modern production does, (Mamet) undermines Chekhov's superb subtlety.

[462] This is rather cryptic. Is he reprimanding her for having succumbed to his charms? He seems somewhat of a prude.

[463] Does he really "break her heart" as one critic suggested? She's powdering her nose while making this avowal of love, hardly a sign of deep feeling.

[464] The "hen house" or "chicken coop" or chicken or however translated is a euphemism, as is herring.

Although, perhaps he's been dipping into Gaev's Kerch herring on the sly.

[465] Staryy dedushka

[466] sokrovishche

[467] In December 1897 Maria wrote to Chekhov: "At Babkino many things are in a state of collapse from the owners to the buildings… the master himself has become an old infant." Three years later the estate was sold, its value greatly enhanced by the completion of a railway line from Moscow which made the land a desirable location for dachas for city dwellers. Alexie Kiselev became a director of a bank at the same salary as Gaev of six thousand rubles. Babkino is the estate where Chekhov spent three summers with the Kiselevs during happier times.

[468] Ranevskaya is, in effect, stealing the money which was sent in trust to buy the estate for the benefit of Anya. Importantly, Anya isn't given any money but expects to work after graduating to help support her mother. The ultimate irony is that the money to save the cherry orchard is to be used so Ranevskaya can return to her decadent lifestyle back in Paris and support the scoundrel who jilted and swindled her.

[469] "Anya will start a new future with her suitor Petya Trofimov, a revolutionary student." Where on earth does Loehlin get this idea from? We are told Anya is going to study, take her exams and help her mother, who she begs to come back. As far as Trofimov's future: "I'll see them off in town and tomorrow I'll go to Moscow."

[470] The depth of Anya's naivety is mind boggling; Ranevskaya is abandoning her to resume her dissolute life in Paris with her lover who robbed and deserted her; stealing the money sent in trust for Anya. Does Anya really believe that her mother is at all interested in reading books with her on autumn evenings?

[471] Mama, priezhai

[472] Priedu, moe zoloto

[473] "In effect, Anya's governess has just criticized the lack of maternal feeling in Lyubov by debunking her motherly reassurance." Sharon Marie Carnicke, Introduction to *Chekhov,*

Anton: The Cherry Orchard (Hackett Classics), Hackett Publishing.

Ranevskaya has abandoned and will continue to abandon, first her son, then her daughter. This throwing down the baby is really a sick bit of business highlighting Ranevskaya and Gaev's utter irresponsibility and perhaps pointing blame at their guilt for the death of Ranevskaya's son. Why does no one once mention who is to blame, and there is never any doubt, there is blame, for that drowning? "…two elements… mark out Chekhov's mature drama: inconsequential conversation acting as a counterpoint to tragic utterances, and a plot which hangs on a character who has died before the action starts and about whom we shall never be told the truth." Donald Rayfield

[474] "Charlotta … destitute and with no passport… In a moment of abrupt gestic clarity Charlotta drops her comic persona and casts her swaddled 'baby' to the floor, where it lies abandoned like herself" Frayn, p. 342. Chekhov wanted his wife Olga Knipper to play Charlotta; often calling her the German lady or the little German. (Her aunt's name was Charlotta). There is no doubt that Chekhov wrote for himself; that his plays are full of allusions that perhaps only he could decipher. "If what is going beyond the obvious shades into the private language of the author, it must be the author himself who is his own primary audience. Could it be that Chekhov did not want the audience to recognize his intimate allusions? This is quite a conundrum." Senderevich p. 23

Harvey Pitcher tells us that Knipper herself did Charlotta's baby ventriloquism trick as a party trick which might lead us to ask if she had some deep psychological reason for performing such a trick. Could this seemingly brutal disappearing baby "trick" refer to the abortion Chekhov suspected his wife of having; or was it a possible ectopic pregnancy, in which he, allegedly, was not the father, which possibly ruined her chances of having Chekhov's baby? Olga's own "miscarriage" is described in her letter to Chekhov of March 31, 1902. This controversy has arisen among scholars as to whether it was a miscarriage, an ectopic pregnancy, or an abortion; and the paternity of the child has been questioned. I reference Hugh McLean and Donald Rayfield in The Bulletin of the North American Chekhov Society XI, 1 (Summer 2003), and letters in subsequent issues. "Rayfield repeatedly insinuates that Olga Knipper was sexually involved with Vladimir Nemirovich-Danchenko, and speculates about the time, place and partner leading to Knipper's pregnancy and her miscarriage on 30 March 1902. Yet it seems more probable that the pregnancy resulted from Knipper's stay with Chekhov in Yalta on 22-28 February 1902; her bleeding began on 26 March, not in 'February'". Gordon McVay, *Anton Chekhov: The Unbelieving Believer*, The Slavonic and East European Review, Vol. 80, No. 1 (Jan., 2002), pp. 63-104

Chekhov was desperate to have a child before he died. Chekhov to Knipper August, 1902: "Don't let's separate so early before we've had a proper life, before you give birth to a boy or girl for me. And when you do, then you can act as you wish." To which Knipper eventually replied: "I shall present you with a good son for next year. You write that if we have a child I can do as I like." A. R. Kugel (pen name Homo Novus): "The most typical Chekhov work combining Chekhov's poetry and his world view is *The Cherry Orchard*. The entire play is permeated by an ironically sad smile directed at himself". A. R. Kugel, Russkie dramaturgi: Ocherki teatral 'nogo Kritika, Moscow, Mir, 1933, P. 119.

[475] She is all alone in the world without identity papers which makes her extremely vulnerable. She is abandoned by everyone … except Lopakhin… except Lopakhin. It is not for nothing that

Chekhov wanted Kniper and Stanislavsky to play these two most important characters.

[476] I wonder what he has in mind. Lopakhin doesn't make trifling statements or empty promises. He has, as far as we know directly, never made or in any way implied any promise to Varya. His marital interest in Varya may exist entirely in the minds or in the wishful thinking of the other characters. ("… but in fact, there's nothing, it's all like a dream".) (While Gaev is a man of entirely empty promises, sworn solemnly to God.) One critic is wrong when he says of Charlotta: "She has no points of contact whatsoever with the central figure of Lopakhin." In fact, she has two extremely important points of contact. And we don't know if she is German, only that she was taken in by a German lady.

[477] He has this backwards; it is he and Ranevskaya who are abandoning everyone: "brosat" (to abandon, to leave, to throw); just as Charlotta throws down the baby.

[478] "Freak of nature" is an unfair translation, aberration perhaps; certainly, there is the idea of being immune to the famous "misfortune" which seems to afflict everyone; or "The wonder of nature."

[479] It should be noted that he is a man of some honor, keeping careful account of the money he has borrowed, unlike Ranevskaya who has absolutely no concern about meeting any of her obligations.

[480] I don't think Lopakhin expected this money back, so it was more in the way of a "gift". One production has Lopakhin counting out money to an unknown party like a usurious money lender; but we have no indication that he has charged Pischik interest or even taken back a note.

[481] And yet we are told it is cold; which is it?

[482] Clay can be mined for many different manufacturing uses. White clay can be used for cosmetics and making fine porcelain china and tile. It suggests the possibility of oil.

[483] The British often appear in nineteenth-century Russian fiction as progressive and enterprising businessmen. They were often hired as estate managers, land surveyors, or experts in livestock. The uncle of the writer Nikolay Leskov was a Scotsman who managed several vast Russian estates for their aristocratic owners.

[484] Richard Peace observes that Pishchik unlike Ranevskaya is willing to come to terms and thus survive the commercial interests bearing down on his class, first by selling land so the railroad can pass through and then selling white clay to an Englishman.

[485] In Mamet's production Pishchik toasts his new wealth and then wipes his mouth with a handful of rubles: a gross oversimplification of the character.

[486] They seem to have forgotten to inform Pishchik that they are leaving just as they forget Fiers.

[487] Richard Peace seems to think this is "an obvious literary 'quotation' from the comic character Bobchinsky in Gogol's play *The Government Inspector.*"

[488] Anya's almost as irresponsible as her mother. Who in their right mind would trust Yasha with anything of importance?

[489] There is profound irony in the fact that Ranevskaya worries about keeping Varya working, like the exploited servant that she always was, though Varya was too blind to see it.

[490] "… only then we can redeem ourselves, by suffering and by unremitting, ceaseless hard work." These are the words of Trofimov who doesn't seem to work much at all. We here it over and over, about the glory of work; Lopakhin craves it and can't stand to be without it. There is irony in Chekhov's talk about

work. What exactly does Varya accomplish by her ceaseless work; her responsibilities are never clearly delineated for us; is she just a lowly "housekeeper"? If she in any way "manages" the estate, she is a total failure. She is unable to exercise authority over Epikhodov, to get him to do any work; and perhaps she has no real authority over him. That an estate of this vast size can't produce any significant income is evidence of the uselessness of her work which is reduced to no more than petty housekeeping. Routine work is often portrayed in Chekhov as a mindless numbing narcotic which swallows up and destroys his characters; routine, repetitive work that is the enemy of living. "Central to all of Chekhov's work is the depiction of an action in which human beings are consciously caught between the petty routines of daily existence and their visionary aspirations for a happier more meaningful life." Richard Risso, [*Chekhov: A View of the Basic Ironic Structures* from Jean Pierre Barricelli, *Chekhov's great plays: a critical anthology*, New York, New York University Press, 1981. Gotham library of the New York University Press, p. 181]

"… along with Wordsworth he [Chekhov] was aware too of the potency of use and custom to establish a 'universe of death'. In most of Chekhov's mature stories a pattern of routine is established which swallows up the characters. 'About six times a day', says the narrator in *In the Ravine* (1900) 'tea was drunk; about four times they sat down at the table to eat. And in the evening, they counted the takings, and then they slept soundly … Sometimes there is insistence on the cold tyranny of the clock as in the second part of *In a Native Corner* (1897) with its dull daily round, the routine of meals, the regularity of guests, the habit of amusements…" W. Gareth Jones, *Chekhov's Undercurrent of Time*, The Modern Language Review, Vol. 64, No. 1 (Jan., 1969), p. 8. Modern Humanities Research Association

Starting in the 1860s Russia saw the popularity of ideologies ecstatically glorifying work, leftist, communist or just idealistic rejections of economic and social structures marked by indolence and exploitation from the upper classes of the grueling labor of the impoverished lower classes. In *The Three Sisters* Irina says: "We come from families who thought they never had to work," Tuzenbach's and Vershinin's celebrating the glories of physical work comes from a confused and credulous wish to expiate the guilt of their "aristocratic" past. Tuzenbach: "there's a storm gathering . . . wild, elemental ... it will clean out our society, get rid of laziness . . . and this prejudice against working." But Irina has only to experience it to change her mind: "Whatever it was I wanted or was dreaming of," ... "this [her work in the telegraph office] is definitely not it. It's work, but there's no poetry in it, no meaning."

This is work as a prison house, routine, mind numbing, soul killing work. "Above all, Chekhov is able to create a feeling of human identity, by dislodging a character from human routine [often a routine of work] as if delicately unpicking a strand from the closely woven cosmic pattern - and letting it unravel." W. Gareth Jones

"Anton could at last live out an idea he had preached periodically, but never practiced: that the prerequisite of personal happiness was idleness." Donald Rayfield

I think "idleness" is the wrong word; Chekhov was referring to a creative "leisure"; a time to rejuvenate and think.

Michael Frayne while recognizing work as one of Chekhov's major themes also recognizes his complex attitude toward it: "Work as the longed-for panacea for all the ills of idleness; work as obsession and drudgery and the destruction of life; work as life, simply. What Sonya looks forward to in heaven for herself and her uncle at the end of Vanya is not finding peace, as some translations have it; what she says, five times over, in plain everyday Russian, is that they will rest." Michael Frayne *Anton Chekhov, Plays, Introduction*, Methuen Publishing Ltd., London "We shall rest" (Mi otdokhnyom). Magarshack insists that otdokhnyom here suggests "not the horror of the rest in the grave, but a serene and happy rest after a task well done." Magarshack, *Chekhov the Dramatist*, London, 1952, p. 224. However, many critics, wrongly find "at peace" a perfectly acceptable translation. But there is no doubt Chekhov believed in work, creative work, the work of the true artist, the work which is engagement with life itself. Ivan Bunin, [Ivan Alekseyevich Bunin, October 22, 1870 –November 8, 1953) was the first Russian writer to win the Nobel Prize for Literature] his friend, quotes this interchange: "'Do you write a lot' he [Chekhov] asked me. I replied that I did not' 'What a shame' he said glumly, in his deep chest voice. 'You must work you know. You must work without stopping… all your life.'"

[491] Varya suffers many of the same defects as Ranevskaya and Gaev. Chekhov describes her as a "crybaby".

[492] Although entirely unenthusiastic about it (translated as "be done with it" or "Let's get it over with" one suspects that Lopakhin, being of good nature, would have gone along with the marriage if sufficiently prodded. Ranevskaya could easily have been more forceful if she really cared about anyone other than herself. Did she really believe that if the two were left alone the proposal would occur?

[493] "Go" in French.

[494] The question is, why does Ranevskaya leave when she easily could have brought this proposal to a consummation? "Liuba, having unsuccessfully attempted to call Varya into the room, makes the fatal mistake of leaving the room to get her. This leaves Lopakhin on his own without the support that he needs in

order to have the nerve to ask Varya to marry him." Borny P. 245. Of course, this failure to propose has nothing to do with a failure of nerve, but Ranevskaya by her presence would have forced the issue.

One of the aspects that isn't discussed often by critics is that Lopakhin's reluctance may have a financial foundation. Wouldn't his marriage to Varya entail his bailing out the Gaevs, her adopted family, and saving the estate for them? Varya comes with a lot of baggage. Can he really dispossess the Gaevs if he marries Varya?

[495] One of the few times she is referred to by her proper name.

[496] He always seems to know the exact time, distance, place and temperature. "Only Lopakhin the businessman in *The Cherry Orchard* is as insistent as Astrov on how many miles it takes to get somewhere." Chekhov, Anton. *The Complete Plays*. W. W. Norton & Company.

[497] "So life in this house is over." One of the most poignant lines in the play. He declares it over only after she tells him emphatically that she is going to the Ragulins. "Where will you go, Varvara Mikhailovna?" How sweet that he uses her proper name; one of the few times we hear it in the entire play. The line can be interpreted as an opening. Would it have been too forward for her to answer: "Well, that depends on you"?

[498] "So life in this house is over": is previously posed almost as a question by Lopakhin and it is Varya that answers it "Yes, life in this house is done . . . There won't be any anymore, ever . . ." She could have kept the question open by simply answering: "That's up to you. It's your house now." or perhaps more noncommittally: "it's such shame to tear down such a beautiful old house and certainly with such an incredibly large orchard, some of the trees can stay."

[499] Magarshack gets the scene wrong: "Face to face with Varya he [Lopakhin] is so conscious of her social superiority that he cannot bring himself to propose to her, while Varya … is quite incapable of disregarding the conventions which demand that the lady has to wait for the gentleman to propose to her." It is Lopakhin, in his fine clothes, now the lord of the manor, and Varya with her sad servant's clothes, "adopted" daughter of the now dispossessed, who is now in the superior social position and cannot bring himself to descend once again. But Borny picks up a different subtext for this intricate "tennis match" of words. Borny P. 246.

[500] It is only after what can be regarded as Lopakhin tentative opening and Varya's closing of it that Lopakhin reveals to her his hiring of Epihodov.

[501] The hiring of Epihodov has to be regarded as a perhaps unintended insult to Varya and thus sabotaging any possibility of a further relationship. He gives Epihodov a position of genuine authority while Varya is once again reduced to a "housekeeper" which is perhaps all she was really capable of, and perhaps she is as responsible as the Noble Gaevs, of blood, for the decline and ruin of this great orchard. Perhaps it is she, the abandoned child of peasants, brought in like a stray dog, who through her gross incompetence and negligence brought down this great house. Chekhov never believed in the efficacy of mind numbing, ceaseless work.

It was Epihodov who had made it clear to Varya that she had no "real" authority over him, an assertion that hit a raw nerve of truth.

[502] "The choice of Yepikhodov, the most inept, accident-prone person in the play, certainly seems a strange choice of character to replace the highly efficient Varya. What Lopakhin seems to be trying to do here is to goad Varya into objecting to Yepikhodov's

appointment. He knows how much she dislikes 'Simple Simon'. All he needs is to get Varya to respond by saying something like, 'How on earth can you think of employing that fool?', and he will be able to respond with something like, 'Well who else is there who can do the job properly?' This in turn is likely elicit the response, 'I can'. Once Lopakhin can engineer some such overt response from Varya to the effect that she wishes to stay, the possibility of his proposing to her becomes much more likely. What actually happens in Chekhov's non-proposal scene is that Varya is too proud to object overtly to Lopakhin's choice of Yepikhodov as manager for the estate:
VARYA. Oh, have you?
(Subtext: 'Surely not? Oh well. If that's what you really want, it's up to you.' Passes ball.) Borny P. 247.
Actually, we have little evidence that Epikhodov is so inefficient at his work, only that he is socially inept, clumsy and a failure with the ladies. It is Varya, the drudge, who works ceaselessly and accomplishes absolutely nothing who is the last person who Lopakhin would want to put in charge of the orchard. Epikhodov admires Lopakhin to such a degree one suspects that he might actually shape up under Lopakhin's stern hand.

[503] The same temperature we started with in Act One.

[504] All of their thermometers are broken. Only Lopakhin seems to know the temperature; also, the time, distance and the lay of the land.

[505] A number of critics including Donald Rayfield regard it as "a probably prearranged call." But Rayfield further groundlessly surmises that this failure to propose indicates "a sheer lack of libido" on Lopakhin's part.

[506] Glinka ascribes the failure of Lopakhin's wooing to that mysterious reticence which governs all Chekhov's characters: "something unseen, something immaterial holds them back; they

are hindered by some psychological trammel." Carol Flath refers to the "well-established Russian literary tradition according to which a man's failure to love actively represents a deeper flaw in Russian society with serious social implications." Carol Flath, *Writing about Nothing: Chekhov's 'Ariadna' and the Narcissistic Narrator,* The Slavonic and East European Review, Vol. 77, No. 2 (Apr., 1999), P. 230. A number of critics have stressed <u>the marriage proposal that does not take place</u> as the central 'non-event' in many of Chekhov's best works including 'U znakomykh', *A Visit to Friends*, 1898. Batyushkof, however, attributes it to Varya and Lopakhin both being "numbskulls", nedotyopa. Both have spent their life on work and left the rest undeveloped.

But I think Lopakhin may be relieved to get away. I don't think this is shyness or a case of nerves or incompetence with the ladies. (See note 300) Their "exchange" is subtle and full of meaning; an opening and then a closing. It might even be regarded as a "proposal" and a rejection. Lopakhin's halfhearted "courtship" of Varya may have resulted from a misplaced and undeserved devotion to Ranevskaya. If Ranevskaya had literally joined their hands together the match would have been made; Lopakhin would have gone along; even to the end he is to some extent under Ranevskaya's spell.

There is also the fact that Lopakhin has, in another sense, finally broken free of the charms of Ranevskaya. He is no longer under her obligation. He has finally usurped her power and become proprietor of the very estate which held sway over him and his fathers.

So, the failure to propose is not a failure, at all. "… by the time of the scene in Act IV the audience has been given the clear impression that Varya is indeed not a suitable match for

Lopakhin, that she is not worthy of him." Vladimir Kataev, p. 272

"When he decides not to propose to Varya in the last act (he knows he has moved passed her into a world in which she does not belong), this is shown to be a positive act, consciously conceived and resolutely carried out." James R. Brandon. *Toward a Middle-View of Chekhov*, Educational Theatre Journal, December, 1960, Johns Hopkins University Press. 12 (4): 270–275.

Well, maybe not conscious or resolute, but certainly not the hindrance of some psychological trammel, either.

Harold Bloom [it is amazing how these icons of criticism so often have absolutely no idea what they're talking about] seems to touch upon Lopakhin's "this seeming infatuation" with Ranevskaya but has somehow gotten hold of a very different *Cherry Orchard*: "Son of a muzhik, Lopakhin has considerable cruelty in him, but his deep feeling is for Lyubov, with whom we can surmise he always will be, quite hopelessly, in love. But then, so are we, with its endlessly mobile and magnificent woman, this large-souled vision of passion on the old, grand, high scale. In his elegy for himself, the lover of women Anton Chekhov has given us his most vivid representation of an embodied Sublime in Lyubov." Bloom, Harold, *Dramatists and Drama,* Chelsea House Publishers, Philadelphia, 2005 p. 184

But Bloom is not alone, Vsevolod Meierkhold's [*The Naturalistic Theater and the Theater of Mood* from A Norton Critical Edition, *Anton Chekhov's Selected Plays*, edited by Laurence Senelick, W. W. Norton & Company New York, London, 2005] vision of Ranevskaya identifies her as the life force. Kataev also: "Lopakhin loves Ranevskaya." Rayfield seems to agree with his positive view of Ranevskaya: "Nobody else (besides

Ranevskaya) expresses ardour, any more than Charlotta's rifle or Epikhodov's revolver ever fire." Donald Rayfield.

Frank Rich in a New York Times review of the Peter Brooks production alludes to this strange bond that Ranevskayia has over Lopkhin which he himself breaks by purchasing the estate. "(Lopakhin) can't help celebrating his purchase, but his half-jig of victory is slowly tempered by the realization that he has forfeited any chance of affection from the aristocratic woman he has just bought out… We're left with an indelible portrait of not one but two well-meaning souls who have <u>lost what they most loved</u> by recognizing their own desires too late."

We should remember that her brother Gaev called her a slut, (perhaps intending Anya to overhear him); that her every movement exuded it. The cruelty is not in Lopakhin but in Ranevskaya whose outward show of gushing sentimental love betrays an egotistical indifference that can only be described as cruel, even if unintentionally so. If this is Chekhov's vivid representative of sublime womanhood, which I believe it is not, then Chekhov would be guilty of the misogyny of which he is accused. (… as early as 1963 Sophie Laffitte argued that he was a misogynist." [*Tchikhov: 1860—1904* (Paris: Galimard, 1963), p. 198].

But Bloom, in his foolishness, may be on to something; because all of these characters are beguiling in spite of, or maybe because of, their seemingly myriad shortcomings. And they are beguiling to actors as well: "The Cherry Orchard is one of those very rare works in which an entire [acting] company can lose itself, ceasing to believe that it is in a theater, believing firmly that this family exists, that this house exists, and that this is life." Jean-Louis Barrault

"Chekhov's objective is to lure the spectator into the events, to give him a desire to hobnob with the characters in his plays…

They constantly make mistakes and yet one desires to be with them: what a tour-de-force Chekhov managed in that." Peter Stein p. 636. But why do we desire to be with them? Why do we enjoy their company? "Its people are alive; they have charm and generosity, they feel as we feel and are foolish as we are foolish, and pretend as we pretend that somehow we will be saved from our follies, from the fate we have created for ourselves." Tobias Wolf, introduction to *Anton Chekhov, Five Plays*, translated by Maria Brodskaya, Stanford University Press, California.

Even though nobility, they do form a kind of "community" with their servants and former serfs; though still in some ways distant, there is a palpable bond, perhaps based on their shared Russianness. "And it was Chekhov's constant and firm position not to divide people into classes or social groups: 'No division is good, for we are all a nation and the best things we do are for the nation'" Polotskaya, Emma, *Chekhov and His Russia: The Cherry Orchard,* p. 178

"…Chekhov is interested not in their social differences, but in the human situation that unites them." Richard Pevear.

"This is what gives a universal and distinctive quality to the picture of the real world that Chekhov is beginning to construct: regardless of who they are, each person comes into the same kind of conflict with life, and finds it inscrutable and incomprehensible." KATAEV, VLADIMIR, *If Only We Could Know!* An Interpretation of Chekhov, translated from the Russian and edited by Harvey Pitcher, IVAN R. DEE, Chicago 2002.

"They live in extended Russian families, where relatives, neighbors, and friends are drawn into the domestic circle. Except perhaps for Tolstoy, no modern writer has been better at depicting the tensions, affections, and profound loyalties of familial life." Milton Ehre "His plays are based not on the contrast between characters but on unity and what they have in common." Kataev P. 273.

Gerhardie speaks of the "extraordinary homogeneity of the Russian people." (However, we should also remember what Tolstoy said just after Chekhov's death: that Chekhov's writings and the characters he creates are close not only to every Russian but to people everywhere, and that this universal quality is the most important thing about Chekhov.) There is nothing more unChekhovian and more repellent than having Lopakhin speak with a low class or Cockney accent, as some British productions would have it; it destroys the play. Kataev seems to point toward this: "'We look down our noses at each other, but life goes by regardless.' Thus, Chekhov's characters are convinced of the absolute value of their opposing 'truths.' The author himself on each occasion points out what they have in common, the concealed similarity that they fail to notice or indignantly reject... *apparent opposition combined with concealed similarity*... Chekhov the writer makes no distinction among them in their collision with reality...." Kataev's italics. TJ underlining. Kataev P. 279.

Many critics have commented on the fact that unlike Shakespeare's tragi-comedy Chekhov does not divide his scenes into high and low comedy; he rather combines both in each scene; and neither does he divide his characters into high seriousness and low comedy. As Karl Guthke comments: "… this device of internal character dichotomy realises its tragi-comic effect by exploring the two sides of the dramatis persona in such a way that they not only offset each other, but impart their aesthetic quality (comic and tragic respectively) to each other." K. S. Guthke, *Modern Tragi-Comedy*, Random House, New York, 1996, p. 84. Or as Borny says: "In Chekhov, there is no clear separation into high and low characters as occurs in a play such as *A Midsummer Night's Dream*. Instead, each character combines traits that are both noble and ludicrous."

"*The Cherry Orchard* does not contain comic characters (such as Charlotta, Yepikhodov, and Varya) who stand apart from the rest. All the characters are assigned the kinds of limitations in thought and behavior—not understanding each other, holding opinions that clash with other people's, drawing illogical conclusions, making inappropriate replies and responses—that may be presented in a comic way." Kataev P. 279 TJ underlining. When contemplating the incredible homogeneity of these characters, of their "apparent opposition combined with concealed similarity", we have to remind ourselves that the Gaevs are nobility.

One English critic [Kenneth Tynan] argued that the Gaevs are country gentry and not the ruined aristocrats that the English audience likes to imagine them. But Tynan is dead wrong; they are exactly that; ruined aristocrats, ruined nobility in plain fact; their aunt is a countess; they travel to Paris, as even their ancestors did, by post-chaise, as Fiers reminds us, and dress smartly in Parisian fashion. In fact, Chekhov objected to the dress and boots that Vanya wore in a production of *Uncle Vanya*, reminding the director that these are educated people who go to Paris, who dress stylishly, Vanya "has a wonderful tie; he is an elegant, cultured man", decidedly not just country gentry. (And the directors will never learn: in Gregory Mosher's 1991 production Vanya dresses like a slob and so does Astrov; these men had servants; they were capable of wearing impeccably clean white shirts. But then, what else can you say about a production which has beautiful Rebecca Pidgeon playing Sonya and the less beautiful Mastrantonio playing the meant to be beautiful Elena.)

[507] What kind of a reaction is that? This isn't upper class reserve or reticence; she's not too reserved to chase after her lover in

Paris. Why should she not say? "Go after him; it's not too late. What is the matter with the two of you?" Or maybe she understands, better than the others, that Lopakhin has moved on and that if she herself forced the subject she would only embarrass herself; and reveal the collapse of her own social position.

[508] This is promising; he manages to dress warmly without Fiers's help; still no fur coat, though.

[509] This is delivered authoritatively. Lopakhin is now in charge. Perhaps Epikhodov will actually shape up under the forceful guidance of Lopakhin, his reluctant mentor, who he in many ways emulates and "unfortunately" mimics.

[510] This may be the observance of an Old Russian custom. Sitting for a few minutes just before a journey was thought to bring good luck and a safe trip. Also, not a bad idea to sit, collect your thoughts and take a second look around the house and make absolutely certain you haven't forgotten anything. (like Fiers)

[511] Trinity Sunday is the first Sunday after Pentecost in the Western Christian liturgical calendar, and the Sunday of Pentecost in Eastern Christianity. Trinity Sunday celebrates the Christian doctrine of the Trinity, the three Persons of God: the Father, the Son, and the Holy Spirit when the Holy Spirit came down to Christ's apostles as a tongue of flames. In Chekhov, time is often measured against and encrusted within Orthodox holy days.

[512] Maybe that infamous roach that he should have been on the look-out for.

[513] Except for Fiers. We can almost see this coming.

[514] "When in Act IV Varya takes up an umbrella rather too violently and Lopakhin feigns fear that he is about to be beaten, the audience is aware not only of Varya's threatened fist in Act I (and the actual beating in Act III) but also of the poignancy of

Lopakhin's non-proposal that preceded it and has injected its own tension into this second non-event." Richard Peace p.120

[515] This is perhaps a profound or absurd existential statement.

[516] How ironically appropriate that this "visionary" should pull on filthy galoshes to lead the charge and usher in his new world.

[517] When he will come back. So it is that Lopakhin, the seeming destroyer of paradise, which wasn't really a paradise, becomes the agent of rebirth and renewal, of a sort.

[518] This way out or There's a way out (Vykhod est'), "Lopakhin had pleaded earlier with respect to his plan to save the estate financially. The 'way out', for the family, in the end turns out to be, 'On your way . . .' or simply, 'Out with you!'" Jackson P.149

[519] Notice how carefully and authoritatively he ushers them out, taking full possession of the old house, only to lock it up.

[520] "Until spring. On your way, gentleman . . . Till the station (Znachit, do vesny [Значит, до весны.] Vykhodite, gospoda [Викходите, Господа]. . . Do svidantsiia [До свидантсииа])," says Lopakhin. He wanted to say "do svidania" (good-bye) but unconsciously conflates the word "stantsiia" (station) with "svidanie (meeting), thus suggesting "until the station," rather than "until we meet again." Jackson P. 149

[521] A powerful word "in despair" (votchayanii [Вотчайании])

[522] "… the audience hears the cheerful voices of Anya and Petya Trofimov, the younger generation being no less infantile in its merriment than the older one in its grief…" Svetlana Evdokimova

[523] In Stanislavsky's later productions Ranevskaya leaves without Gaev realizing it; when he turns to speak to her she is gone. "He is about to break into violent sobbing when suddenly he stuffs his handkerchief in his mouth like a schoolboy caught laughing. As he turns his back and goes out we see the twitch of the big shoulders and it is almost more than an impressionable playgoer

can bear." Heywood Broun, "The New Plays," New York World, January 23, 1923, Clippings, The New York Public Library, Performing Arts Research Collections, New York. Quoted by Sharon Marie Carnicke. One can understand why Chekhov so objected to Stanislavky's sense of tragic melodrama. There is no indication in Chekhov's own script that Gaev is left alone on stage and certainly no indication that he stuffs a handkerchief in his mouth. But this melodrama resonated. American director Harold Clurman: "I shall never forget the heartbreak—not without its humour—when Stanislavsky, as Gaev in the original production, reached ineffectually for his handkerchief." Harold Clurman, *The Naked Image: Observations on the Modern Theatre* (New York: Collier-Macmillan Ltd., 1966) This is the kind of scene stealing hamyness that Stanislavsky seemed to live for.

[524] "Death puts in an almost personal appearance at the play's end in the dying servant Firs, but it is present symbolically throughout." Michael Henry Heim.
Chekhov playfully, self-consciously, teased the Symbolists in Kostya's play and in the dead seagull he lays before Nina. ("I suppose it's a symbol," Nina says, "but I'm sorry, I don't understand it.") The supreme irony is that though he mocked the symbolists we cannot escape his own symbols, which are symbols without exactly being symbols.
"Except the seagull I can recall no other example in Tchekhof's plays of a symbol of the artless kind that can be stored in the property-room. But there is a more beautiful and recondite Symbolism, one that harmonizes better with the realistic method, and that is the Symbolism by which the events of the Drama are not merely represented for their own sake but stand also as emblems and generalizations about life at large." Calderon

"Tchekhof did not often use symbols in the old-fashioned sense, material objects adumbrating immaterial meanings, designed to catch attention by their superficial irrelevance, like the lambs and lilies of pictured saints." Calderon

[525] J. L. Styan: "A final prick of comedy is felt in his irritation as he mutters under his breath, 'These young people . . .' Time and his great age have reduced the whole family equally to the level of children who do not know what they are doing."

I have adopted Styan's translation in this note but I translate it as "These children." Fiers emphasizes this point by treating his "master", Gaev, as though he were a child, which he is, ironically, which reverses the patriarchal conventions of earlier Russian literature, where the landowner was depicted as father and the servants as his children. Maxim Gorky: "Here they are, the weepy Ranevskaia and the other former masters of the Cherry Orchard, as egotistical as children and as flabby as senile old men."

There is little that is innocent in these old children; we forget that the myth of childhood is a relatively modern phenomenon. We live in an age which romanticizes childhood even raising silly childish games to the delusionary level of "manly" sports. Freedom from incessant work has allowed us to become big children; like Gaev and Ranevskaya, playing games, (vint) entertaining ourselves, engaging in mindless socializing in which we talk ignorantly about nothing. Only Lopakhin understands that he has been corrupted by these idlers; that he must get back to work. Perhaps these interludes, these interruptions, are his work, his attempt to turn the cherry orchard into plots for dachas, to create a new life while saving a part of the old.

"Childishness, therefore, by definition centers on the inherent incongruity of child-like behavior in someone who is expected to be a 'grown-up.' It exposes man's disregard for the passage of time and his inability or unwillingness to complete the rite of passage, that is, to realize fully the transition from the age of innocence to the state of knowledge and maturity. <u>It is in this sense that one can link childhood to a golden age and maturity to the Fall</u>. Childishness, then, is a form of atavism that represents the recurrence of child-like characteristics in the post-lapsarian world of adulthood. A childish individual is one who not only feels nostalgia for paradise lost but who actually never fully realizes the transition from innocence to knowledge, from the bliss of carelessness to the burden of responsibility, <u>from childish impotence to adult sexuality.</u>" Svetlana Evdokimova (TJ Underlining) More than one critic has observed that carnal love does not fit into the Russian image of paradise. It is Ranevskaya who is cast out of paradise to return to the West and her carnal lover.

[526] But Ranevskaya has also "let life slip away". In a discarded ending to Act II, Chekhov had Charlotte help Firs look for items that Lyuba had dropped. While looking, she had commented: "Lyuba Andreyevich is forever losing things. She's <u>thrown</u> her life away the same way." Another perfect change. I think Chekhov realized this was too heavy handed; we can conclude this for ourselves.

[527] An absurd final realization, recognizing the futility of his lifelong devotion to the Masters, calling himself what he repeatedly called the others, nedotyopa: numbskull, dimwit. *The Cherry Orchard* has been called the first modern play in the Theater of the Absurd. To be absurd is not to be ludicrous. But these characters never succumb to the absurdity as perhaps would be expected; they even recognize it. Each of the characters in his own way is undefeatable or even indefatigable, determined "to keep going despite everything"; as "unchastened" as Ranevskaya; "…<u>nor do they seem threatened by the blankness of</u>

<u>a metaphysically meaningless existence… and they seem never to question the human value of energy, purposive activity and work</u>…" Hahn p. 4. TJ underlining. Would it be too corrosively ironic to suggest that Epikhodov, in his own absurd way, exemplifies this quintessentially admirable, very Russian trait: "He, like a truly tragic figure, is a stoic in the face of adversity: 'Every day something or other unpleasant happens to me. But I don't complain; I'm accustomed to it, I even laugh at it.'" Peace, Richard, *Chekhov, A Study of the Four Major Plays,* Yale University Press, New Haven and London, 1983, P. 126 Epikhodov always carries a gun, but he does not shoot himself, does not shoot himself. What is it that gives so much power to the repeated line: "There goes Epikhodov."? Followed by the ominous words of Gaev: The sun's gone down, ladies and gentlemen. And Charlotta, that most admirable, "unfortunate" and indestructible of characters, even finds Epikhodov's whining insufferable.

"Chekhov makes his work an extraordinary compound of morality and reality, rebellion and acceptance, irony and sympathy— <u>evoking a singular affirmation even in the darkest despair</u>." Robert Brustein, *Theatre of Revolt,* Little, Brown and Co., 1964, TJ underlining.

Valency is wrong when he states: "[Chekhov] had no theory of life to expound, no point to make, no thesis. It is quite unnecessary for the understanding of his drama to discuss his world view. If he had anything of the sort, it was irrelevant to the subject of his art. His great talent lay in his sensitive depiction of life around him, the physical and psychic landscape in which he lived." Chekhov may not have been possessed of a traditional philosophy, but he is the most moral of writers without being, and in fact refusing to be moralistic and dogmatic. It is his very refusal to judge so neatly and so easily that raises him to this higher moral plane. Linkov noted Chekhov's disinclination to pass judgement on his characters as pinpointing the author's "moral discipline". V. Linkov, *Skepticism i vera Chekhova,* Moscow: Izdatel'stvo Moskovskogo universiteta, 1995. Chekhov maintained that his conception of the short story genre requires "speaking and thinking in the spirit and tone" of his heroes for the duration of the narrative, and precludes subjective evaluation: "… it would be nice to combine sermonising with art, but for me it would be difficult and nearly impossible because of the stipulations of my technique…" Letter to Suvorin, April, 1890. *The Cherry Orchard* resembles theater of the absurd but wedded to a dogged determination that might be taken for optimism. *Our situation may be absurd, as is the world, but we will endure. We will pick ourselves up and dust ourselves off as best we are able. Chekhov's is a testament to human will, to give meaning where there is no meaning.*

"They are not wastelanders; nor do they seem threatened by the blankness of a metaphysically meaningless existence." Hahn, P.4. TJ underlining and italics. And this is perhaps the lightness, the comedy that Chekhov insists upon; these characters, despite all the evidence, will not accept their own defeat; though beaten, outcast and abandoned, they will not lie down and die. As Gottlieb put it so well: "… the tragic view of human impotence in the face of seemingly inevitable forces implies an *acceptance* of the world order as it manifests itself and works out its design in the characters on stage. The assumption of human impotence, the acceptance of 'that which is', the belief in ungovernable external forces, and the insistence on 'absolutes', all become part of a retrograde world view. This philosophy, I would suggest, was complete anathema to Chekhov, whose concern as a scientist and as a writer was with the exposure of contradictions, and not an annulment or denial of contradictions. His aim was to expose,

<u>and not to tranquillize</u>, what Coleridge called, 'the lethargy of custom.'" TJ underlining. Matthias Freise asserts that the Chekhovian hero: "faced by a total collapse of meaning in his everyday life, *<u>emerges from despair and nothingness via an indomitable, if illusory, search for meaning (or yearning for transcendence).</u>* [TJ underlining, italic] Speaking of *Uncle Vanya* it is Freedman who said, not flippantly: ".... perhaps the only meaning in life is to be found in looking for meaning in life". Freedman, M., 'Chekhov's Morality of Work', Modern Drama, Vol. 5, No. 1, 1962

In many of Chekhov's stories, religion bears hope for transcendence, for absolute meaning "but this does not make Chekhov a religious writer. His prose does not understand human existence as a movement towards God. On the contrary, it understands religion as a concretisation of the existential hope for meaning" (p. 299). *Die Prosa Anton Cechoov*s, Freise quoted and summarized by Gordon McVay

Chekhov is different in kind from those who followed and even claimed his influence. He is unique. He has few descendants. The critics misinterpret.

"…Chekhov's writings, however objective in technique and tone, are anything but morally neutral. They dramatize Chekhov's sympathy for the powerless and his loathing of oppression, not only the oppression of one class by another but also of wife by husband and husband by wife, servants by their masters, truth by falsehood, gentleness by violence. He hated bullies. And as much as he hated bullies, he hated the cowardice that creates them, that make us cringe before the possibilities of life. Chekhov was not a cynic; he believed in those possibilities. He did not always believe in our power to achieve them, but they gleam at the edges of even his darkest work, throwing light on the faces of the just and the unjust, giving them a wistful, expectant, familiar look."

Tobias Wolf, Introduction to *Anton Chekhov, Five Plays*, translated by Maria Brodskaya, Stanford University Press, California.

Senelick says that Chekhov "is a synecdoche for all modern drama." One critic called this final scene with its nightmarish locked room, a Sartrean room with no exit. "Death, in an ending which heralds Samuel Beckett, is banal: a senile servant is forgotten in a locked house." Donald Rayfield, *Anton Chekhov: A Life*

"In his old livery and tall hat… the impression of this scene as given by the Moscow Artistic Theatre is overwhelming," says Glinka. "Life has passed on, gone by, forgotten him… The old life has cast him aside; the new life will have nothing to do with him. It goes hurrying on somewhere, knocking and jostling, hastening to reach the future happiness of mankind. And yet Firs is a man too." "His being abandoned makes us think, all at the same time, of mortality, chance, the end of things, the beginning, change." Gillman p. 241

"They are sure to find out soon and send back for him… but the author wanted to show to what a pitch of thoughtlessness people can go who, from their childhood up, have never once faced the realities of life." Batyushkof

I'm not as optimistic as Batyushkov; however, we might rest a little easy knowing that Epikhodov is now in charge and will be in possession of those famous keys and might well find old Fiers. What are the chances of that? Do we laugh or cry or both, at the very same time?

Michael Frayne sees only tragedy: "In his [Magarshack's] book *Chekhov the Dramatist* he urges the view that *The Cherry Orchard* is simply a funny play in its entirety. He even manages to find the last scene funny, where Firs is left locked into the empty house for the winter. He argues that the stage-direction says merely that Firs is lying motionless, not dying, and that someone will shortly realize what has happened, and come back and release him. This seems to me frankly preposterous. No doubt Firs is not clinically dead at the fall of the curtain, but anyone who believes he has a serious chance of emerging from that room alive has clearly never considered the practicalities of playwriting, let alone the effects of extreme cold upon extreme old age. In the course of the last act Chekhov establishes not once but three times, in a brilliantly escalating confirmation of misunderstanding, that the family believes Firs to have been taken off to hospital already; not once but four times that the house is to be closed up for the winter; and even twice that the temperature is already three degrees below zero [below freezing]. If you can believe that after all this there remained in Chekhov's mind some unexpressed hope that Gaev, say, might get the next train back from town, or that Yepikhodov might for some reason suddenly take it into his head to unlock the house again and inspect its contents, then you can believe that Wagner hoped the local Boy Scouts might put out the fire at the end of Gotterdammerung and give Siegfried and Brunnhilde artificial respiration."

If we're going to play these games, we can go on and on; obviously Fiers knows the house and could very well find an alternate way out; he may have the strength to start a fire; there might very well be some fire wood left behind or refuse that could burn; there is still some furniture left, piled to the side; from Chekhov's letters we know that this was supposed to be very expensive furniture; it is not made clear whether Lopakhin now owns this furniture or whether Gaev, who is only a short way away in town intends to have it picked up or sold. There is also the letter that was not sent with Fiers which they may follow up on and discover he never arrived at the hospital. Also, since

Epikhodov is left behind as manager it is probable that he is in residence somewhere on the property ("I'm leaving Epikhodov here in charge of the property.") in one of its outbuildings and certainly would notice smoke coming from the chimney, if Fiers does manage to start a fire; also someone has to stay to supervise the tree cutters, presumably Epikhodov; and doesn't Lopakhin mention that it's good weather for building; why waste time; the building could start immediately and a hundred other possibilities which Chekhov opens up. Lopakhin: "Here we are and it's already October, but it might as well be summer it's so sunny and it's calm like summer. Good weather for building." It is not "already" three degrees below freezing; that's the morning temperature which will quickly rise on this calm, summerlike, sunny day in early October. It is Pishchick, the old Russian, who complains: "It's hot in here." It is also Pishchick who exclaims about the "wonderful weather".

Chekhov has seduced us into believing in the separate continuing reality of this play; it takes on a life of its own; quite probably Chekhov didn't know the outcome himself.

Maurice Valency: "Chekhov's plays are not finished. When the curtain has fallen, the play goes on; there is still the sense of flux."

"The open-endedness of Chekhov's plays—of his work as a whole, for that matter—results from a conviction that the writer's job is not so much to provide the proper answers as to pose the proper questions." Michael Henry Heim, *Anton Chekhov: The Essential Plays: The Seagull, Uncle Vanya, Three Sisters & The Cherry Orchard, Translated, with an Introduction and Notes, by Michael Henry Heim* (Modern Library Classics) Random House Publishing Group.

This final scene must be presented with the greatest subtlety and understatement otherwise it can easily devolve into the cheapest sort of melodrama, as with so many productions, starting with Stanislavsky. I can understand Gerhardie's reservations: "…the Cherry Orchard, whose only blemish, by the way, is perhaps the introduction of the old servant at the end, whose final mutterings one would wish had been left out: there is just a touch of stage-effect in his having been locked up, by an oversight." But it is only a blemish if played as melodrama. This very situation is prefigured in Chekhov's vaudevilles which may offer a "key". Zingerman: "The vaudevilles give us the key to Chekhov's dialectic, and through them to all his playwriting." B. Zingerman, *Chekhov's Vaudevilles,* in Voprosy tealra 72. Sbomik statey i material) Theatrical Matters 72: Collection of Articles and Documents) (Moscow, 1973)

Many great writers started their careers by writing worthless pulp for the consumption of a popular audience: "Oh, with what trash I began; my God, with what trash!" Chekhov confessed that he had never spent more than a day writing a story: "the way reporters write notices of fires: mechanically, half-consciously, without caring a pin either about the reader or myself." "The word newspaper-writer means, at the very least, a scoundrel. I am one of them; I work with them; I shake hands with them; I'm even told that I've begun to look like one. But I shan't die as one." Typically, the self-deprecating Chekhov overstates the case; his early work often seemed to be laying the groundwork for his final masterpieces. More than one critic has recognized prefigurations in his early characters of those who come alive in his latter works: Bugrov in 'A Living Chattel' (1882) predicts Lopakhin in *The Cherry Orchard* (1904). In the kind of small comic publications that Chekhov originally wrote for: "Authors were free to write in any manner, invent new techniques, modify the old conventions and experiment with new forms." Chudakov P. 7

"Many of the artistic principles, explored by Chekhov in his first five years as a writer, remained constant for the rest of his career. There were preliminary expositions of the situation, no excursions into the characters' past, or similar introductions to the narrative – it always began instantly. It is the characters who create the action, and there is no explanation or, more accurately, exposition, as to the causes of these actions." Alexander Chudakov, *Chekhov in Context, Dr. Chekhov: a biographical essay (29 January 1860–15 July 1904)* from *The Cambridge Companion to Chekhov*, Gottlieb, Vera and Allain, Paul, editors, The Cambridge University Press, 2000. Chekhov was inevitably influenced by his earlier work especially his stories; but furthermore, Chekhov had just finished compiling, editing and in some cases reworking his earlier work for a collected works published by Marks; so, almost his entire oeuvre was fresh in his mind. "Most of Chekhov's time in the last four years of his life was spent selecting and revising his work for republication in his collected works: this proves how prominent his earlier work was in composing his last pieces." Rayfield P. 45

[528] "I propose that Chekhov introduces the snapping string as a *memento mori*, to signal the presence of death in life." Michael Henry Heim

[529] "Still, the chopping down of the cherry orchard is so clearly an allegory of the demise of the landowning class in Russia—the play's main Russian issue—that it fairly begs to be extended symbolically to death in general." Michael Henry Heim

[530] Old cherry trees were very valuable as a source of hardwood and extremely popular with cabinetmakers. Cherry wood is easy to work, fine textured, strong and durable. Considering the size of the orchard Lopakhin would more than recoup his whole investment from the sale of this wood alone. Since chopping down the entire orchard would flood, and thus depress the market

in cherry wood, perhaps Lopakhin, the shrewd businessman, will come to his senses and only chop down a small portion of it. Ivan Bunin hated Chekhov's play and inexplicably thought cherry orchards were ugly (I can assure you from personal experience that there is nothing more beautiful than a cherry orchard in bloom). But even Bunin could see: "It's also quite implausible that Lopakhin should have these profitable trees cut down with such stupid haste before the former owner has even left the house."

Chekhov was a knowledgeable and skillful plantsmen and horticulturalist; the dimensions he gives are purposeful. There can be little doubt that it is the largest cherry orchard in the world, 2500 acres, with its very real 100,000 trees capable of producing 4 million pounds of cherries; it is meant to embody symbolic and mythical scopes.

www.ingramcontent.com/pod-product-compliance
Lightning Source LLC
Chambersburg PA
CBHW050551170426
43201CB00011B/1658